Why We Buy

THE SCIENCE OF SHOPPING

Paco Underhill

SIMON & SCHUSTER

089-T5-03

SIMON & SCHUSTER
Rockefeller Center
1230 Avenue of the Americas, New York, NY 10020

Copyright © 1999 by Obat, Inc.
All rights reserved,
including the right of reproduction
in whole or in part in any form.

SIMON & SCHUSTER and colophon are registered
trademarks of Simon & Schuster Inc.

Manufactured in the United States of America

1   3   5   7   9   10   8   6   4   2

Library of Congress Cataloging-in-Publication Data
Underhill, Paco.
Why we buy : the science of shopping / Paco Underhill.
p.   cm.
Includes index.
1. Marketing research. 2. Consumer behavior. 3. Shopping. I Title.
HF5415.2.U53   1999
658.8'34—dc21   99-12125
CIP
ISBN 0-684-84913-5

DEDICATION

Since 1987, I have had a core group of colleagues who helped turn a good idea into a viable business. While Envirosell employs about twenty full-time and fifty part-time workers around the world, these six have made my life possible. This book is dedicated to them.

Tom Moseman

Barbara Weisfeld

Tony Trout

Craig Childress

Lee Smith

Anne Marie Luthro

I am grateful for their commitment to building Envirosell, and their patience and contributions to this book.

CONTENTS

I

INSTEAD OF SAMOA, STORES: THE SCIENCE OF SHOPPING

II

WALK LIKE AN EGYPTIAN: THE MECHANICS OF SHOPPING

III

MEN ARE FROM SEARS HARDWARE, WOMEN ARE FROM BLOOMINGDALE'S: THE DEMOGRAPHICS OF SHOPPING

IV

SEE ME, FEEL ME, TOUCH ME, BUY ME:
THE DYNAMICS OF SHOPPING

I

Instead of Samoa, Stores: The Science of Shopping

A Science Is Born

ONE

C omfortable shoes, the American commercial camouflage uniform—khaki pants, olive polo shirt, no aftershave and good, thick, dun-colored socks.

Okay, stroll, stroll, stroll . . . *stop.*

Get out the clipboard and pen.

Shhh. Stay behind that potted palm. This is the first track of the day.

The subject of study is the fortyish woman in the tan trench coat and blue skirt. She's in the bath section. She's touching towels. Mark this down—she's petted one, two, three, four of them so far. She just checked the price tag on one. Mark that down, too. Careful, her head's coming up—blend into the aisle. She's picking up two towels from the tabletop display and is leaving the section with them. Get the time. Now, tail her into the aisle and on to her next stop.

It's another day of fieldwork; the laboratory, another troubled department store. The focus of our analysis is the domestic department as per the science of shopping. But let's start by addressing a fundamental question: Since when does such a scholarly discipline even exist?

Well, if, say, anthropology had devoted a branch to the study of modern shoppers in situ, a fancy Latin way of saying shoppers out shopping, interacting with retail environments (not only stores, but also banks and restaurants), including but not limited to every rack, shelf, counter and table display of merchandise, every sign, banner, brochure, directional aid and computerized interactive informational fixture, the entrances and exits, the windows and walls, the elevators and escalators and stairs and ramps, the cashier lines and teller lines and counter lines and restroom lines, and every inch of every aisle—in short, every nook and cranny from the farthest reach of the parking lot to the deepest penetration of the store itself—that would be the start of the science of shopping. And *if* anthropology had already been studying all that . . . and not simply studying the store, but what, exactly human beings do in it, where they go and don't go, and by what path they go there; what they see and fail to see, or read and decline to read; and how they deal with the objects they come upon, how they *shop*, you might say—the precise anatomical mechanics and behavioral psychology of how they pull a sweater from a rack to examine it, or read a box of heartburn pills or a fast-food restaurant menu, or deploy a shopping basket, or react to the sight of a line at the ATMs . . . again, as I say, *if* anthropology had been paying attention, and not just paying attention but then collating, digesting, tabulating and cross-referencing every little bit of data, from the extremely broad (How many people enter this store on a typical Saturday morning broken down by age, sex and size of shopper group?) to the extremely narrow (Do more male supermarket shoppers under thirty-five who read the nutritional information on the side panel of a cereal box actually buy the cereal compared to those who just look at the picture on the front?), well, then we wouldn't have had to try to invent the science of shopping.

But anthropology didn't pay attention to those details, and so down the hall from my office is a room containing around fifty cameras, mostly video but with some still and digital cameras and a couple of old-fashioned Super 8 time-lapse film cameras thrown in. Next to them are piled cases of blank 8mm videotapes, two hours per tape, five hundred tapes to a case. We go through about fourteen cases, seven thousand tapes, a year. (In 1992, when we shot a lot of time-lapse Super 8 film—about $60,000 worth—Kodak told us we were the single largest consumer of Super 8 film in the world.) We also have maybe a dozen handheld computers on which we take down the answers from the thousands of shopper interviews we conduct, and there are some odd laptops in there, too, plus all manner of tripods, mounts, lenses and other camera accessories, including lots of duct tape. Oh, and hard-shell cases for everything, because it all travels. A lot. We have enough gear in that room to equip a major university's school of social anthropology or experimental psychology, assuming the university has a deserved reputation for generating tons of original research gathered all over the globe.

Despite all that high-tech equipment, though, our most important research tool is a low-tech piece of paper we call the track sheet, in the hands of the individuals we call trackers. Trackers are the field researchers of the science of shopping, the scholars of shopping, or, more precisely, of *shoppers*. Essentially, trackers stealthily make their way through stores following shoppers and noting everything they do. Usually, a tracker begins by loitering inconspicuously near a store's entrance, waiting for a shopper to enter, at which point the "track" starts. The tracker will stick with the unsuspecting individual (or individuals) as long as the shopper is in the store (excluding trips to the dressing room or the restroom) and will record on the track sheet virtually everything he or she does. Sometimes, when the store is large, trackers work in teams in order to be less intrusive.

Befitting a science that has grown up in the real world, meaning far from the ivory towers of academia, our trackers are not all taken from the usual researcher mold. In the beginning we hired graduate environmental psychology students, but we found they were sometimes unsuited to the work and tended to come to the job burdened with textbook theories they wanted to apply. As a result, they often didn't possess the patience necessary to simply watch what shoppers do. The other problem we had with grad students involved stamina: While we don't work in the dusty heat of Mesopotamia, twelve hours on your feet under the fluorescent lights at Kmart is no picnic either. Fieldwork in any physical or social science is difficult. We found that, for our purposes, smart, creative people—artists, actors, writers, a puppeteer—often have what it takes. Beyond the fact that they have no theories to uphold or demolish, their professional skills are often rooted in their ability to observe. Also, it does not hurt that they have flexible schedules, so that when that Brazilian brewer or Australian tampon manufacturer or American fast-food operator happens to call, they have the open calendar and curiosity to be willing to go take a look.

When we find someone we think has the temperament and the intelligence for this work, we first put him or her through a training session. There's a lot to learn—how do I watch and simultaneously take notes, for instance, or how can I tell whether someone is reading a sign or just staring at the mirror next to it? We have to teach the most important tracker skill of all: How do I stand close enough to study someone without being noticed? It's crucial to our work that shoppers don't realize they're being observed. There's no other way to be sure that we're seeing natural behavior. Fact is, we're all still surprised by how close you can stand to someone in a store and still remain invisible. We find that positioning yourself behind the shopper is a bad idea—we all know the sensation that we're being watched. But if you stand to the side of a shopper, his or her peripheral vision "reads" you as just another customer—harmless, in other words, and barely worth noticing. From that position you can get close enough to see exactly what a shopper is doing. You can be sure that he's touched, say, nine golf gloves, not eight or ten. Then we throw the tracker hopefuls out into the real world, in a store setting, to see them in action. Most of them wash out at this point—you can teach technique, but not the intelligence or the slight case of fascination required to do this work well. Over half of our core group of thirty U.S. trackers have been with us for more than five years, some for a decade or more. It's hard work, but addictive, too. In teams of three to ten people, led by a member of our staff, they crisscross the United States and Canada, as well as Europe, South America and Australia, visiting every kind of retail business imaginable, from banks to fast-food restaurants to high-fashion boutiques to hangar-size discounters and everything in between. To make our international work easier and more efficient, for three years we have had research teams based out of Milan, Italy, and for two years out of Sydney, Australia.

In addition to measuring and counting every significant motion of a shopping trip, the trackers must also contribute incisive field notes describing the nuances of customer behavior, making intelligent inferences based on what they've observed. These notes add up to yet another, this time anecdotal, layer of information about a given environment and how people use it.

The forms our trackers use have evolved over the two decades we've been doing this research. They are the key to the entire enterprise, an achievement in the art of information storage and retrieval, nondigital division. Our earliest track sheets could record maybe ten different variables of shopper behavior. Today we're up to around forty. The form is reinvented for every research project we undertake, but typically it starts with a detailed map depicting the premises we're about to study, whether it's a store, a bank branch, a parking lot (for a drive-thru project) or just a single section or even just one aisle of a store. The map shows every doorway and aisle, every display, every shelf and rack and table and counter. Also on the form is space for information about the shopper (sex, race, estimates of age, description of attire) and what he or she does in the store. Using the system of shorthand notation, a combination of symbols, letters and hash marks, a tracker can record, for instance, that a bald, bearded man in a red sweater and blue jeans entered a department store on a Saturday at 11:07 a.m., walked directly to a first-floor display of wallets, picked up or otherwise touched a total of twelve of them, checked the price tag on four, then chose one, moved at 11:16 to a nearby tie rack, stroked seven ties, read the contents tags on all seven, read the price on two, then bought none and went directly to the cashier to pay. Oh, wait, he paused for a moment at a mannequin and examined the price tag on the jacket it wore. We'd mark that down, too, just as we'd note that he entered the cashier line at 11:23 as the third person in line, waited two minutes and fifty-one seconds to get to the register, paid with a credit card and exited the store at 11:30. Depending on the size of the store and the length of the typical shopper's stay, a tracker can study up to fifty shoppers a day. Usually we'll have several trackers at a site, and a single project may involve the simultaneous study of three or four locations in separate cities over a series of different weekends.

By the end of a job, an incredible amount of information has been crammed onto those sheets. They come back to the office where the job captain spends a day "cleaning" the forms—making sure that each hash mark is visible and that every box that should be filled out has been. Then our data department spends another day or so entering all the information, every single notation on every track sheet, into a data base.

Over the years we've spent tens of thousands of dollars and countless frustrating hours with computer programmers, trying to come up with a data base system that could handle the kind of work we do. The big problem is that while we crunch the same numbers in the same ways from job to job, each project usually requires us to do something a little differently—to collect different kinds of data, or to devise new comparisons of facts we've uncovered. We've hired fancy consultants who've spent six months at a crack with us, trying to build us a computer system. They ask us to list everything we want our program to do, but every week we add six new things to the list that negate all their work from the previous month. And, of course, our turnaround time must be swift, so there's no time to change the system completely for each job—we may need to do one new comparison for a project today and then not have to perform that function again for seven months.

Until recently, most of our work was done in Microsoft Excel. Excel is not a data base program but a spreadsheet program, intended to help accountants do relatively simple flat calculations. Excel's beauty is its open architecture—you can get in there under the hood and tinker, and soup it up. And that's exactly what we've done. It's as though Microsoft built a very nice bicycle ten years ago and we've turned it into a data-busting all-terrain vehicle. Today we run much of our work in File-Maker and SPSS, but still vet it in Excel.

When the videotapes come back from the sites, it's someone else's job to screen every foot. Depending on the size of the store, we may have ten cameras running eight hours a day trained on specific areas—a doorway, for example, or a particular shelf of products. We videotape around twenty thousand hours' worth of store time annually. The video produces even more hard data; if, for example, a study is meant to determine in part how a particular cash register design affects worker fatigue, we may use the video and a stopwatch to time how long it takes for a clerk to ring up a sale at 10 a.m. compared to 4 p.m.

The list of particulars we're capable of studying—what we call the deliverables—grows with every new project we take on. At last count, we've measured close to nine hundred different aspects of shopper-store interaction. As a result of all that, we know quite a few facts about how human beings behave in stores. We can tell you how many males who take jeans into the fitting room will buy them compared to how many females will (65 percent to 25 percent). We can tell you how many people in a corporate cafeteria read the nutritional information on a bag of corn chips before buying (18 percent) compared to those lunching at a local sandwich shop (2 percent). Or how many browsers buy computers on a Saturday before noon (4 percent) as opposed to after 5 p.m. (21 percent). Or how many shoppers in a mall housewares store use shopping baskets (8 percent), and how many of those who take baskets actually buy something (75 percent) compared to those who buy without using baskets (34 percent). And then, of course, we draw on all we've learned in the past to suggest ways of increasing the number of shoppers who take baskets, for the science of shopping is, if it is anything, a highly practical discipline concerned with using research, comparison and analysis to make stores and products more amenable to shoppers.

Because this science has been invented as we have gone along, it's a living, breathing field of study. We never quite know what we'll find until we find it, and even then we sometimes have to stop to figure out what it is we've seen.

For example, we discovered a phenomenon known as the butt-brush effect almost accidentally. As part of an early study for Bloomingdale's in New York City, we trained a camera on one of the main ground-floor entrances, and the lens just happened to also take in a rack of neckties positioned near the entrance, on a main aisle. While reviewing the tape to study how shoppers negotiated the doorway during busy times, we began to notice something weird about the tie rack. Shoppers would approach it, stop and shop until they were bumped once or twice by people heading into or out of the store. After a few such jostles, most of the shoppers would move out of the way, abandoning their search for neckwear. We watched this over and over until it seemed clear that shoppers—women especially, though it was also true of men to a lesser extent—don't like being brushed or touched from behind. They'll even move away from merchandise they're interested in to avoid it. When we checked with our client, we learned that sales from that tie rack were lower than they expected from a fixture located on a main thoroughfare. The butt-brush factor, we surmised, was why that rack was an underperformer.

As I was delivering our findings to the store's president, he jumped up from the conference table, grabbed a phone, called down to the floor of the store and had someone move that tie rack immediately to a spot just off the main aisle. A few weeks later the head of store planning called me to say that sales from the rack had gone up quickly and substantially. Since that day we've found countless similar situations in which shoppers have been spooked by too-close quarters. In every case, a quick adjustment was all that was needed.

Another such "accident" of patient observation and analysis happened during a supermarket study we performed for a dog food manufacturer. When we staked out the pet aisle, we noticed that while adults bought the dog food, the dog treats—liver-flavored biscuits and such—were often being picked out by children or senior citizens. We realized that for the elderly, pets are *like* children, creatures to be spoiled. And while feeding Fido may not be any child's favorite chore, filling him up with doggie cookies can be loads of fun. Parents indulged their little ones' pleas for treats here just as they did over in the cookie aisle.

Because no one had ever noticed who exactly was buying (or lobbying for the purchase of) pet treats, they were typically stocked near the top of the supermarket shelves. As a result, our cameras caught children climbing the shelving to reach the treats. We witnessed one elderly woman using a box of aluminum foil to knock down her brand of dog biscuits. Move the treats to where kids and little old ladies can reach them, we advised the client. The client did so, and sales went up overnight.

Even the plainest truths can get lost in all the details of planning and stocking a store. A phrase I find myself using over and over with clients is this: The obvious isn't always apparent.

While studying the cosmetics section of a drugstore chain, we watched a woman in her sixties approach a wall rack, study it carefully and then kneel before it so she could find the one item she needed—concealer cream, which, because of its lack of glamour, was kept at the very bottom of the display. Similarly, in a department store we watched an overweight man try to find his size of underwear at a large aisle display—and saw him stoop dangerously low to reach it, down near the floor. In both cases, logic should have dictated that the displays be tailored to the shoppers who use them, not to the designers who made them. Move the concealer up, we advised, and put something aimed at teen shoppers down near the floor—the teens will find their products wherever they're stocked.

In some studies, we synthesize every bit of information we can possibly collect into a comprehensive portrait of a store or a single department. A major jeans manufacturer wanted to know how its product was sold in department stores, so in one weekend we descended on four sites, two in New England and two in Southern California. Each department was similar—the jeans section was a square area that held from eight to twelve tabletop displays and some wall shelving. We started by drawing a detailed map of each, showing the displays and the aisles leading into and out of the sections, but also where any signs or other promotional materials were posted. During that weekend we tracked a total of 815 shoppers and observed many more on camera, both video and time-lapse. We paid particular attention to the "doorways"—our term for any path leading into or out of an area of a store.

Until the client knew which paths were most popular, it was impossible to make informed decisions about where to stock what, or where to place the merchandising materials meant to lure shoppers.

By the time our study was completed, we could say which percentage of customers used which paths into each of the sections. Once we knew that, it was clear, for instance, that much of the signage was misplaced—common sense dictated that it be positioned to face the main entrance of the store, but we found that most jeans shoppers came upon the section from a completely different direction. Even the client's big neon logo and a monitor showing rock videos were facing the wrong way if their job was to signal the greatest number of shoppers. We tracked shoppers from table to table, seeing where they stopped, what signs they read, whether they noticed the video monitors, and how they handled the merchandise, including whether they took anything to the dressing rooms. If they seemed to be showing jeans to a companion, we noted that, too. Some of the shoppers captured on video were also questioned by our interviewers, so that their demographic information and their attitudes and opinions could be correlated with their behaviors—to see, for example, whether young shoppers with high school educations who say they depend on name brand when choosing jeans read price tags. After the research is done and the numbers are crunched and analyzed, we see what sense can be made of what we've learned. For example, if we were to find that a high percentage of male shoppers buy from the first rack of jeans they encounter, and that shoppers tend to enter the section through the aisle leading from men's accessories rather than from the women's side of the store or from the escalator, then we would advise our client to ask for the display table nearest men's accessories. Or maybe there's another determining factor—maybe men who are accompanied by females and entering the section from the women's department buy more jeans than men who are alone. In that case, the best table would be nearest the women's merchandise. But no one knows for sure until we collect the data.

In other instances we're hired to study some small retail interaction in great detail. One such project was commissioned by a premium shampoo maker that wanted to know about the decision-making process of women shoppers who buy generic or store-brand beauty products. The client was interested in the "value equation" women bring to each shopping experience—how does the shopper who buys from the generics section at the supermarket in the morning and then from Nordstrom in the afternoon decide which product she'll buy where? Does she judge that her skin deserves the premium brand but her hair can settle for the generic? Once upon a time only the budget-conscious bought store brands, but now you find them in everyone's shopping basket. Let's call her shopper number 24, a thirtysomething woman in yellow pants and white sweater, accompanied by a preschool girl, who enters the health and beauty aisle of a supermarket at 10:37 a.m. on a Wednesday morning. She has a handbasket, not a shopping cart, and has already selected store-brand vitamin C capsules, a large container of Johnson's Baby Powder and a packet of snapshots she picked up at the photo-processing booth. She is also holding a shopping list and the store circular. She goes directly to the shampoo shelves and picks up a bottle of Pantene brand, reads the front label, then picks up a bottle of the store brand and reads the front label, then reads the price tag on the Pantene, then reads the price on the store brand, and then puts the store brand in her basket and exits the section forty-nine seconds after she entered it. In that brief encounter, there was lots of data to collect—what she touched, what she read and in what order, about twenty-five different data points in all. If, in one day, we track a hundred shoppers in that store's health and beauty aisle, it can amount to 2,500 separate data entries. As the woman exits the section, we interview her, asking twenty questions in all. So each of the twenty-five data points has to be cross-tabulated with each of her twenty answers—a cross-tab challenge, take it from me.

No university, to my knowledge, has ever attempted behavioral research in the retail environment to the degree that we have. My old colleagues in the world of academia regard what we do with envy and horror—envy because we get to do what we do and get paid for it, horror because we actually stick our necks out and are held accountable for the success or failure of our suggestions. After almost twenty years of work, our client list is as blue-chip as they come, and while we do get it wrong sometimes, three-quarters of our clients who buy us once come back for more.

I make much of the "accidental" nature of my involvement in the science of shopping. More than twenty years ago I was a student and admirer of one of America's most esteemed social scientists, William H. Whyte, author of such highly influential books as *The Organization Man, The Last Landscape, City—Rediscovering the Center* and *The Social Life of Small Urban Spaces.* He was also the founder, in the early '70s, of the Street Life Project and, in 1974 with Fred Kent and Robert Cook, of the Project for Public Spaces, or PPS, where I worked for two years. PPS, based in New York City, continues to make significant contributions to the preservation and ongoing good health of the urban landscape.

William H. Whyte, or "Holly," as he is known, was, in his active days, a quixotic, beloved figure. He had the gray hair and aristocratic mien of an old-fashioned WASP banker, yet he had fallen in love with the streets of New York City and worked hard to learn how people might best use them. Whyte's greatest contribution was his research into how people use public spaces—streets, parks, plazas and so on. Using time-lapse photography, hidden trackers and interviews, he and his associates would stake out some urban plaza or mini-park, say, and study it, minute by minute, over the course of several days. By the time they finished, they could tell you everything about every bench, ledge, path, fountain and shrub, especially how people interacted with them, using them as places to lunch, sun, socialize, people-watch, nap or just happily and peacefully loiter. Whyte and his colleagues would measure everything—the ideal width of a ledge for sitting, how sunlight, shade and wind affect park use and how a public space's surroundings, the office towers or construction sites or schools or neighborhoods, determine the quality of life there.

Whyte was, essentially, a scientist of the street—one of the first, which is amazing when you think of how long streets existed before he came along. His work has been used to make public spaces better and more useful to citizens, which in turn has made cities better. Whyte's methods were a kind of lens through which a physical environment could be studied and improved, and my work on behalf of shopping owes a great deal to his methods and to my early work with PPS.

Back in 1977 I was a part-time instructor at City University of New York, teaching courses in fieldwork techniques for the department of environmental psychology. I was also working in an establishment of which I was a part-owner, the Ear Inn, a bar in downtown Manhattan. There I had a friend and customer who had been hired to design a system of signage at Lincoln Center, the performing arts complex that's home to the Metropolitan Opera House, the New York State Theater, Avery Fisher Hall and a number of other performance venues. He told me they needed someone to look into the usage and circulation patterns of the underground concourse that connected all the buildings to parking garages and the subway. There was a small, makeshift gift shop down there at the time, but Lincoln Center wanted to see if a larger store might be viable there. First, though, they needed to make sure that a store wouldn't create congestion in the pedestrian walkways. With my friend's help, I got the job.

So I recruited a few of my students to help and we took some cameras, staked out our observation spots and went to work counting and mapping. The crowding question was easy enough to answer—we roped off an area exactly the size of the store they wanted to build, then watched and filmed pedestrians streaming through during the busiest times. Four weeks after I started, the report was submitted and the board of directors at Lincoln Center approved the construction of a complex of shops and tour facilities in the underground concourse. It prospers to this day.

Lincoln Center took most of my suggestions. One recommendation I made was to place benches in the concourse, particularly for Lincoln Center's senior visitors. My client declined to take this advice at first, but within six months, in response to seniors' complaints, the benches were installed. I also strongly recommended that they double the size of the ladies' room, and Lincoln Center's male management declined to take that advice. Today, twenty years later, the line at the ladies' room still goes out the door during busy times. Shameful.

As I was compiling the data to write the report and looking at the many hours of film I had shot, I realized that from one of the camera positions I was able to examine the functionality of the temporary gift shop, from browsing to purchase. There, as I watched, two customers lined up to pay. One looked to be a wealthy woman, probably an operagoer, who had piled a small tower of boxes on the counter. Next to her was a teenage girl whose purchase required just one small brown paper bag. I couldn't see enough to tell exactly what was going on, but I was intrigued.

I visited the shop next day and talked to the clerk, who told me that the woman was the wife of a Mexican diplomat who had decided to buy some fancy music boxes as gifts to take home with her. The boxes were expensive, and she was buying about a dozen of them, for a total sale of close to $9,000. She needed to pay quickly, before intermission ended, and she had to arrange to have the boxes delivered to her. There was also the matter of having the sales tax waived owing to her diplomatic status. A complicated transaction, to say the least.

But this had to wait while the clerk handled the transaction with the teenage girl, who had arrived at the register first bearing her selection—a ballerina pen.

It was clear even to an academic like me that the cash register procedure could stand a little reorganization and clarification. These two transactions should not be competing for the same clerk's attention. And then the lightbulb clicked on. Why not take the tools of the urban anthropologist and use them to study how people interact with the retail environment?

A few years earlier I had witnessed an argument between the esteemed sociologist and author Erving Goffman and Jack Fruin, the chief engineer of the Port Authority of New York and New Jersey, who was at that moment in the midst of a gigantic undertaking, the planning and construction of Newark International Airport. Jack was expressing his frustration with the world of academia—he was attempting to get scholar-experts to help his engineers and architects in their work, but instead of the clear-cut advice he had hoped to receive, he was getting buried under the academics' discomfort at applying their knowledge to practical design problems. Goffman held the intellectual high ground in their argument, but I clearly remember thinking, I'd have a lot more fun working for Jack than for Erving. Erving's hiding in his ivory tower. Jack is out there *doing* stuff.

Not long after the Lincoln Center assignment, I was sitting with some friends at a nightclub in Greenwich Village. One of the guys at our table was a young executive with Epic Records, a division of CBS, and I described to him my bright idea of measuring what happens in stores—the thought that there might be something worth learning by turning scientific tools on shopping. And over the course of a few beers my idea must have sounded interesting because the guy said, "Send me a proposal!"

Full of ambition the next morning, I rose early, dragged out my typewriter and drafted a plan. I sent it over, then waited. For, oh, about a year. Of course I tried writing again and telephoning during that time, but no one ever returned my calls. These were the dark ages of the science of shopping, remember.

And then, out of the blue, I heard from a woman who was in charge of market research for CBS Records. She said that they had found my proposal in a dusty file somewhere and were all quite fascinated by it, and was I still interested in studying a record store?

Sure, I said, inwardly rejoicing that a major American corporation was actually going to underwrite—to the tune, I think, of about $5,000—my research into the habits of the modern shopper. I immediately called a few of my students, assembled some notebooks and time-lapse cameras and made my way to a record store in a northern New Jersey mall.

Now, almost two decades and several hundreds of thousands of hours of videotape and much personal observation later, that study seems almost charmingly rudimentary. But at the time it felt as though the discoveries came flying fast and furious.

For instance, in the late '70s, when the study was being done, traditional singles—45 rpm records—were still big sellers. The store, wisely, displayed the *Billboard* magazine chart of best-selling singles near the racks of records, as a stimulus to sales. But our film showed that most buyers of 45s were young adolescents—and the chart was hung so high on the wall that the kids had to stand on their toes and crane their necks to see what exactly was at the top of the chart. We suggested to the manager that the chart be lowered, and a week later he called to say that sales of 45s had gone up by 20 percent. Just like that! Lower the chart! It worked!

We spent a lot of time that weekend watching people in line to pay at what the retail industry calls cash/wraps. Regardless of what store designers and merchandise managers think, in many ways the cash/wrap area is the most important part of any store. If the transactions aren't crisp, if the organization isn't clear at a glance, shoppers get frustrated or turned off. Many times they won't even enter a store if the line to pay looks long or chaotic.

At this store there were several big displays of new releases as soon as you walked in—just a few feet from the cashier. Which was fine as long as the store was empty, but if customers were in line, their bodies completely hid the displays. Put up a stanchion and a velvet rope to keep the line off to one side, we suggested, and again our advice had an instant effect—sales of records from the displays went up immediately.

Doesn't all this sound just the least bit obvious? It does to us, too, especially after we've spent so much time watching and filming and timing and interviewing and so on. Until then, however, these are the kinds of problems that remain hidden in plain view.

While watching the record store customers, we noticed an odd pattern: The LP section (this was pre-CD, remember) was always more crowded than cassettes, but sales were split evenly between the two formats. As we followed customers, the reason became clear—because the LP covers were bigger, it was easier to read the song lists and see the photos, so cassette shoppers would browse in LPs, make up their minds and then go to the tapes section to find their choices. Our suggestion was to make the aisles wider in LPs, so that shoppers wouldn't feel crushed and rushed, a definite sales-killer. Also, we thought the store should invest in more durable carpet for the sections that got significantly more traffic.

My final memory from that study comes from a film clip I still show to audiences: a young man shoplifting classical music tapes. Only after watching him take the tapes over and over on the film did I notice that the bag he slipped them into was from a chain that had no location at that mall. I passed on that tidbit to the client's security executive and told him that they should be watchful whenever such "wrong" bags were spotted in their stores. I got back a note saying that they had discovered several thousand dollars in theft using that method of detection.

That first attempt at understanding how stores worked turned up enough to make me realize I was on to something. To my surprise, things that seemed logical and obvious to me were delightful insights to my clients. It was clear that I had stepped into a world of business where what I did had value, but I knew nothing of the consequences or, really, the context. At that point, almost twenty years ago, I knew a science existed—all I had to do was start looking for it. Somewhere out there was something the retail world was going to call the science of shopping.

Before the science of shopping existed, there were at least two other ways to measure what takes place in a store. The most common way of viewing a store is to simply examine "the tape"—the information that comes from the cash registers, which tells what was bought, when and how much of it. This is how virtually every retail undertaking, from the largest, most sophisticated multinational chain to the corner newsstand, does it. It's a fine way to see how the store as a whole has done this quarter, or this year, or on any given day, or even time of day, and is, in the end, the measure of a store's overall health and growth (or decline) that counts. The information that comes out of a register has gotten distinctly more sophisticated over the past two decades. Thanks to scanning of universal product codes, the development of customer loyalty cards and links to credit card receipts, stores and marketers know a lot about what sells and who buys it. However, register-based data has two basic problems. The first is that the industry is much more adept at collecting it than at designing systems or processes to use that data in a timely fashion. The second is that the view from the register back into the body of the store is distinctly myopic.

When businesspeople attempt to infer too much from the tape, it can be downright misleading. Here's a good example, from a chain drugstore in an enclosed regional mall in Massachusetts. This was one of the first mall stores owned by this particular company, so management was eager to see the results. Based solely on total sales, our client was pleased overall, and in particular with how the analgesic section of the store was performing.

But based on our many previous studies of both drugstores and the analgesic category, one crucial figure was on the low side. The closure rate—the percentage of shoppers who bought—was below what we expected. In other words, plenty of customers stopped at the aspirin section and picked up and read the packages, but too few of them actually bought aspirin. The conversion rate for aspirin is usually high—it's not the kind of product you idly browse; you tend to go to that aisle only when you're in need. So we spent some time tracking and videotaping the aspirin shelves.

Over the course of three days, a pattern emerged. The aspirin was displayed on a main aisle of the store, on the path to some refrigerated cases of soft drinks, which tended to draw a great many customers to that part of the store. That might lead one to expect that the aspirin would sell well, but just the opposite happened. The main customers for cold drinks were teenagers, and our observation showed many of them entering and making a beeline for the coolers. In fact, this was a favorite place for the mall's young employees to grab a quick cold soda during breaks.

These young shoppers were supremely uninterested in aspirin. The shoppers, often seniors, who *did* want aspirin stood a little nervously at the shelves, searching for their usual brand or figuring out which was the better deal while trying to stay clear of the teenagers racing down the aisle on ten-minute breaks. In fact, a substantial number of aspirin shoppers became so irritated or rattled by the teenagers that they would prematurely break off their browsing and walk away empty-handed. It was a modified version of the butt-brush effect—the shoppers weren't being jostled exactly, just a little rattled. You could see it plainly on the video-tape—some customers were practically cringing and hugging the shelves, not the ideal shopping position. And when we timed shoppers, we found that they were spending less time at the shelves than our experience led us to expect.

This is something that comes up in our work all the time: A store has more than one constituency, and it must therefore perform several functions, all from the same premises. Sometimes those functions coexist in perfect harmony, but other times—especially in stores selling diverse goods, like cold drinks and patent medicines—those functions clash. A perfect example is a Harley-Davidson dealership—where a roughly 3,000-square-foot showroom has to make room for well-off male-menopause victims looking to recover their virility by buying bikes, blue-collar gearheads who are there for spare parts and teenage dreamers interested in the Harley-logo fashions. All three groups want nothing to do with one another. When a premise's functions clash, a way must be found to accommodate as many uses as possible. In this drugstore, we advised our client about what we had learned and suggested a counterintuitive move—that the over-the-counter drug section be relocated to a quieter corner of the store. Fewer total customers would come upon it, we knew, but more aspirin would be sold. When they moved the shelves, sales rose by over 15 percent. We also recommended moving the snack food section closer to the front of the store—a move that has now become a drugstore industry standard.

We performed research for a large bookstore that had recently put a large table of discounted books just inside the entrance, where every customer would see it first thing. And it performed admirably—almost everyone stopped for at least a cursory browse, and the percentage who bought at least one book was high. Which meant that, according to the cash register tape, the table was a resounding success.

Except that as we tracked shoppers, we found that the number who would go to the table and then travel through the rest of the store was lower than it should have been. In a case like this, every hour on the hour a tracker would hurry through the entire store and note how many shoppers were in each section, including the register area, the coffee shop and so on. This is the density check that we perform as part of every store study, and it tells us a great deal: It gives an instant snapshot of the store's "population" and where people are drawn or not; it suggests when something about the architecture or the layout may be inhibiting shoppers from visiting certain areas; it shows how shoppers move (or fail to) through the premises. And, in fact, taken section by section, the number of shoppers who were penetrating the rest of the store was uniformly down. Also, our track sheet maps of customer travels began showing a telltale shallow loop—shoppers would enter, hit the bargain table, then maybe visit one or two more displays, but never stray far from the front of the store before heading to the cashier. This was no coincidence, needless to say—customers were choosing from the discount table, then going directly to the register, paying for their bargains and leaving without even browsing the best-sellers or any of the other books selling at the normal profit margins. Our shopper interviews turned up an unfortunate side effect, too: Thanks to the prominence of the bargain table, the store was gaining a reputation as a discounter rather than as the place to go for the hot new book. The success of the table was causing the failure of the rest of the store.

So much for what can be learned from the register tape.

The second means of discovering information, employed by most of the rest of the world interested in market research, is to poll or simply ask people questions (on the phone or in person) about what they just saw, or did, or considered doing. Then, after a long list of questions, basic demographic information is taken (age, education, income, sex, race, and so on). From those two, a big fat binder full of suppositions is assembled: Forty-year-old Caucasian college-educated married mothers of two living in Northeast suburbs and driving station wagons would prefer Jif even more if it were low-fat, for example. Or, men who buy Coke at convenience stores say they would notice their brand less often if it were any color but red. Or, one-quarter of all college graduates eat pasta once a week. The possibilities for cross-referencing are endless, and there is much marketing wisdom to be gotten from such studies. But they don't really reveal much about what happens in a store, when shoppers and goods finally come together under the same roof. There are surveys that do ask customers for information about what they saw and did inside a store, but the answers are often suspect. Sometimes people just don't remember every little thing they saw or did in a store—they weren't shopping with the thought that they'd have to recall it all later. In a fragrance study we performed, some shoppers interviewed said they had given serious consideration to buying brands that the store didn't carry. In a study of tobacco merchandising in a convenience store, shoppers remembered seeing signs for Marlboro even though no such signs were in that store.

If we went into stores only when we needed to buy something, and if once there we bought only what we needed, the economy would collapse, boom.

Fortunately, the economic party that has been the second half of the twentieth century has fostered more shopping than anyone would have predicted, more shopping than has ever taken place anywhere at any time. You almost have to make an effort to avoid shopping today. Stay out of stores and museums and theme restaurants and you still are face-to-face with Internet shopping twenty-four hours a day, seven days a week, along with its low-rent cousin, home shopping on TV. Have to steer clear of your own mailbox, too, if you're going to duck all those catalogs.

As a result, every expert agrees, we are now dangerously overretailed—too much is for sale, through too many outlets. The economy even at its strongest can't keep up with retailing's growth. Judging from birthrates, we are generating stores considerably faster than we are producing new baby shoppers.

Retailers are not opening stores in the United States to serve new markets anymore. They are opening stores to try to steal someone else's customers. As the competition gets heated, there is a need for an edge—a science, if you will.

There's another reason that the science of shopping s a force today.

Generations ago, the commercial messages intended 'r consumers' ears came in highly concentrated, reliable form. There were three TV networks, AM radio only, a handful of big-circulation national magazines and each town's daily papers, which all adults read. Big brandname goods were advertised in those media, and the message got through loud, clear and dependably. Today, we are nearing a hundred TV channels, and we have remote controls and VCRs to allow us to skip all the ads if we choose to. There's FM radio now, a plethora of magazines catering to each little special interest, a World Wide Web of infinitely expanding sites we can visit for information and entertainment and a shrinking base of daily newspaper readers, all of which means that it is harder than ever to reach consumers and convince them to buy anything at all.

Simultaneously, we are witnessing the erosion of the influence of brand names. Not that brands don't have value, but that value is not the blind force it used to be. A generation or two ago, you chose your brands early in life and stuck by them loyally until your last shopping trip. If you were a Buick man, you bought Buicks. If you were a Marlboro woman, you smoked Marlboros. You chose your team—Coke or Pepsi, Maytag or Speed Queen, Camay or Ivory—and stayed with it. Today, in some ways, every decision is a new one, and nothing can be taken for granted.

That means that while branding and traditional advertising build brand awareness and purchase predisposition, those factors do not always translate into sales. The standard tools of marketing work, they just don't work anywhere near as well as they used to. Many purchasing decision are made, or can be heavily influenced, on the floor of the store itself. Shoppers are susceptible to impressions and information they acquire in stores, rather than just relying on brand-name loyalty or advertising to tell them what to buy.

As a result, an important medium for transmitting messages and closing sales is now the store and the aisle. That building, that place, has become a great big three-dimensional advertisement for itself. Signage, shelf position, display space and special fixtures all make it either likelier or less likely that a shopper will buy a particular item (or any item at all). The science of shopping is meant to tell us how to make use of all those tools: How to design signs that shoppers will actually read and how to make sure each message is in the appropriate place. How to fashion displays that shoppers can examine comfortably and easily. How to ensure that shoppers can reach, and want to reach, every part of a store. It's a very long list—enough to fill a book, in my opinion.

Finally, our studies prove that the longer a shopper remains in a store, the more he or she will buy. And the amount of time a shopper spends in a store depends on how comfortable and enjoyable the experience is. Just as Holly Whyte's labors improved urban parks and plazas, the science of shopping creates better retail environments—ultimately, we're providing a form of consumer advocacy that benefits our clients as well.

What Retailers Don't Know

TWO

It might be useful right about now to pause and look at the science of shopping from the perspective not of the scientist but of the practitioner—that is, the retailer. He or she is certainly part of the equation we're studying, the provider of shopping experiences, as it were. The retailer is also the one who's expected to absorb all our lessons and then apply the principles of what we've learned. And since it's his or her own store we study, it's fair to ask: How much doesn't the retailer already know?

Well, more than you might think. For example, it's testament to the still vastly uncharted state of the untamed retail environment that an extremely intelligent and able man, a senior executive in a multibillion-dollar chain could be so very wrong when asked this simple question:

How many of the people who walk into your stores buy something?

You'd know that, wouldn't you, if you were he? You think so, but, trust me, this fellow is no slouch in the knowing department. He knows quite a bit that goes on in his chain's thousands of stores, and he learns more on a daily basis—genuinely important things like total tickets (number of transactions *and* their dollar value), and average sale amount, and sales in any given store compared to sales on the same day the year before, and sales within the various regions, and profitability by item and category and store and maybe even phase of the moon.

He knows all that.

When I asked how many of the people who walk into his stores buy something, his answer was: All of them, pretty damn near. And when I say it was his answer, I mean it was also the answer of the huge, PC-networked, data-chewing, number-crunching, cipher-loving organization at his command. Everybody there agreed: What we call the conversion or closure rate—the percentage of shoppers who become buyers—was around 100 percent. After all, this corporation reasoned, their outlets were destination stores, so people didn't go there unless they had some very specific purchase in mind. Hence, they believed, the only time shoppers *didn't* buy was when their selection was out of stock.

In fact, the very concept of conversion rate, implying as it does that shoppers need to be somehow transformed—"converted"—into buyers, was alien to this man and this corporation (as it still is to many other successful companies and executives).

I was asking the question because we had just performed a large-scale study of this chain's stores. And I knew the conversion rate, based on our having spent hundreds of hours counting, among other things, the number of shoppers who entered and the number who made purchases. It was a very good conversion rate for stores of this kind. But it was about half of what this man thought it was. To be precise, 48 percent of shoppers bought something.

The man, because he believes in the value of information, was taken aback but eager to hear more. Some in his organization, though, were incredulous, outraged, insulted and certain that we had made a terrible miscalculation. So they performed their own homegrown version of our study, standing at the door of a store or two, counting the number of people who went in and the number who emerged holding bags.

Their result was identical to ours. Which, in the end, was very positive news for them. It meant that a good company could change some very specific things and become even better. If you talk to the executive, he'll say that our study brought about "a fundamental change in some of the long-held beliefs and opinions of this company." At any rate, they've begun to do some things differently in store layout, display, merchandising and staffing, and I have no doubt that they'll improve their conversion rate and make more money as a result.

Our findings were also important to that company's big picture. We showed that meaningful growth—which Wall Street demands and everybody else is pretty fond of, too—can be stimulated at the store level without having to expand the empire, an expensive strategy that always runs out of gas sooner or later.

Conversion rates vary wildly depending on what kind of store or product we're talking about. In some sections of the supermarket, conversion rate probably *is* around 100 percent (I'm thinking of dairy or toilet paper here). In an art gallery full of big-ticket paintings, maybe one shopper in a hundred will buy something, and that's plenty. Whatever's being sold, though, I think it's impossible to dispute that conversion rate is a critically important measure of performance. Marketing, advertising, promotion and location can bring shoppers in, but then it's the job of the merchandise, the employees and the store itself to turn them into buyers. Conversion rate measures what you make of what you have—it shows how well (or how poorly) the entire enterprise is functioning where it counts most: in the store. Conversion rate is to retail what batting average is to baseball—without knowing it, you can say that somebody had a hundred hits last season, but you don't know whether he had three hundred at-bats or a thousand. Without conversion rate, you don't know if you're Mickey Mantle or Mickey Mouse.

Still, a great many businesspeople don't know from conversion rate. It's not one of the ways of measuring a business that business schools emphasize. It's not about profit margins or return on investment or money supply or any of that. It's all about what happens within the four walls of the store. I can think of other underutilized ways to measure what happens inside a store.

Once I asked a major cosmetics executive how much time women actually spent shopping for makeup per store visit.

"Oh, about ten minutes," he said.

"Hmm," I replied, knowing from the study we had just completed for him that the average shopper spent two minutes in the cosmetics section. The average shopper who bought something spent only thirty seconds more.

Now, the amount of time a shopper spends in a store (assuming he or she is shopping, not waiting in a line) is perhaps the single most important factor in determining how much she or he will buy. Over and over again, our studies have shown a direct relationship. If the customer is walking through the entire store (or most of it, at least) and is considering lots of merchandise (meaning he or she is looking and touching and thinking), a fair amount of time is required. In an electronics store we studied, nonbuyers spent 5 minutes, 6 seconds in the store, compared to 9 minutes and 29 seconds for buyers. In a toy store, buyers spent over 17 minutes, compared to 10 for nonbuyers. In some stores buyers spend three or four times as much time as nonbuyers. A great many factors contribute, one way or the other, to length of shopping trip, and studying them is most of what we do. The majority of the advice we give to retailers involves ways of getting shoppers to shop longer. But you've got to know how long people spend shopping your store or your product before you can know how to increase it.

Here's another good way to judge a store: by its interception rate, meaning the percentage of customers who have some contact with an employee. This is especially crucial today, when many businesses are cutting overhead by using fewer workers, fewer full-timers and more minimum-wagers. All our research shows this direct relationship: The more shopper-employee contacts that take place, the greater the average sale. Talking with an employee has a way of drawing a customer in closer.

We studied a large clothing chain where the interception rate was 25 percent, meaning that three-quarters of all shoppers never spoke a word to a salesperson. That rate was dangerously low—it meant that in all probability customers were becoming frustrated wandering the stores, lost or confused or just in need of information, trying (and *trying*) to find a clerk with an answer. It also meant that employees couldn't have been spending much time actively selling anything. They were stocking the shelves and ringing up transactions and not finding time to do much in between. This was practically a guarantee that the store was underperforming. It was also a telling clue as to why.

Here's a final measure, a real simple one: waiting time. This, as we discuss elsewhere, is the single most important factor in customer satisfaction. But few retailers realize that when shoppers are made to wait too long in line (or anywhere else), their impression of overall service plunges. Busy executives hate to wait for anything, but some don't realize that normal people feel the same way. One housewares chain's vice president was startled when we showed him video in which a woman who had just spent twenty-two minutes shopping in his store joined a very long checkout line, stood there until it dawned on her that she was in cashier hell, and abandoned her full cart and exited the place. We weren't surprised—we see this happen all the time. We once did a job for a bank that was about to institute a policy where customers made to wait five minutes or more would receive $5. After studying the teller lines over the course of two days, we informed the client that this policy would cost them about triple what they had set aside. They dropped the plan and went to work on shortening the wait.

This final matter doesn't involve any particular way to measure a store, but it's a remarkable example of businessperson ignorance: They often don't really know who their shoppers are. I've already discussed the pet treats manufacturer whose product was typically stocked high on shelves, unaware that its main buyers were old people and children. We studied a chain of family-style restaurants whose outlets had too many tables for two and not enough tables for four, which caused headaches during busy times—all because no one had ever bothered to count the size of dining groups. In another family-style chain we studied, each restaurant devoted roughly 10 percent of its floor space to counter seating. During slow times it went unused because lone diners preferred tables, where they could read newspapers or magazines. During busy times it went unused because parties of two, three or four wanted to sit at tables. The counters were empty even as groups of diners stood in line waiting for tables.

The matter of retailers not knowing who shops in their stores comes up all the time. A newsstand in Greeley Square in New York City wanted to increase sales and planned to do so by expanding the space devoted to magazines. We pointed out that a large percentage of its customers were either Korean—the square borders on a large Korean enclave—or Hispanic. Stock Korean-language magazines (Korean papers already sold well) and soft drinks popular in the Latino market, we advised, and sales rose immediately.

This related issue comes up all the time in New York, Los Angeles and other big cities: foreign shoppers in need of a break from stores and restaurants. Almost no accommodation is made for Asian shoppers, despite their numbers and tendency to spend a lot of money on luxury goods. But there are no sizing conversion charts, no currency exchange rates posted, not even a little sign or two in Japanese or Korean telling shoppers which credit cards are accepted. Smart retailers would reward employees who learned a little Japanese, German, French or Spanish—even just a handful of phrases would make a difference, as anyone who has shopped in a foreign country would realize. Restaurants should have menus in Japanese and German on hand.

But it doesn't have to involve anything so exotic for retailers to be woefully clueless about who's in their stores. I loved visiting the national chain drugstore branch in Washington, D.C., where there was a large assortment of dye and other hair products for blonds—in a store where over 95 percent of shoppers are African-Americans. I also was amused in a Florida-based drugstore chain's Minneapolis branch, where a full assortment of suntan lotion was on prominent display—in October.

II

Walk Like an Egyptian:
The Mechanics of Shopping

The first principle behind the science of shopping is the simplest one: There are certain physical and anatomical abilities, tendencies, limitations and needs common to all people, and the retail environment must be tailored to these characteristics.

In other words, stores, banks, restaurants and other such spaces must be friendly to the specifications of the human animal. There are all the obvious differences in shoppers based on gender, age, income and tastes. But there are many, many more similarities. This fact, and the accompanying thought—that stores should reflect the nature of the beings who must use them—seems too obvious to bear mentioning, doesn't it? After all, who designs and plans and operates these premises but human beings, most of whom are also at one time or another shoppers themselves? You'd think it would be easy to get everything right.

Yet a huge part of what we do is uncover ways in which retail environments fail to recognize and accommodate how human machines are built and how our anatomical and physiological aspects determine what we do. I'm talking about the absolute basics here, such as the fact that we have only two hands, and that at rest they are situated approximately three feet off the floor. Or that our eyes focus on what is directly before us but also take in a periphery whose size is determined in part by environmental factors, and that we'd rather look at people than objects. Or that it is possible to anticipate and even determine how and where people will walk—that we go in predictable paths and speed up, slow down and stop in response to our surroundings.

The implications of all this are clear: Where shoppers go, what they see, and how they respond determine the very nature of their shopping experience. They will either see merchandise and signs clearly or they won't. They will reach objects easily or with difficulty. They will move through areas at a leisurely pace or swiftly—or not at all. And all of these physiological and anatomical factors come into play simultaneously, forming a complex matrix of behaviors which must be understood if the retail environment is to adapt itself successfully to the animal that shops.

The overarching lesson that we've learned from the science of shopping is this: Amenability and profitability are totally and inextricably linked. Take care of the former, in all its guises, and the latter is assured. Build and operate a retail environment that fits the highly particular needs of shoppers and you've created a successful store. In the five chapters that follow, we'll see how the most elemental issues—the holding capacity of the human hand, the limits to what a being in motion can read, even the physical needs of the nonshopper—go into determining the shopping experience.

The Twilight Zone

THREE

top.

Stay here with me a minute. Don't ask. Just watch.

I *know* we're standing in the middle of the parking lot. That's the point.

Do you notice how everybody's moving at a pretty brisk clip toward the store? Is it because they're all so darned excited to be going there? Well, maybe, but I've spent a lot of time watching people move through parking lots, and this is how they all do it—fast. A parking lot isn't the place for a leisurely stroll. It's not Fifth Avenue or even Main Street. It's speeding cars, exhaust fumes and asphalt, with the usual elements on top—rain, wind, cold, heat. Every parking lot in the world has terrible weather all the time.

Okay, so let's join everybody rushing for the store. What do you see ahead? Windows. And what's in them? Stuff. Or is it signs? Or is it stuff *and* signs? It's hard to tell, exactly, because of how the sunlight glares off the glass. Or because it's dark out and the lighting is too low. Most retailers don't change the lighting depending on whether it's day or night, meaning that visibility must be pretty bad during at least one of those periods, if not both.

For the sake of discussion, let's say we can tell what's in the windows: some kind of display—mannequins or a still life. Whatever it is, though, the scale is wrong. There are too many small things there that we can't quite see from this distance. Bear in mind, too, that the faster people walk, the narrower their field of peripheral vision becomes. But by the time we get close enough to see the goods or read the signs, we're in no mood to stop and look. We've got that good cardiovascular parking-lot stride going, and it's bringing us right into the entrance. So forget whatever it is those windows are meant to accomplish—when they face a parking lot, if the message in them isn't big and bold and short and simple, it's wasted.

Boom. We hit the doors and we're inside. Still got that momentum going, too. Have you ever seen anybody cross the threshold of a store and then screech to a dead stop the instant they're inside? Neither have I. Good way to cause a pileup. Come over here, stand with me now and watch the doors. What happens once the customers get inside? You can't see it, but they're busily making adjustments—simultaneously they're slowing their pace, adjusting their eyes to the change in light and scale, and craning their necks to begin taking in all there is to see. Meanwhile, their ears and noses and nerve endings are sorting out the rest of the stimuli—analyzing the sounds and smells, judging whether the store is warm or cold. There's a lot going on, in other words, and I can pretty much promise you this: These people are not truly in the store yet. You can see them, but it'll be a few seconds more before they're actually *here*. If you watch long enough you'll be able to predict exactly where most shoppers slow down and make the transition from being outside to being inside. It's at just about the same place for everybody, depending on the layout of the front of the store.

All of which means that whatever's in the zone they cross before making that transition is pretty much lost on them. If there's a display of merchandise, they're not going to take it in. If there's a sign, they'll probably be moving too fast to absorb what it says. If the sales staff hits them with a hearty "Can I help you?" the answer's going to be, "No, thanks," I guarantee it. Put a pile of fliers or a stack of shopping baskets just inside the door: Shoppers will barely see them, and will almost never pick them up. Move them ten feet in and the fliers and baskets will disappear. It's a law of nature—shoppers need a landing strip.

When I talk to clients they invariably point to our findings on the transition zone as among our most meaningful, useful work. It is also perhaps the most startling news we deliver. I think that's mostly because our counsel defies the most ingrained human yearnings about the front: We all want to be there, at the front of the pack, the head of the line, the top of the class. To the front-runner goes the spoils.

In the retail environment, however, up front is sometimes the last place you want to be. For instance, retailers will charge manufacturers for placing their name on the front door, which sounds like a smart use of the marketing dollar—everybody sees the front door. And then you realize that when shoppers approach a door, all they're looking for is a handle and some sign of whether to pull or push. We've yet to see a shopper stop his or her progress to read what's on a door. There's only one time when anyone pauses to study what's written there: when the store is closed. Which may be worth something, as marketing tools go, but not a lot.

Today many stores have automatic doors, which make life easier for customers, especially those with packages or baby strollers. But the effortlessness of entering only serves to enlarge the transition zone—there's nothing to even slow you down a little. Some stores, especially smaller ones, benefit from having the entrance provide more of a threshold experience, not less. Even a gestural one—a slightly creaky door or a squeaky hinge does the trick. Special lighting on the doorway also clearly marks the divider between out there and in here.

A big store can afford to waste some space up front. A smaller one can't. In either case, store merchandisers can do two sensible things where the transition zone is concerned: They can keep from trying to accomplish anything important there, and they can take steps to keep that zone as small as possible.

A good lesson in what *not* to do with the entrance and transition zone comes courtesy of a big, sophisticated company. In the early '80s,

Burger King was testing a new salad bar. To introduce it with a bang, they decided that they'd switch the entrances and exits on their test restaurant. Until then, the door closest to the parking lot was always the entrance. They turned that entrance into an exit and put the salad bar just behind the big window next to it, so you'd walk from your car, go to the old entrance, see the salad bar and be so tempted by it that when you entered—through the *new* entrance—you'd head straight for the lettuce.

But here's what happened: Customers went to the old entrance and tried to find the handle—which had been removed as part of the reconfiguration. They would then back up, scratch their heads and begin searching for a way to get into the place. They weren't looking at the salad bar—they were too busy looking for a door! And once they found it, and burst into the restaurant feeling hungry and frustrated, all they wanted to do was find the counter and order their usual burgers and fries. In that atmosphere, the salad bar never had a chance.

Another bad idea for the transition zone was invented at an athletic goods chain where management decreed that every incoming shopper had to be greeted by a salesclerk within five seconds of entering the store. Here's how that played in the real world: You'd walk in and come face-to-face with a lineup of eager clerks hovering just inside the entrance like vultures, ready to pounce with a hearty hello.

We discovered another misuse of the zone a few years ago, when we tested an interactive computerized information fixture that had been designed for Kmart by a division of IBM. It had a touch screen and a keyboard, and you'd ask it where men's underwear was, for example, and it would give you a map of the store and maybe a coupon for T-shirts or socks. A terrific idea, executed well. It helped customers and spared the store from having to pay someone to stand behind a desk and tell people where boys' sweaters were—seventy-two times a day.

It wasn't long, though, before store executives discovered a little glitch: Few shoppers used the fixtures. The problem was that no one admits, six steps into a store, that they don't know where they're going. At that point you haven't even looked around long enough to realize you're lost. Placing the computers too close to the door had turned them into very expensive pieces of electronic sculpture. The store gave up on them right away, but I'm certain they could have worked just fine—maybe a third of the way into the store, at about the point where customers really *do* realize they need help.

What *can* you do with the transition zone? You can greet customers—not necessarily steer them anywhere but say hello, remind them where they are, start the seduction. Security experts say that the easiest way to discourage shoplifting is to make sure staffers acknowledge the presence of every shopper with a simple hello. Sam Walton's homespun observation was that if you hire a sweet old lady just to say hello to incoming customers, none of them will dare steal.

You can offer a basket or a map or a coupon. There's a fancy store in Manhattan, Takashimaya, where the uniformed doorman proffers a handsomely printed pocket-size store directory as he ushers you in. Just to the right of the entrance, within the transition zone, is the store's flower department. As you enter, you see it from the corner of your eye, but you don't usually stop in—instead, you think, Hmm, flowers, good idea, I'll get them on my way out. Which makes perfect sense, because you wouldn't want to shop the rest of the store carrying a bouquet of damp flowers.

Right inside the door at The Gap and its younger, trendier sibling, Old Navy, there's what's known as a power display—a huge, horizontal bank of sweaters, for instance, or jeans that acts as a barrier to slow shoppers down. Kind of like a speed bump. It also functions as a huge billboard. It doesn't necessarily say, "Shop me." It says, "Pause a second to look at what you're walking in on."

Another solution, which I saw at Filene's Basement, is to totally break the transition zone rule. Not just break it, but smash it. There, just inside the entrance, they've placed a large bin of merchandise that's been deeply discounted, a deal so good it stops shoppers in their tracks. That teaches us something about rules—you have to either follow them or break them with gusto. Just ignoring a rule or bending it a little is usually the worst thing you can do.

I'd love to see someone try this out-of-the-box strategy: Instead of pulling back from the entrance, push the store out beyond it—start the selling space out in the parking lot. After all, football fans make elaborate use of parking lots in even the worst weather, barbecuing and eating and drinking and socializing on asphalt. Drive-in movies everywhere are turned over to flea markets during daylight hours, proof that people will comfortably shop al fresco. Some supermarkets will bring seasonal merchandise out into the parking lot during summer; I visited one in a seashore resort that had all barbecue supplies, beach toys, suntan lotion and rubber sandals in a tent outfitted with a clerk and a cash register—allowing beachgoers to pull up, grab a few necessities and drive away, all without having to drag their sandy selves through the food aisles and long checkout lines. Pushing the store outside also begins to address an interesting situation in America—the fact that so much of the country has been turned into parking lots. Buildings can be put to a variety of uses—a clothing store can sell electronics or groceries or even be converted into office space. But our vast plains of asphalt will require more imaginative thinking.

Our findings that being first isn't necessarily best extend beyond the transition zone and into the store proper. In any section of a store, the first product customers see isn't always going to have an advantage. Sometimes, just the opposite will happen. Allowing some space between the entrance of a store and a product gives it more time in the shopper's eye as he or she approaches it. It builds a little visual anticipation. Someone making a study of, say, the computer section of a store is highly unlikely to stop at the very first model and buy it with no further comparisons. By the time he reaches the midpoint of the computer section, though, he may feel confident and informed enough to decide. At trade shows, the booths just inside the door may seem most desirable, but they're pretty bad locations. Visitors zoom past them on their way into the hall, or, even worse, they arrange to meet friends by the entrance, thereby creating the (false) impression that there's a crowd at the first booth, thereby scaring off genuine clients. Besides, just inside the door is usually drafty. It feels as though you're in the vestibule.

Cosmetics and beauty product firms don't usually want to occupy the first counter inside the entrance of a department store's makeup bazaar—they know that women, when reinventing themselves before a mirror, prefer a little privacy. That's not the only reason to wish for a little peace and quiet. If you were one of the two major players in the home hair-coloring market, you'd want the best position possible in drugstores. Now, young women tend to buy hair color as a fashion statement—they've got some occasion coming up that requires a little extra glamour, or they've been wanting to change something so they'll try a new shade. Older women, however, buy it as a staple—they've been using a particular color for fifteen years now, and more gray is coming in every day, so it becomes as regular a purchase as soap. As a result of that difference, older shoppers just find their color, grab it and go, while younger ones need to study the rack and the packaging awhile before they buy. In hair care, for example, we found that older women shop one-third fewer products than their younger counterparts, 2.1 to 3.1. So in a store where younger shoppers predominate, hair color will do best away from the bustle and the crowding, which usually means away from the front of the store. If most shoppers are older women, however, closer to the entrance is better for hair color—these shoppers won't be browsing for long anyway.

Finally, there's a famous (around our offices) story about a very elaborate and costly supermarket display for chips and pretzels—a handsome fixture featuring the cartoon character of Chester the Cheetah, who, aided by a motion-detector device, would say, "If you're looking to feed your face, you're in the right place" every time a shopper walked past. The fixture's owner paid a great deal of money to have the displays stationed up front in some supermarkets. They were effective—so much so that the greetings ran constantly, which soon maddened the cashiers who had to listen to the drawling voice for eight hours straight. Before long, at least one market's employees solved the problem neatly—they disconnected Chester, rendering him instantly agreeable but forever mute.

You Need Hands

FOUR

I t's a chilly day and the shopper is a woman. What does that tell us?

It says that at the very least she's carrying a handbag, and that she's wearing a coat, which she'll probably want to remove once she's inside the store, meaning she'll have to carry that, too. God gave her two good hands. But she's shopping with one.

If she selects something, the free hand carries it. Now she's down to no hands. Maybe, if it's small and light, she can tuck the purchase under one arm. Perhaps she'll sling the handbag over a shoulder or forearm. Then she'll have—let's call it a hand and a quarter. If she picks one more thing, though, she'll run out of hands. Only an extremely motivated buyer will persevere. Human anatomy has just declared this shopping spree over.

This is a classic moment in the science of shopping. The physical fact (most shoppers have two hands) is fairly well known. But the implications of that fact go unimagined, undetected, unconsidered, unaccommodated, unacknowledged. Ignored.

I first paid close attention to the hand-allotment issue while studying a newsstand at that great crossroads of humanity, New York's Grand Central Station. We pointed our cameras at the stand and watched it during the busiest times, the morning and evening rush hours.

The success of the business depended on one crucial task—its ability to process large numbers of transactions during the periods when everybody is in a hurry, either rushing from train to job in the morning or from job to train at night. Commuters on the run glance over at the newsstand to see how crowded it is. If it looks as though they can breeze in, buy a paper or magazine or cigarettes or gum, and then be on their way, they'll stop. If it looks swamped with customers waiting to pay and nervously checking their watches, they'll keep going. They'll say to themselves, Too much of a hassle, I'll miss my train, it'll be faster to get it elsewhere.

The other, related fact of newsstand life we noticed was that every customer had one hand already occupied, either with a briefcase or a tote bag or a purse or a lunch. Almost no one goes to work empty-handed nowadays. When you think about it, it's a rare moment in the modern American's life when both hands are completely free. Even the ubiquitous backpacks and fanny packs that many of us now use don't free our hands—they just enable us to carry more than before. Humans are like two-legged pack animals, and it amazes me what we feel we need to have with us everywhere we go.

The final factor in our study was the stand itself, which was of typical design—a low shelf where the day's newspapers go, above which were racks holding magazines, above which were shelves holding candy and chewing gum and mints, and inside the circular structure, above it all, the cashiers.

Thanks to the videotape, we could break each transaction down into its smallest components. Here's what we saw: Carrying your briefcase, you'd approach the stand, bend and pick up, say, a newspaper. Then you'd straighten up and brandish the paper so the clerk could see your choice. At that point you'd either put your briefcase on the floor or you'd put the paper under your briefcase arm, and, with your free hand, you'd hold out the money. (If you were a last-minute type, you'd have to reach into your pocket, find the money and hand it over.) You would then stand tilting slightly toward the clerk, waiting with free hand out-stretched for your change. The change goes into the pocket and you pick up your briefcase—or, the paper goes from the briefcase armpit to the free hand—and then you turn and depart, squeezing through the rest of the throng trying to buy something.

The stand's designer obviously believed that the best possible structure was the one that displayed the most merchandise. Maybe the stand's owner believed that, too. But from the customer's point of view, the design was all wrong. There should have been a shelf at about elbow height—someplace where customers could rest their briefcases or purses or their purchases while digging out their money and waiting for change. A counter, in other words.

Instead, the only horizontal surface was at about shin height, which displayed newspapers just fine but turned each transaction into an awkward ballet starring a tilted one-handed commuter. As a result, the typical purchase involved more steps than were needed, and so required more time to complete—even split seconds add up—which in turn limited the number of transactions possible during rush hour. Which caused congestion, scared away customers and ultimately cost the newsstand sales. A better design—one that took human anatomy into consideration—might have displayed less merchandise but accommodated more customers.

That woman I began this chapter by describing could have been shopping at a big discount drugstore. It was during a study we did for one such chain that we thought of one simple but very effective solution to the hand shortage.

The eureka moment came on a sultry August night in my office as I listened to the Yankees on the radio and watched videotape of people shopping in the drugstore. I was viewing footage from the camera we had trained on the checkout line, witnessing a shopper trying to juggle several small bottles and boxes without dropping one. That's when it dawned on me: The poor guy needed a basket.

Why hadn't he taken one? The store had plenty of them, placed right inside the door. Maybe people don't associate drugstores with shopping baskets. Perhaps they come in thinking they need just one or two items and only later do they realize they should pick up a few more things. The biggest culprit, of course, was the transition zone—the baskets were so close to the entrance that incoming shoppers blew right by without even seeing them down there. I immediately began to scan all three days' worth of checkout line video and saw that fewer than 10 percent of customers used baskets, meaning there were quite a few amateur jugglers shopping at the store. And, I thought, if someone gave these people baskets, they'd probably buy more things! They wouldn't buy fewer items, that's certain. But here we were, allowing the arm and hand capacity of human beings to determine, ultimately, how much money they spent.

We suggested that all employees be trained to offer baskets to any customer seen holding three or more items. Management gave it a shot. And because people tend to be gracious when someone tries to help, shoppers almost unanimously accepted the baskets. And as basket use rose instantly, so did the size of the average sale—up just like that. In retail, the easiest way to make more money is to sell more stuff to your existing customer base.

The issue of shopping baskets is a perfect example of something I mentioned earlier, the complex matrix of anatomical traits and human behaviors that determine how we shop. In a very successful bookstore near my office, there is a pile of shopping baskets in the usual erroneous place—in a corner just inside the door. Transition zone aside, this is bad planning for another reason, one that shows how totally retailers fail to comprehend what shoppers do in stores. This failure is remarkable, considering that businesspeople are themselves shoppers at least some of the time and so should be able to see the world from that perspective. Instead, there's a fatal disconnect.

Judging by where the baskets are kept here, you'd think that retailers think that shoppers enter bookstores saying to themselves, Well, today I plan on buying four books, a box of arty greeting cards and a magazine, and so first thing I will take a basket to hold all my purchases. Whereas common sense tells us that people don't work that way—more likely somebody walks in thinking about one book, finds it, then stumbles over another that looks worthwhile. In such moments the very heart of retailing lies, and if shoppers suddenly ceased to buy on impulse, believe me, our entire economy would collapse. For many stores, add-on and impulse sales mean the difference between black ink and red.

Anyway, when our book shopper stumbles upon a second worthy volume, she then begins wishing she had a basket to make life a little easier. And if at that exact moment a basket suddenly materialized—in plain sight, and easy to reach *without stooping*—then she would probably take one. And then, perhaps, go on to buy books number three and four. Maybe even a bookmark.

The lesson seems clear: Baskets should be scattered throughout the store, wherever shoppers might need them. In fact, if all the stacks of baskets in America were simply moved from the front of the store to the rear they would be instantly more effective, since many shoppers don't begin seriously considering merchandise until they've browsed a bit of it. The stack should be no lower than five feet tall, to make sure the baskets are visible to all, yes, but also to ensure that no shopper need stoop to get one, since shoppers hate bending, especially when their hands are full.

The baskets themselves also need to be rethought. This store uses shallow, hard plastic ones with hinged steel handles, the same as supermarkets and convenience stores offer. They're perfect if you're buying bottles, jars or crushable items, but make no sense for books, office supplies or clothes. When the contents grow heavy the handles become uncomfortable in your hand, but you can't sling the basket over your arm or shoulder, as common sense might wish you could. As a result, you don't want to let that basket get too full. How do we usually carry books? In bags, tote bags especially. A rack of canvas or nylon tote bags would be much better here, and would have the added advantage itself of being salable merchandise. The clerk could unload the bag, total up the damages, ask if the customer wants to buy the tote, and then reload everything and save on plastic to boot.

The cleverest use of baskets I've seen yet is at Old Navy in Manhattan. I always take visiting retailers to see that store—it's one of the liveliest, most energetic shopping experiences in the city. As soon as you step inside there's a gregarious, smiling employee greeting you and proffering a black mesh tote bag to carry your purchases. The bags are cheaper, lighter and easier to store than plastic baskets, and they look a whole lot better. In fact, when you bring yours to the checkout, the cashier will ask if you want to buy the bag, and a fair number of people say yes, adding one final sale at the last possible moment.

The least clever use of baskets was one I witnessed in a southern department store during Christmas season. There was a large rack of mesh totes perfectly positioned just inside the entrance. But some merchandising wizard decided to place in front of it an even larger display of stuffed Santas—rendering the bags totally invisible to entering shoppers. (Exiting shoppers saw them just fine.) I don't know how many Santas were sold, but it couldn't have been enough to offset that bad decision.

When we studied its stores, the tabletops maker and retailer Pfaltzgraff was already providing baskets as well as shopping carts to its customers. But at checkout, we noticed that many of the carts were filled to capacity with dishes and bowls, and so on. The company immediately replaced the carts with new ones that were roughly 40 percent larger. Just as fast, the average sales per customer rose.

This all serves as a reminder of one of the most crucial big-picture issues in the world of retailing: You can't know how much shoppers will buy until you've made the shopping experience as comfortable and easy and practical as possible.

There's a rather elaborate way of keeping customers' hands free that I'd love to see some retailer try. This plan would keep shoppers feeling 100 percent unburdened until it was too late—after they had reached the exits.

The idea would be to create a combination coat check–package call system. Customers could unload all encumbrances as soon as they enter the store. And instead of carrying their selections around with them, they'd instruct salesclerks to dispatch the bags and boxes to the will-call desk near the exit. After a full session of vigorous, hands-free shopping, the customer would head for the door, pick up coat and hat and purchases, and be gone, into car or taxi or waiting limousine.

Sometimes even that isn't enough. The big souvenir shop at Disney-land is still working on this problem. There, all day long the store is vir-tually empty, since visitors wisely don't want to shop and then have to lug their purchases around the park all day. But by 4:30 p.m. it's a mad-house of souvenir lust. A will-call desk was established so that shoppers could buy in the morning, leave the store empty-handed and then drop by the will-call desk to retrieve their purchases at day's end. The only problem is that a great many shoppers forget to come by for their pur-chases. Perhaps the store could deliver them to the buyers' hotels.

My fullest vision of such a service was one I suggested to Blooming-dale's. In the flagship store in Manhattan, the eighth floor is not terribly well suited to selling, owing to its hard-to-reach location. So I suggested that the floor be turned into a kind of semi-private retreat for better cus-tomers, complete with attended restrooms, ATMs, a cafe, a concierge and other similar amenities—including, of course, the coat check–will-call desk. If shoppers are just visiting New York, delivery could even be made to their hotels. In fact, I envisioned that membership to this semi-private club could be sold to hotels, which would then pass along the benefits to their guests. This kind of service would be most profitable on an even bigger scale. Someday soon a mall or shopping center developer will institute such a system to serve all tenants, doing his part to drive up sales—and, of course, his own take, too.

It's hard to overemphasize the importance of the hand issue to the world of shopping. A store can be the grooviest place ever, offering the finest/cheapest/sexiest goods to be had, but if the shopper can't pick them up, it's all for naught. In Chapter 12 I explain the crucial matter of touch, trial and other sensory aspects of shopping. If shoppers can't reach out and feel certain goods, they just won't buy. So it's not simply a matter of making sure shoppers can carry what they wish to take. They won't even get close to making that decision if their hands are full. It's why, in many cases, flat tabletop displays are better for showing apparel than hangers on racks: It's a struggle to examine something on a hanger if you've got only one hand free, whereas you can place your burdens on the tabletop and unfurl that sweater to get a good, close look and feel.

The most amusing manifestation of the hand issue was in a super-market I visited. Like just about every retailer in America today, this market had decided to put in a coffee bar, where shoppers could sit and drink, if they wished. This wasn't the first coffee shop I'd seen in a su-permarket, but it was the first one to truly understand how the whole thing should work: It had also put in cup holders on the shopping carts, meaning that you could drink and drive. That clever little touch sells coffee, I'll bet.

How to Read a Sign

FIVE

"**W**ell," he says to me, "what do you think?"

And with that, the graphic design executive unveils the sign that's about to go into five hundred or so stores.

I'm seated in a comfortable chair, in a climate-controlled conference room with perfect lighting. The sign is right before my nose, at the ideal viewing distance, beautifully printed on expensive paper, which has been exquisitely matted by professionals. There's a kind of hush all over the room.

"Gee," I answer, "I don't know what I think."

Worried glances all around. They're not worried about me—they're worried *for* me.

"What do you mean you don't know?" the executive asks. "You're *supposed* to know."

And that's when I try to explain.

I start by saying that unless every customer is going to come upon the sign under the exact same conditions that I first saw it, it's impossible for me to know if it's the greatest sign ever designed or a tragic waste of time, space and money. I attempt to remind everybody that people in stores or restaurants or banks are almost never still; they're moving from one place to another. And they're not intent on reading signs—in fact, they're usually doing something else entirely, like trying to find socks, or seeing which line is shortest, or deciding whether to have the burger or the chicken. And there's that brand-new sign somewhere in the distance, off at a sharp angle, partially hidden by a tall man's head, and the lighting isn't even so hot, and anyway somebody's talking to the customer and distracting her.

In other words, I end by saying, showing me a sign in a conference room, while ideal from the graphic designer's point of view, is the absolute worst way to see if it's any good.

To say whether a sign or any in-store media works or not, there's only one way to assess it—in place. On the floor of the store.

Even there it's no picnic. First you've got to measure how many people looked at it. Then you've got to be able to say whether they looked long enough to read what it says, because if they're not reading it, even the best sign won't work. Now, the difference between an inadvertent glance at a sign and a thorough reading might be two or three seconds. So you can see what kind of challenge this is for our researchers. They've got to discreetly position themselves just so, behind the sign itself, and then watch a shopper's smallest eye movements while simultaneously keeping track of the stopwatch, just to be able to say with absolute scientific certainty that this man focused on that sign for four seconds, and then his eyes shifted to that poster and looked at it for three seconds. We watch shopper after shopper for hours on end, hundreds of people, thousands of minutes, and then assemble all our findings before we can say whether a sign is any good.

Go try. It ain't easy.

But there's no other way. As far as I know, we're the only firm in the country doing this kind of work. There are companies that will measure sign readability by putting subjects into high-tech helmets that measure the smallest eyeball movements, then holding signs before them. But even that won't tell you if you've put the right sign in the wrong place, which happens all the time (and which, by the way, is actually worse than putting a so-so sign in the perfect place). And it surely can't predict whether shoppers will read and respond to a sign on the floor of a store, where distractions abound.

Once you know whether people are reading a sign, you can begin to measure its influence on their behavior. But not until. So the first thing you've got to do is get the hell out of that conference room.

The most common mistake in the design and placement of signs and other message media is the thought that they're going into a store. When we're talking signs, it's no longer a store. It's a three-dimensional TV commercial. It's a walk-in container for words and thoughts and messages and ideas.

People step inside this container, and it tells them things. If everything's working right, the things they are told grab their attention and induce them to look and shop and buy and maybe return another day to shop and buy some more. They are told what they might buy, and where it is kept, and why they might buy it. They're told what the merchandise can do for them and when and how it can do it.

A great big three-dimensional walk-in TV commercial.

And just as if scripting and directing a TV commercial, the job is to figure out what to say and when and how to say it.

First you have to get your audience's attention. Once you've done that, you have to present your message in a clear, logical fashion—the beginning, then the middle, then the ending. You have to deliver the information the way people absorb it, a bit at a time, a layer at a time, and in the proper sequence. If you don't get their attention first, nothing that follows will register. If you tell too much too soon, you'll overload them and they'll give up. If you confuse them, they'll ignore the message altogether.

This has always been so. The main reason it's so important today is that more and more purchasing decisions are being made on the premises of the store itself. Customers have disposable income and open minds, and they're giving in to their impulses. The impact of brand-name marketing and traditional advertising is diffuse now because we all absorb so much of it. The role of merchandising has never been greater. Products now live or die by what happens on the selling floor. You can't waste a chance to tell shoppers something you want them to know.

And shoppers are more pressed for time than ever. They're not dawdling the way they used to. They've grown accustomed to stores where everything for sale is on open display, and they expect all the information they need will be out in the open, too. Nobody wants to wait for a clerk to point them in the right direction, or explain some new product. Nobody can find a clerk anyway. Once upon a time you went into a coffee shop and the only thing to read was the menu and the *Daily News*. Now you go into even the smallest Starbucks and there are eleven distinct signing positions communicating everything from the availability of nonfat eggnog to the tie-in with Oprah's Book Club.

So you can't just look around your store, see where there are empty spots on the walls and put the signs there. You can't simply clear a space on a counter and dump all your in-store media. Every store is a collection of zones, and you've got to map them out before you can place a single sign. You've got to get up and walk around, asking yourself with every step: What will shoppers be doing *here*? How about *here*? Where will their eyes be focused when they stand here? And what will they be thinking about over *there*? In this zone people will be walking fast, so a message has to be short and punchy—arresting. Over there, they'll be browsing around, so you can deliver a little more detail. In this area they'll be thinking about, oh, let's say we're standing near the motor oil shelf, so they'll be thinking about their cars. So maybe it's a good opportunity to tell them something about replacement windshield wipers. Over here by the registers they will be standing still for a minute and a half, a perfect window for a longer message. And then they'll be on their way out of the store, but you can use the exit path to give them a thought for the road.

Each zone is right for one kind of message and wrong for all others. Putting a sign that requires twelve seconds to read in a place where customers spend four seconds is just slightly more effective than putting it in your garage.

I'm forever walking around and adding to my mental list of places shoppers stand around doing nothing, where some message might be appropriate. One struck me the other day: In a shoe department you tell the clerk what you want and he or she goes off to find your size. At that point you've already examined all the shoes, so what do you do? It's probably a good spot for a sign promoting other merchandise. You'd probably welcome something to read right then and there. Maybe something about handbags.

Here's another good spot for signs currently being neglected: escalators. That struck me as I ascended from the tracks on the underground, in London. There you spend a lot of time rising slowly.

It isn't enough simply to figure out the general vicinity where a sign should go. We once studied shoppers who came upon a banner hanging directly over the cash/wrap area of a store. Good placement, no? No. A very low percentage of shoppers even saw it. Nobody stands around in a store looking straight up in the air. We recommended that the banner be moved four feet away, and the number of people who saw it doubled. When it comes to positioning a sign, the difference between an ideal viewing spot and a terrible one is often just a few feet. For maximum exposure, a sign should interrupt the existing natural sight lines in any given area. So you've got to stand in a spot and determine: Where am I looking? That's where the sign goes. It's no surprise that the number-one thing people look at is other people. That's why some of the most effective signs in fast-food restaurants are the ones sitting atop the cash registers—more or less at the level of the cashier's face. Smart sign placement simply tries to interrupt the shopper's line of vision and intercept her gaze.

Sometimes, though, you've got to get creative with message placement. Toro made an in-store video to promote its automatic mulching mower. Naturally, it was going into home and garden-supply stores, but where? In the mower section? Where shoppers would see the monitors going but then realize that they'd have to stand still for ten minutes to watch the whole thing, and not only that but they'd have to stand in the middle of an aisle and quite possibly get mowed down (and mulched) by shoppers on their way to barbecue accessories? Instead, the video went into repair department waiting areas, where it played before cap-tive audiences grateful for even the slightest distraction. Everyone who visits the repair department of a home and garden-supply store is going to buy a new mower *someday*. For some reason, we find that even retail-ers who pile on the signs elsewhere will fail to appreciate the possibili-ties for communication in waiting areas, where people tend to be bored to tears. We once studied a car dealership's service area waiting room that offered not one word of reading material—not a single piece of promotional literature. Not an issue of *Car and Driver* or *Road and Track*. Not even an old *Reader's Digest*.

Nobody studies signs like the fast-food industry. Even if you don't plan on owning a Burger God franchise, it's instructive to see how they do it.

They realize that you can put an effective sign in a window or just in-side a doorway, for example, but it has to be something a customer can read in an instant. Just two or three words. We've timed enough people to know that such signs get, on average, less than two seconds of expo-sure per customer.

I was once asked to evaluate a door sign that had ten words on it.

"How much can you read in a second and a half?" I asked the designer.

"Three or four words, I guess," he admitted.

"Hmm," I replied.

Fast-food restaurants used to hang all kinds of signs and posters and dangling mobiles in and around doorways to catch customers' atten-tion fast until studies showed that nobody read them. When you enter a fast-food restaurant, you are looking for one of two things: the counter or the bathroom.

There's no point in placing a sign for people on their way to the bath-room to see. They've got more important things on their minds. But a sign facing people as they leave the bathroom works just fine.

As people approach the counter, they're trying to decide what they're going to order. In the fast-food arena, that means they're look-ing for the big menu board. But they're not going to read every word on it—they're just going to scan until they see what they're looking for. If

they're regular customers (as most customers are), they probably already know what they want and aren't even looking at the menu.

If there's a long line, customers will have lots of time to study the
menu board and anything else that's visible. After the order is placed
the menu board and counter area signs still receive prolonged customer
attention. McDonald's found that 75 percent of customers read the
menu board *after* they order, while they wait for their food—during the
"meal prep" period, which averages around a minute and forty seconds.
That's a long time, and that's when people will read almost anything—
they've already paid and gotten their change, so they're not preoccupied. That's a perfect window for a longer message, something you
want them to know for the next time they come.

Then they either leave or they go to the condiments. You can place
promotional materials over the condiment bar, though it's pointless to
advertise burgers there—it's too late. But it's a good opportunity to tell
diners something about dessert. This is a lesson in the logical sequencing
of signs and fixtures. There's no point in telling shoppers about something when it's too late for them to act on it. For instance, it's a good idea
to position signs for shoppers standing in line to pay, but it's a bad idea if
those signs promote merchandise that's kept in the rear of the store.

After the condiment bar, diners go to their tables to eat. A few years
ago there was a move in the fast-food business to banish all dining area
clutter—the hanging signs, mobiles, posters and "table tents" (those
three-sided cardboard things that keep the salt and pepper company).
That was a mistake, it turned out, one that was made because the store
planners failed to notice what was going on in their own restaurants,
specifically the social composition of the typical fast-food meal.

We tested table tents in two types of restaurant—the "family"
restaurant and the fast-food establishment. In the family place, the table
tents were read by 2 percent of diners.

At the fast-food joints, 25 percent of diners read them.

The reason for that dramatic difference was simple: At family restaurants, people usually eat in twos, threes or fours (or families!). They're
too busy talking to notice the signs. But the typical fast-food customer is
eating alone. He's dying for some distraction. Give him a tray liner with

lots of print and he'll read that. Give him the first chapter of the forth-coming Stephen King novel, and he'll read *that*. One of our clients, Sub-way, was printing napkins with the boast of how much healthier their sandwiches were than burgers. Go a step farther, we advised—print the napkins with a chart comparing grams of fat. In the seating area of a fast-food restaurant you can practically guarantee that customers will read messages that would be ignored anywhere else. There's an obvious role model: the back of the cereal box.

You can see, then, how a fast-food restaurant is zoned: The deeper in you are, the longer the message can be. Two or three words at the door; a napkin filled with small type at the tables. I passed a fast-food place the other day with a perfect window sign. It bore this eloquent phrase: "Big Burger." Only when you entered the place did you come upon another sign explaining the details of the teaser. (They were selling . . . big bur-gers.) That's smart sign design—breaking the message into two or three parts, and communicating it a little at a time as the customer gets far-ther into the store. Thinking that every sign must stand on its own and contain an entire message is not only unimaginative, it's ignorant of how human brains operate. It even takes the fun out of signs—remem-ber how the sequencing made those old Burma Shave billboards such icons of American humor?

Another lesson in sign language comes courtesy of the United States Postal Service, for which we performed a huge study to help design the post office of the future.

In one of the prototype stores we studied, hanging behind the cashiers were large banners promoting various services. Fourteen per-cent of customers read those banners, our researchers found, for an average of 5.4 seconds each. There were also posters pushing stamp collecting hung on the walls to either side of the cashiers. Fourteen per-cent of customers read those, too, for an average of 4.4 seconds each.

Which is pretty good in the sign world. And not unexpected, be-cause when you're in line at the post office, what else is there to do? The area behind or to the side of the cashiers is almost always the hottest signage real estate.

The post office also hung signs meant to be seen by customers using the writing tables. Those signs were read by just 4 percent of customers, for an average of 1.5 seconds each. Mobiles hanging over the weighing stations were read by just one percent of customers, for an average of 3.3 seconds each. Which was no surprise—when you're writing or weighing, you're not reading. Those signs were as good as nonexistent.

Banks also expend a lot of energy trying to figure out which signs work and which don't. Banks, fast-food restaurants and the post office have this in common: lots of customers standing still and facing the same direction—ideal opportunities for communication. The difference is that banks are some of the worst offenders in the art and science of sign placement. I can take you to branches of the world's biggest and most sophisticated financial institutions where placement of merchandising and informational materials is laughably inept. There are church bake sales and kiddie lemonade stands that exhibit better signage sense than some banks I can name. Five minutes from my office is a branch of the Chase Manhattan Bank where you can find this merchandising innovation: a round table covered by the cheapest blue plastic tablecloth you've ever seen, atop which were tossed some brochures for car loans and mortgages, joined by a TV monitor, once intended perhaps for showing in-branch videos but now unused and completely covered by a blanket of dust. The table was jammed into a corner in the front of the bank, just a few feet from the customer service desk. It's so bad that it's funny. A lot of bank signage can claim that distinction.

A California bank client decided—correctly—that it would be smart to promote its new free checking policy by hanging outdoor banners visible from the heavily traveled road beyond its door. And then it decided—incorrectly—that the banners should say, "Please come in and ask a friendly banker to explain our wonderful new free checking policy" or something to that effect. Drivers would have had to pull over to read the sign, it was so verbose. On a highway, two words—maybe something catchy, like "Free Checking"—must be made to suffice.

We did a study for a Canadian bank that had just installed some very sophisticated backlit displays on the customer writing tables. These exhibits detailed the various services and investments the bank offered.

They were quite beautiful. Nobody read them.

Again, when you're filling out a deposit slip or endorsing checks, you're concentrating too hard to think about anything else. And once you've filled out the paperwork, you race to get into line.

We delivered our sad findings, and the bank's president said, "God, you just saved us from wasting about a million bucks on those damn things." He still spent the million bucks on in-branch media, of course—but on things that would make a difference.

It was also at a bank that we discovered one of our easiest and most effective fixes ever. We were hired to study all aspects of a bank branch, including the large rack that held brochures describing the money market funds, certificates of deposit, car loans and other services and investments offered. The rack was hung on the wall to the left of the entrance, so you'd pass it on your way in.

Everyone passed within inches of it. No one touched it.

Again, the reason seems obvious: You enter a bank because you have an important task to perform. Nobody goes into a bank to browse. And until you perform that task, you're not interested in reading or hearing about anything else. The fact that the rack was to the left side of the doorway, when most people walk to the right, only made it worse.

We took that rack and moved it inside, so that customers would pass it as they exited rather than entered, and we had a tracker stand there and watch. With no other change, the number of people who saw the rack increased fourfold, and the number of brochures taken increased dramatically. Banks aren't the only place where task-oriented behavior must be reckoned with. We enter a drugstore intent on seeing the pharmacist and turning over our prescription, and we don't notice a single sign or display we pass until that mission is accomplished. Then we've got some time to kill, only we're in the rear of the store, and all the signs and fixtures are positioned to face shoppers approaching from the front. Or we've gone to the post office for a roll of stamps, and we're not slowing down until we've secured our position in line. Or we're at the convenience store, hot on the trail of barbecue starter fluid, and until we're sure they have it, we won't be distracted by anything else. In all those instances, it's futile to try to tell shoppers anything until after they've completed their task. So in that drugstore, for instance, two separate signage strategies must be mapped out—one for shoppers walking front to back, and the other for shoppers walking back to front, from the pharmacist to the front.

At a bank client's branch we studied there was a standing rack of brochures located in the general vicinity of the teller lines. But it was positioned a little too far away—customers standing behind the ropes could barely read the brochure titles, let alone grab them.

"Whose job is it to set up the ropes and stanchions and the brochure rack?" we asked the branch manager.

"Well," he said, "the cleaning staff mops up every night, and when they're through they put all that stuff back on the floor." And sure enough, that cleaning crew didn't know squat about signage.

There's one arena of American life where sign design and placement isn't just a somewhat important issue, it's a matter of life or death. I'm speaking about our roads, especially our interstate highway system. There, signs are almost as important as surface and lighting to maintaining safe, well-ordered conditions. As a result, engineers make sure to get the signage right. The principles seem simple enough: no extra words; the right sign at the right place; enough signs so that drivers don't feel ignored or underinformed; not so many signs that there's clutter or confusion. The fact that you can be driving in a place you've never been and know for sure that you're heading in the right direction—without stopping for directions or even slowing down to read a message—is a testament to the power of a smart system of signs.

Look at the most common road signs in the country: Stop and One Way. A big red octagon with bold white capital letters—what else could it mean? If you couldn't read it, you'd still stop. One Way is a perfect marriage of words and symbol—you catch it from the corner of your eye and you know what it means. The arrow keeps you going in the right direction without forcing you to slow down or even pause to read it. On the road we use a vocabulary of icons, the universal language, that tells us what we need to know without words. When you see a sign with a gas pump, or a fork and spoon, or a wheelchair, you understand at a glance. That's the best way to deliver information to people in motion. Also on road signs, the technical aspects are usually perfect—the color combination provides enough contrast, the lettering is large, the lighting is good and the positioning is just so.

Back in my urban geographer days I took part in a study of the directional signs in the underground concourse at Rockefeller Plaza in New York City. Down there you have no bearings except for what signs provide, so they're very important. On film, we saw how people moved along until they began to worry that they were getting lost, or until they saw a fork up ahead where they'd have to choose a direction. Then you'd see their heads begin to swivel and their pace begin to slow. Just before that spot, then, was the logical place for a directional sign—something to head off their confusion and worry.

We also saw that their main concern was not to bump into other people while walking. So if they had to really scour the area for a sign, or if the type was so small that they had to get real close to read it, or the sign was small or badly placed, walkers would be torn between looking at the sign and watching where they were going. Anytime pedestrians had to slow down or stop, we concluded, it was because the signs had failed to do their job. That's what really taught me the similarity between people walking and drivers driving—the best sign in either case is one you can read fast, and positioned so you can read it while moving. And the only way to achieve that, in most instances, is to break the information down into pieces and lay them out one at a time, in a logical, orderly sequence.

Of course, the only way we discovered all that was by watching lots and lots of pedestrians move through the space. Otherwise, all the signage decisions would have been made by the concourse planners themselves—the only people in the world who *didn't* need signs to find their way around down there.

I'm still trapped in this conference room.

So if I can't get out, I'll make life for this sign as difficult as possible. I'll put it on the floor, leaning against the wall, then I'll take ten paces away and see how it looks. I'll stand practically alongside it and see if it catches my eye. I'll stride by it at my normal pace and see if it registers. I'll turn down the lights. If the sign doesn't work in an imperfect world, it doesn't work. Believe me, real life is even tougher on signs than I am.

We're now arriving at a state of communication overload, and most of the problem is due to commercial messages. Little advertising stickers stuck to your apples and pears are either the cleverest thing ever or the most obnoxious defacement of God's bounty, depending on your point of view. There are too many words telling us too many things, and people are getting mad as hell and they're not going to read it anymore. Even as some opportunities for communication are being missed, many are being cluttered with so many messages that none stands out. One display or sign too many and you've created a black hole where no communication manages to get through.

Here's a personal example. I spend a lot of time in airports waiting for planes, and like most road warriors I work while I wait. Lately, though, my concentration is always being broken by Airport TV—the CNN-produced programming for air travelers. Try as I do, I can't find a way to have it turned off. Even when I'm the only person in the gate lounge, it must remain on. And so I burn quietly and vow never to watch CNN again. But there is a place in airports where even the busiest road warrior stands around dumbly waiting rather than working: near the baggage carousel, praying for luggage. There, before the suitcases begin to roll, we're all grateful to get a little Wolf Blitzer.

In general, the state of commercial messages is haphazard. Half of all signs that are shipped to stores, banks and restaurants never even make it onto the floor, according to one study. All over America, retail managers end long, tiring days by sitting in storage rooms, unloading huge cartons of signs and other point-of-purchase materials sent by a merchandising manager who may never even have seen their particular store. Believe me, those tired, overworked store managers aren't agonizing for too long over which sign goes where.

Conversely, once some signs make it onto the floor, it's hell getting rid of them. Every February I make a game of seeing how many liquor store windows still bear holiday-themed displays and signs. It's always quite a few. We once studied a major New York bank branch where bits and pieces of twenty-seven different promotions were all still evident. In a car dealership's window, we once found a sign announcing the arrival of the new cars—the *previous* year's new cars.

Some signs are perfectly fine, except they're in places they were never intended to go. You'll pass a drugstore display window and see a stack of cough syrup boxes with a tiny sign showing the sale price, a sign that was obviously meant to go on the shelves, where shoppers are a foot or so away, not in a window facing a busy street. Often, retailers simply ask too much of a sign—more than any sign can deliver. A fast-food chain tested a sign system explaining one version of its "meal deals," then tried to make the signs clearer, then tested them again and fixed them again until they realized that it wasn't the signs that were bad—the meal deals were just too complicated to be explained. The deals were changed and the signs worked just fine. We did a study for a department store in the South that blanketed the place with signs announcing big discounts. The only problem was that you practically had to be a mathematician to figure out what you'd save. Even the sales-clerks had trouble keeping all the percentages straight. That store didn't need signs to explain the discounts, it needed textbooks.

The world of signs today is actually enjoying something of a renaissance. Just look at what's happened to billboards. Thirty years ago Lady Bird Johnson was going to outlaw them as part of her American beautification scheme. Today, even in post-literate America, some billboards are our most visually exciting, inventive and clever form of commercial expression. They're more stylish than print ads, hipper than TV commercials and more fluent in the language of imagery and graphics than anything you'll find on the Web. Some billboards are to print ads what MTV is to network TV—the edge of the envelope, the lab for experimenting with new ideas in communication. Technology has given us three-part shifting billboards, video JumboTrons, rotating sports arena message boards and digital menu boards featuring flying french fries. At a fast-food restaurant we studied, a moving digital menu board panel was read by 48 percent of customers, compared to 17 percent for the same menu board—a nonmoving version—tested earlier. Those numbers have held up over many tests we've done comparing moving and nonmoving signs.

But a sign need not be on the cutting edge of technology to leave an impression. Not long ago I entered the elevator of a hotel in the financial district in New York. On the wall was a mirror, below which were these words: "You Look Famished." And below that were the names and brief descriptions of the hotel's restaurants. I guarantee that sign gets close to 100 percentage exposure, and that everyone who sees it smiles, then checks in with their stomachs to see if they really *are* famished. A good sign.

Shoppers Move Like People

SIX

—

Anatomically speaking, the most crucial aspect of shopping is the one that looks the simplest—the matter of how exactly human beings move. Mainly, how we walk.

Now, people move pretty much as their bodies allow them to move, as is most natural and comfortable. This gets tricky only when you realize that a good store is by definition one that exposes the greatest portion of its goods to the greatest number of its shoppers for the longest period of time—the store, in other words, that puts its merchandise in our path and our field of vision in a way that invites consideration. It's fairly simple to measure whether a store accomplishes this or not: We simply chart the path of shoppers and then determine which parts of the store are going undervisited. We routinely perform an hourly "plot" of a store—on the hour, a tracker quickly breezes through every part of the store, counting how many shoppers are in each. If a store's flow is good, if it offers no obstacles or blind spots, then people will find their way to every nook and cranny. If there's a problem with flow, some flaw in the design or the layout, then we'll find some lonesome corners. The

smart store, then, is designed in accordance with how we walk and
where we look. It understands our habits of movement and takes advantage of them, rather than ignoring them or, even worse, trying to
change them.

Here's a simple example: People slow down when they see reflective
surfaces. And they speed up when they see banks.

The reasons are understandable: Bank windows are boring, and nobody much likes visiting a bank anyway, so let's get past it quickly; mirrors, on the other hand, are never dull. Armed with this information,
what do you do? Well, never open a store next to a financial institution,
for when pedestrians reach you they'll still be moving at a speedy clip—
too fast for window shopping. Or, if you can't help being next to a bank,
you can make sure to have a mirror or two on your facade or in your
windows, to slow shoppers down.

Here's another fact about how people move (in retail environments
but also everywhere else): They invariably walk toward the right. You
don't notice this unless you're looking for it, but it's true—when people
enter a store they head rightward. Not a sharp turn, mind you, more like
a drift. (The right bias is also tied to which side of the road we drive on.
In Britain and Australia, for example—in spite of what I believe is a biological predisposition to the right—Brits and Aussies walk on the left.)

This is a profound truth about how humans make their way through
the world, and it has applications everywhere, in all walks of life. It took
us awhile to see this pattern, and ever since we've collected data that
bears it out. But how can a retail environment respond?

We performed a study for a department store where just to the right
of the entrance was the menswear department. And by our count, the
overwhelming majority of shoppers in the store were female. Having
menswear there meant that women shoppers would simply sail
through the section, barely looking at the merchandise, determined to
get to their main destination—ladies' clothing—first. In fact, because
the front door was in the center of the store rather than to one side, our
trackers charted lots of women who walked in, stepped right, looked
around and saw that they were in menswear, then veered off sharply to
the women's apparel sections on the left side of the store—never again

to return to the right side, even to the right rear, where the children's clothing was displayed. Not coincidentally, our track sheets showed that children's clothing was the least visited section in the entire store; fully half of the main floor was going undervisited owing to this error in planning.

A similar situation held at an electronics store we studied. There, the cash/wrap was against the left-hand wall, near the front of the store. Shoppers would enter, head right, but then see the register and the clerks, and turn sharply left so they could examine the merchandise there or ask where to find what they had come for. In some cases, those shoppers headed toward the rear to browse the displays there, but few of them ever made it back to the right half of the store. They were moving in a kind of question-mark track. To alter that, the register was moved to the right-hand wall and farther back, about halfway into the store. That then became the main hub. A second area of high shopper interest, a telephone display, was installed on the right wall but closer to the front. The hope was that shoppers would enter, walk right toward the cash register area, then visit the phone displays. Those moves shifted the store around to a configuration more natural to how people move, and instantly, the circulation patterns improved—more people saw more store. Because American shoppers automatically move to the right, the front right of any store is its prime real estate. That's where the most important goods should go, the make or break merchandise that needs 100 percent shopper exposure. That's one way to take advantage of how people move.

All shoppers reach right, most of them being right-handed. Imagine standing at a shelf, facing it—it's easiest to grab items to the right of where you stand, rather than reaching your arm across your body to the left. In fact, as you reach, your hand may inadvertently brush a product to the right of the one you're reaching for. So if a store wishes to place something into the hand of a shopper, it should be displayed just slightly to the right of where he or she will be standing. Planograms, the map of which products are stocked where on a shelf, are determined with this in mind: If you're stocking cookies, for instance, the most popular brand goes dead center—at the bull's-eye—and the brand you're trying to build goes just to the right of it. (Again, in Britain and Australia the drive-left-reach-right rule creates conflicts in design that we do not have in North America.)

An even simpler aspect of how people move is the one that raises the greatest number of logistical issues for stores. In fact, this particular peculiarity of human ambulation can be said to render nearly every retail space seriously ill suited to its purpose. It's this: People face and walk forward.

The implications of this are enormous only because the normal retail environment is designed for those nonexistent beings who walk sideways—who sidle like the figures drawn in ancient Egyptian hieroglyphs—rather than place one foot in front of the other. Picture it: If you're walking straight down a store aisle, you're looking ahead. It requires an effort to turn your head to one side or the other to see the shelves or racks as you pass them. That effort even makes you vaguely uncomfortable because it requires you to train your eyes somewhere other than where you're walking. If it's a familiar environment (say, your favorite supermarket) and the setting feels safe (wide aisles, no boxes or other obstacles on the floor to trip you up), then maybe you'll turn your head as you walk and take in the merchandise. In a less familiar setting, you'll see less—subconsciously, you've got your peripheral vision on the lookout so that you don't trip over a box or a small child and fall on your nose. If, as you walk, a display gets your attention, you may stop in your tracks and look upon it as it was meant to be seen, straight in the eye, as it were. But only then.

This issue is not limited to a store's shelves. On the street, how do you approach a display window? In almost every instance, from an angle—as you're walking toward the store from the left or the right. But most display windows are designed as though every viewer is just standing there staring into them head-on. Which is almost never the case. This comes up regarding outdoor signs, too. Near my office there's a new restaurant that spent a lot of money on a very handsome hanging sign, but instead of positioning it perpendicular to the building, so it is visible to pedestrians approaching from either side, it hangs parallel to it, so it can be read only from directly across the street.

Which is how maybe 5 or 10 percent of possible customers approach the facade.

Obviously, that sign could be rehung in an hour and the problem would be solved. Windows can easily accommodate how people approach them: Displays must simply be canted to one side so that they can be more easily seen from an angle. And because we walk as we drive—to the right—window displays should usually be tilted to the left. Such a move instantly increases the number of people who truly see them.

But how can our insistence on walking and looking forward be accommodated inside the typical store? One method is used in almost every store already. Endcaps, the display of merchandise on the end of virtually every American store aisle, are tremendously effective at exposing goods to the shopper's eye. Almost every kind of store makes use of them—in record stores you'll see one particular artist's CDs, or some discounted new release; in supermarkets there's a stack of specially priced soft drinks or a wall of breakfast cereal. An endcap can boost an item's sales simply because as we stroll through a store's aisles we approach them head-on, seeing them plainly and fully. Endcaps are also effective because they make up much of our exposure to the main drive aisles in the supermarket. In a sense, that mountain of Oreos serves as a billboard, both reminding us of cookies and giving us the option of buying right then and there.

Of course, there's a built-in limitation to the use of endcaps: There are only two of them per aisle, one at each end. But there's another effective way to display goods so they'll be seen. It's called chevroning—placing shelves or racks at an angle, like a sergeant's stripes, so more of what they hold is exposed to the vision of a strolling shopper. Instead of shelves being positioned at a ninety-degree angle to the aisle, they're at forty-five degrees. A huge difference, and an elegant solution, too. There's only one catch: Chevroning shelves takes up about one-fifth more floor space than the usual configuration. So a store can show only 80 percent as much merchandise as it can the traditional way. The big question is, will chevroning more than make up for that loss with increased sales? Can a store that shows less sell more, if the display system is superior? And I can't answer that. We've suggested chevroning schemes to a number of clients, but no one wants to take the total plunge. It's certain, however, that especially for products that benefit from long browsing time, chevroning works.

How we walk determines to a great degree what we'll see, but so too does where our eyes naturally go. If you can see only a tabletop full of sweaters when you're standing right in front of it, then its effectiveness is limited. If you don't see a display from a distance—say, ten or twenty feet—then you won't approach it except by accident. That's why architects have to design stores with sight lines in mind—they must ensure that shoppers will be able to see what's in front of them but also be able to look around and see what's elsewhere. It's also why printed display fixtures should bear their message on every surface, so no shopper confronts a blank side.

Once sight lines are taken into consideration, retailers must take care not to place merchandise so it cuts them off. This happens all the time: A freestanding display is placed in front of wall shelves, blocking whatever's there from the shopper's vision. Or a sign obscures the goods it's meant to describe. Ideally, a shopper should be able to examine goods but then look up and notice that over there, fifteen feet away, there's something just as appealing. It's a pinball effect—the felicitous dispersal of merchandise bounces shoppers throughout the entire store. In that way, the merchandise itself is a tool to keep shoppers flowing. That's how good stores operate: You feel almost helplessly pulled in by what you see up ahead, or over there to the right.

We have studied how much of what is on display in supermarkets is seen by shoppers—the so-called capture rate. About one-fifth of all shoppers actually see the average product on a supermarket shelf. There's a reliable zone in which shoppers will probably see merchandise. It goes from slightly above eye level down to about knee level. Much above that or below and they probably won't see it unless they happen to be looking intently. This, too, is a function of our defensive walking mechanism, for if you're looking up you can't see your feet.

This means that a huge amount of retail selling space is, if not quite wasted, then seriously challenged. If a store can avoid displaying goods outside that zone, fine. But most stores don't have that luxury. One thing stores can try is to display only large items above or below the zone. It's easier to spy the economy-size Pampers down by your ankles than it is the Tylenol caplets. If the bottom shelf tilts up slightly, that helps visibility, too. This issue can also be addressed effectively by packaging designers. Every label, every box, every container should be designed as though it will be seen from a disadvantageous perspective—either above the shopper's head or below her knees. Packaging should also be made to work when seen from a sharp angle rather than just head-on. We'd see a lot more large, clear type in high-contrast colors if that happened. This also has implications in stores where merchandise is stored on the selling floor instead of in stockrooms. I'm thinking here of computers, telephones, personal stereos and other consumer electronics that are sometimes stacked from the floor to over one's head. The boxes haven't been designed to be on display, but that's exactly how they end up. That alone should make no-frills packaging—brown kraft paper, no images, little description of the contents—obsolete. Boxes should be thought of as signs or as posters for a product—same as a box of cereal. Typically, package designers will place the manufacturer's name at the top of a label, thereby satisfying corporate egotism, and the product ID on the bottom, but this is exactly the wrong decision if the box is ever stored down near the floor. When it's down there, shoppers will see the brand name easily but not the description of what is in the box. And since no designer has control over where or how a box is stored, the product ID should *always* be on top, and the label should always look a little like a billboard—clean, high-contrast, with a visible image and large-enough type.

Another matter of concern is something we call the boomerang rate. This is the measure of how many times shoppers fail to walk completely through an aisle, from one end to the other. It looks at how many times a shopper starts down an aisle, selects something, and then, instead of proceeding, turns around and retraces her or his steps. We'll call it a half-boomerang, say, when the shopper makes it halfway down an aisle before turning back. Typically, he or she heads down the aisle in search of one or two things, finds them and then heads back without even looking around (or, if she looks, she doesn't see anything worth

stopping for). What do you do about that? The obvious answer for retailers is to position the most popular goods halfway down the aisle.
Manufacturers should attempt to do just the opposite—to keep their
products as near the end of the aisle as possible.

But there are also ways to try to keep shoppers interested. One of
the newest and most effective of these requires the presence of kids,
which is why it's been used so well in the cereal aisles, where Mom and
Dad typically want to grab and run. There, we've seen a floor graphic
of a hopscotch game work extremely well to nail shoppers down for a
while. In one store we studied, the average time kids played games in
the aisle was almost fourteen seconds—a long time to be standing in
front of cereal without buying some.

Retail masterminds have always sought ways to keep shoppers in
aisles, and most of them are unsuccessful. At Blockbuster, an attempt
was made to interest new releases shoppers in the earlier movies of
their favorite stars. For example, if Bruce Willis had a new movie on
video, next to where it was displayed there would be a big cardboard
Bruce stocked with some of his greatest hits. Kind of like a speed bump,
except that shoppers jumped right over it with barely a notice. The
moral: When you want that new film now, nothing else will do. The
larger lesson is that no amount of merchandising can deter a shopper
from his or her mission. The best you can do is go along for the ride.

There's one aspect of how shoppers move that most people are familiar with—the quest to get us all the way to the back of a store.
Everyone knows why supermarket dairy cases are usually against the
back wall: because almost every shopper needs milk, and so they'll pass
through (and shop) the entire store on the way to and from the rear.
That is pretty effective, too, or at least it was, but it also created a terrific
opportunity for a competitor. In fact, the convenience store industry exists because of its ability to put milk and other staples into shopper
hands quickly, so they can run in, grab and go. Some new supermarkets
now feature a "shallow loop"—a dairy case up near the front of the
store, so shoppers can grab and go there, too.

Large chain drugstores use the pharmacy in the same way—that section is almost always on the back wall, so customers will be forced to

visit the rest of the store, too. But a special accommodation must be made for those customers, lest the strategy backfire. When shoppers are headed for the pharmacy, they typically have a serious task at hand, so they're not interested in browsing the shelves of the store on their way back. Therefore, drugstores must be merchandised from the rear as well as from the front—at least some signs, displays and fixtures must be positioned so that they are visible to shoppers walking from the back of the store to the front. It's almost like planning two different stores on the same site, but it must be done because the pharmacy is so effective at pulling shoppers through the store.

In the opening chapter, I mentioned a drugstore that was the location of choice for young mall employees who needed a quick soda during their breaks. To take advantage, the store placed the coolers in the rear, which forced the kids to race in, hurry to the sodas and race back out so that they could enjoy their fifteen minutes off. Those teenagers were never going to buy shampoo or alarm clocks or talcum on their soda runs. Again, as I mentioned in the opening chapter, the store humanely decided to move the coolers up front, as a favor to loyal soda drinkers who might have found another, more convenient place to fuel up on breaks.

Still, getting shoppers to the back wall of any store is usually a challenge. Blockbuster Video has trained its customers to go directly to the back wall—because that's where the new releases are kept. That long expanse of the most desirable movies creates a peripheral track, which is a highly efficient way to shop videos. As a result, shoppers head directly for the rear, make their choices, then come down the main center aisle to the cash/wrap. That predictable path creates high traffic for Blockbuster's impulse item displays—the center aisle is where the popcorn, candy, soft drinks, movie magazines and other high-margin goods are sold. Wisely, most retailers don't sell their bread-and-butter merchandise from the back wall. Still, every square foot of selling space is equally expensive to rent, heat and light. A store that flows interestingly and smoothly from one section to another will automatically draw shoppers to the farthest reaches. If, from the front of the store, shoppers perceive that something interesting is going on in back, they'll make their way there at least once. A simple solution is to have what amounts to a mandala hanging on the rear wall, a large graphic, for instance, or better yet, something back there that makes some visual or auditory noise, that gives shoppers the sense that something interesting's going on. They may not head there the second they enter, but they'll drift that way, as if pulled by a magnet. Anything is better than the sense you get in most large stores—that the rear wall is the dead zone.

The front of a store has utmost importance in determining who enters. When RadioShack determined to increase the percentage of women shoppers, it did so in part by devoting itself to the telephone business. But it made sure to display phones near the front of its stores, in order to lure women in most effectively. In fact, we advise some clients to change the front-of-store merchandising several times in the course of a day, to attract the different shoppers passing by. At a mall bookstore, for instance, we realized that in the morning, most shoppers were stay-at-home mothers with baby strollers. So we told our client to position books on child care, fitness and family up front. (We also advised that there be enough room for all those strollers to maneuver.) In the afternoon, kids getting out of school ran wild in the mall, so there should be books on sports, pop music, TV and other adolescent subjects. After 5 p.m. was when the work crowd streamed through, so there should be books on business and computers. And because the mall was used very early in the morning by senior citizens getting their walking exercise, we told our client that before the store closed for the night its windows should be stocked with books on retirement, finance and travel. In fact, the store bought large, cylindrical display fixtures that could be turned around depending on the time of day and which books needed to be shown. Supermarkets are jam-packed up front from Friday to Sunday, so the space is designed to handle the crush. On Monday and Tuesday, though, it's mellow up there. We've advised clients to turn the area just before the registers into a new selling zone, kind of a small bazaar of impulse items rather than just the usual rack or two.

How often shoppers move through your store is also something to be accommodated. If the average customer comes every two weeks, then your windows and displays need to be changed that often, so they'll always seem fresh and interesting. Here's another example of how design and merchandising must work hand in hand: If windows are made so they are easy for employees to get into, the displays will be changed more often than if it's a pain in the neck. If something about the design makes carrying merchandise into the window a burden, or if display racks block access to the windows, they'll suffer from a lack of attention, I guarantee.

Some facts of shopper movement can't be turned into universal principles, but they certainly have had their impact in specific environments we've studied. We did a study of a branch of a major family restaurant chain with a location on Sunset Boulevard in Los Angeles. By day the fact that its restrooms were just inside the front door seemed to be perfectly sensible. By night, however, when the street outside came alive with, among other things, the trade of some friendly neighborhood streetwalkers, the ladies' room location was a definite liability. It became a kind of hookers' lounge, a place they could wash, put their feet up and chat a spell between engagements. Not the greatest thing for the rest of the diners.

Some Hallmark card stores feature custom-printed stationery departments, places where brides-to-be can go for invitations, and so on. The design of the department, a writing table with shelves for the large stationery sample books, was perfectly adequate. But in one busy New Jersey mall, the station was located in the front of the store, just beyond the cash register, perhaps the noisiest, most populated part of the room. The sole person using it was filling out a job application.

Dynamic

SEVEN

S tand over here. *Behind* the underwear.

What do you see? A couple? How old? Sixties? Anything special? Just your average slightly tubby mom and pop out on the town, at Kmart or some such place, about to splurge on new briefs for the old guy, am I right?

Hold on—what's he saying?

"Now, where's my size?"

What's she saying?

"Over here."

Now what's he saying?

"I guess I'll just get this three-pack."

Fascinating. What did she just say?

"No, get the six . . . .I can wear 'em, too."

Whoa. What kind of weirdness is going on here? I can't even bear to picture it, the two of them rolling around in only their—

Hey, stop that. You just missed an invaluable lesson in the true dynamic nature of shopping and buying. You don't even have to be a scientist of shopping to figure out what just happened, though if you're a woman it might help, especially an overweight woman, especially an overweight woman whose choices in underwear were limited to styles with thin, biting elastic bands at the waist and the legholes—an uncomfortable prospect, I can only imagine (reluctantly).

Since that event, which happened a few years back, women's underwear styles have come to resemble men's, with their wide, flat (nonconstricting) elastic and soft cotton fabrics, thereby solving our woman's particular problem and keeping her out of his drawers. Still, this is a good illustration of shoppers making the ultimate determination of how they will use the retail environment and the products that are sold in it. Product designers, manufacturers, packagers, architects, merchandisers and retailers make all the big decisions about what people will buy and where and how they will buy it. But then the shoppers themselves enter the equation, and they can turn nice, neat theories and game plans into confetti.

In this particular case, was the general unsuitability of most underwear for ladies of size known to the designers and makers of said garments? Maybe not. Maybe they knew it but didn't know what to do. Maybe they assumed that women wouldn't wear briefs that looked like men's underwear, although, clearly, the general drift in women's clothes has been toward a more masculine ideal. If some underwear executive had been standing in that aisle next to our researcher, maybe he would have realized that this woman was teaching him something extremely important about his own product. Perhaps the revolution in women's underwear would have started earlier than it did.

Then again, maybe not.

Here's another example of shoppers forcing the retail environment to bend to their will. It involves what is perhaps *the* major issue in the design and furnishing of public spaces: seating.

I love seating. I could talk about it all day. If you're discussing anything having to do with the needs of human beings, you *have* to address seating. Air, food, water, shelter, seating—in that order. Before money. Before love. Seating.

In the majority of stores throughout the world, sales would instantly be increased by the addition of one chair. I would remove a display if it meant creating space for a chair. I'd rip out a fixture. I'd kill a mannequin. A chair says: We care.

Given the chance, people will buy from people who care.

This happened in a large, well-known women's apparel store. One that was providing insufficient seating for the men who wait for the ladies who shop. How do we know it was insufficient? Because the husbands and boyfriends were led to improvise, which human beings will always do when a need is going unmet. Whenever you encounter shopper improvisation in the retail environment, you have found poignant evidence of one person's failure to understand what another person requires.

(If I may digress for a good illustration: In the casino hotels of Atlantic City, New Jersey, where kindness is, shall we say, not excessively idealized, you see lots of people who have wagered and lost but must linger until their tour buses depart. The casinos, for obvious reason, wish these people would wait in the gaming area, parked in front of a slot machine or a dealer. To encourage that, there are no chairs in the hotel lobbies. How do the visitors respond? They sit glumly on the floors, dozens and dozens of sour-faced losers in a row, not a sight that evokes the opulent gaming ambience of Monte Carlo for the incoming suckers. These people need chairs!)

In apparel stores, too, the need is plain. While women shop, men wait, and when men (or women) wait, they prefer to sit. Is any truth truer? Is any nose on any face plainer than that fact? Still, designers of commercial spaces screw up royally when it comes to seating. In my days as an observer of parks and plazas, with the Project for Public Spaces, we spent a great deal of our time thinking about how to improve outdoor benches—where they should go, how wide they should be, whether they should be in shade or sunlight, how close they should be to the main thoroughfares, whether they should be wood or stone (stone gets awfully chilly in winter). A bench, we realized, might double the distance an older pedestrian could cover—someone might walk awhile, tire slightly and consider turning back, but then there'd be an inviting bench in the shade. Once restored, the pedestrian would continue forth. In the retail environment, a chair's main purpose is slightly different: When people go shopping in twos or threes, with spouses or children or friends along for the trip, seating is what keeps the nonshopping party comfortable and contented and cared for and off the shopper's back.

In that apparel store, the womenfolk were shopping but the menfolk were not—they were waiting for the womenfolk. They'd have loved a place to sit, but this store chose not to provide it. Why not? Maybe there wasn't enough space for chairs. Maybe there was a chair and it broke. Maybe somebody decided that a bunch of guys hanging around would spoil the decor.

Did that mean the men would stand? Of course not—it meant they'd invent seating. In this case, they gravitated toward a large window that had a broad sill at roughly the height where a bench would be. And the sill became a bench.

And where exactly was this ad hoc bench? Through no one's fault or design, it was immediately adjacent to a large and attractive display of the Wonderbra, the architectural marvel that gave life such a lift a few years back. It seems easy in hindsight to predict what happened next: Women approached the display, began to study the goods and then noticed that they were being studied by the guys on the windowsill. On the day we visited the store, there were two elderly gents loitering there, unabashedly discussing the need for Wonderbras of every woman who was brave enough to stop and shop.

Did I mention that few Wonderbras were purchased there that day?

Now, everyone knows that adjacencies are of huge importance to every product, especially something like the Wonderbra, which is newfangled and so requires a little examination and consideration and then a try-on. Great retail minds churn themselves into mush trying to unravel the mysteries of which products should be sold near one another for maximum spark and synergy. And here, completely without intention, a very bad adjacency was created (bad for the shoppers, bad for the store, not so bad for the guys) by human beings who were forced by a retailer to improvise.

Here's another instance where shoppers rightly confounded the narrow-minded agenda of shoppees.

There's an ongoing struggle afoot between the makers of cosmetics and the users. Women want to test cosmetics before buying, which is understandable considering how expensive makeup is and how it differs in appearance depending on the skin of the wearer. Cosmetics makers, on the other hand, wish that women would not sample their products quite so liberally, since even slightly used products are rarely purchased. There are many plans and systems that provide testers to shoppers, but none of these has been so flawlessly successful that it has become the industry standard. And so the game goes on.

A few years ago a makeup maker thought it had devised a foolproof lipstick—one that couldn't be twisted open without breaking a tape seal. This, the maker thought, would allow women to peer into the tube to see the color but not touch the lipstick itself. The boys in packaging were certain that this was going to save the company millions. We were hired to observe how women interacted with the prototype. We watched shoppers remove the cap, look inside and unsuccessfully attempt to twist it open—at which point they lowered their pinky fingernails into the tube and gouged out a dab to have a look. The experts were foiled again. Their mistake was in even trying to stop women from testing lipstick. The more progressive cosmetics makers recognize that testing leads to buying, so they encourage testing by making it possible without turning women into outlaws. To my mind, the best solution would be one that came with a profit motive—simply package small samples of each season's new colors in lipstick, blusher and face powder, enough for two or three applications of each, and charge a dollar or two.

Not every form of improvisation requires remediation. Most of us are familiar with the weekend crush at the video store to find a copy of the popular new release. On such business, Blockbuster thrives. We noticed that quite a few of the truly expert searchers among their clientele head not for the new releases section but for the returns cart, the trolley where incoming videos go before they are filed. There's no reason for Blockbuster to attempt to alter that behavior—it saves some clerk a little labor, which is a good thing. But an ongoing quest in the video business is the search for a way to get customers to rent more non–new releases (since their cost has already been amortized, each rental is pure profit). To help that effort, we urged Blockbuster to begin spiking the trolleys with older videos, thereby making them seem current and desirable and placing them directly into the hands of the most avid movie-watchers.

Here's a final example of customers using stores in ways other than were intended, this time to the complete benefit of the business. More than half of all fast food is purchased at the drive-thru window, and we (along with everyone else) assumed that those diners either ate as they drove off or took the food back to their offices or elsewhere and downed it there. During a series of recent studies, though, we noticed something odd: Around 10 percent of drive-thru customers would get their food and then park right there in the lot and eat in their cars. Curiously, the drivers who did this tended to be in newer cars than the restaurants' average customers. Were they elitist burger-lovers who were simply embarrassed to be seen in a humble grease pit? Or did they enjoy the luxury of eating in an environment where they could talk freely on their cell phones, listen to their own music and sit in their own seats? Either way, it's a segment of fast-food diners that's worth accommodating—after all, these customers bring their own chairs. As a result, we now advise fast-food restaurants to make sure their parking lots are visible from the street, so that drivers can see that there's space for them. We also emphasize the importance of maintaining pleasant conditions—shade, with a view of something other than the Dumpster—for cars as well as people. (In one restaurant we studied, all the best parking spots were taken by employees, many of whose cars would remain in place for eight-plus hours at a pop, a very dumb practice.) Finally, our finding affirms the overall trend among fast-food restaurants to shrink the size of the building and increase the size of the drive-thru and the parking lot, thereby allowing customers to have it their way—which, in nearly every case, is as it should be.

III

Men Are from Sears Hardware,
Women Are from Bloomingdale's:
The Demographics of Shopping

As we've seen, the simplest aspects of humanity—our physical abilities and limitations—have quite a bit of say in how we shop. But nothing as interesting as shopping is ever quite so simple. We all move through the same environments, but no two of us respond to them exactly alike. This sign may be tastefully rendered, perfectly legible, exquisitely positioned, but you read signs and I do not. The store flows beautifully, and all the merchandise is easily within my grasp, except that I hate buying clothing and would rather be fishing. No shopping baskets were ever more conveniently located, only you're strapped for cash right now, or you're just constitutionally incapable of buying more than two books at a time.

Certainly, we're all aware of how shopping means different things to different people at different times. We use shopping as therapy, reward, bribery, pastime, as an excuse to get out of the house, as a way to troll for potential loved ones, as entertainment, as a form of education or even worship, as a way to kill time. There are compulsive shoppers doing serious damage to their bank accounts and credit ratings who use

shopping as a cry for help. (Then they shop around for twelve-step pro-
grams.) And how many disreputable public figures end up arrested for
shoplifting small, inexpensive items? It seems we get two or three a
year, always in Florida.

In the '80s, Eastern European émigrés who came to America were
awestruck by the abundance on display in a typical suburban supermarket. The stores symbolized how free-market democracy comes down to
simple freedom of choice—lots and lots of choices. It was in a supermarket that I, too, had an emotionally cathartic shopping experience.
This was maybe fifteen years ago, a time when it began to seem as
though Envirosell might succeed as an ongoing concern. Up until that
point, though, it was an open question—I was borderline broke all the
time, working like a dog but plowing every nickel I had back into the
company. Things were tight: If I had a meeting in Florida, for instance,
I would take the last flight of the day down there to get the cheapest
ticket, arriving in the middle of the night. Then I'd pick up my rental
car, drive to my destination, sleep in the car, shave and brush my teeth
in a gas station bathroom, and go to my appointment trying my best to
impersonate a successful research firm founder. *Tight.* Anyway, on the
day in question it became clear that I and my company were going to be
all right. And on that day I just happened to visit the Pathmark supermarket near South Street Seaport in New York City. Standing in the imported goods aisle, it suddenly hit me that I could afford to buy
anything there I wanted. If, say, I wished to try some of the English gin-
ger preserves I remembered from my youth, I could just pick up a jar
and pay for it, heedless of the fact that it cost maybe *four or five bucks.* I
no longer had to sweat over my food budget, I realized, and at that moment I began to cry. Right there in front of all those imported jellies,
jams and preserves.

But doesn't *everybody* cry in supermarkets? Much of our work at Envirosell has to do with identifying differences in shoppers, trying to
come up with types and generalizations that might be useful to the retailers and others who control our shopping spaces. Not surprisingly, in
a world where "men are from Mars, women are from Venus" is a commonplace, we pay close attention to how men and women behave dif-

ferently in stores. Some of the distinctions are what you'd expect—women are better at it, men are loose cannons. But as men and women (and relations between them) change, their shopping behaviors do, too, which will have huge implications for American business. The other great distinction we study has to do with the age of the shopper. Once upon a time children in stores were seen but not heard. Those days are long gone, and now even the smallest among them must be considered and accommodated in the retail equation. At the other extreme, older shoppers are also more important than ever, if only because there are more of them, and they have a lot of money to spend and time to spend it. Their presence will transform how products are sold in the twenty-first century. Enormous cultural and demographic shifts are coming into play on the eve of a new millennium; in the four chapters that follow, we'll see how shoppers differ, and how those differences are reflected in the world of shopping.

Shop Like a Man

EIGHT

W hen they were a client I used to tell Woolworth's, if you would just hold Dad's Day at your stores once a week, you'd bring in a lot more money.

They didn't listen. You may have heard.

Men and women differ in just about every other way, so why shouldn't they shop differently, too? The conventional wisdom on male shoppers is that they don't especially like to do it, which is why they don't do much of it. It's a struggle just to get them to be patient company for a woman while she shops. As a result, the entire shopping experience—from packaging design to advertising to merchandising to store design and fixturing—is generally geared toward the female shopper.

Women do have a greater affinity for what we think of as shopping—walking at a relaxed pace through stores, examining merchandise, comparing products and values, interacting with sales staff, asking questions, trying things on and ultimately making purchases. Most purchasing traditionally falls to women, and they usually do it willingly—even when shopping for the mundane necessities, even when the experience brings no particular pleasure, women tend to do it in dependable, agreeable fashion. Women take pride in their ability to shop prudently and well. In a study we ran of baby products, women interviewed insisted that they knew the price of products by heart, without even having to look. (Upon further inquiry, we discovered that they were mostly wrong.) As women's roles change, so does their shopping behavior—they're becoming a lot more like men in that regard—but they're still the primary buyer in the American marketplace.

In general, men, in comparison, seem like loose cannons. We've timed enough shoppers to know that men always move faster than women through a store's aisles. Men spend less time looking, too. In many settings it's hard to get them to look at anything they hadn't intended to buy. They usually don't like asking where things are, or any other questions, for that matter. (They shop the way they drive.) If a man can't find the section he's looking for, he'll wheel about once or twice, then give up and leave the store without ever asking for help. You can watch men just shut down.

You'll see a man impatiently move through a store to the section he wants, pick something up, and then, almost abruptly, he's ready to buy, having taken no apparent joy in the process of finding. You've practically got to get out of his way. When a man takes clothing into a dressing room, the only thing that stops him from buying it is if it doesn't fit. Women, on the other hand, try things on as only part of the consideration process, and garments that fit just fine may still be rejected on other grounds. In one study, we found that 65 percent of male shoppers who tried something on bought it, as opposed to 25 percent of female shoppers. This is a good argument for positioning fitting rooms nearer the men's department than the women's, if they are shared accommodations. If they are not, men's dressing rooms should be very clearly marked, because if he has to search for it, he may just decide it's not worth the trouble.

Here's another statistical comparison: Eighty-six percent of women look at price tags when they shop. Only 72 percent of men do. For a man, ignoring the price tag is almost a measure of his virility. As a result, men are far more easily upgraded than are women shoppers. They are also far more suggestible than women—men seem so anxious to get out of the store that they'll say yes to almost anything.

Now, a shopper such as that could be seen as more trouble than he's worth. But he could also be seen as a potential source of profits, especially given his lack of discipline. Either way, men now do more purchasing than ever before. And that will continue to grow. As they stay single longer than ever, they learn to shop for things their fathers never had to buy. And because they marry women who work long and hard too, they will be forced to shoulder more of the burden of shopping. The manufacturers, retailers and display designers who pay attention to male ways, and are willing to adapt the shopping experience to them, will have an edge in the twenty-first century.

The great traditional arena for male shopping behavior has always been the supermarket. It's here, with thousands of products all within easy reach, that you can witness the carefree abandon and restless lack of discipline for which the gender is known. In one supermarket study, we counted how many shoppers came armed with lists. Almost all of the women had them. Less than a quarter of the men did. Any wife who's watching the family budget knows better than to send her husband to the supermarket unchaperoned. Giving him a vehicle to commandeer, even if it is just a shopping cart, only emphasizes the potential for guyness in the experience. Throw a couple of kids in with Dad and you've got a lethal combination; he's notoriously bad at saying no when there's grocery acquisitioning to be done. Part of being Daddy is being the provider, after all. It goes to the heart of a man's self-image.

I've spent hundreds of hours of my life watching men moving through supermarkets. One of my favorite video moments starred a dad carrying his little daughter on his shoulders. In the snacks aisle, the girl gestures toward the animal crackers display. Dad grabs a box off the shelf, opens it and hands it up—without even a thought to the fact that his head and shoulders are about to be dusted with cookie crumbs. It's hard to imagine Mom in such a wanton scenario. Another great lesson in male shopping came about watching a man and his two small sons pass through the cereal aisle. When the boys plead for their favorite brand, he pulls down a box and instead of carefully opening it along the reclosable tab, he just rips the top, knowing full well that once the boys start in, there won't be any need to reclose it.

Supermarkets are places of high impulse buying for both sexes—fully 60 to 70 percent of purchases there were unplanned, grocery industry studies have shown us. But men are particularly suggestible to the entreaties of children as well as eye-catching displays.

There's another profligate male behavior that invariably shows itself at supermarkets, something we see over and over on the video we shoot at the registers: The man almost always pays. Especially when a man and woman are shopping together, he insists on whipping out his wad and forking it over, lest the cashier mistakenly think it's the woman of the house who's bringing home the bacon. No wonder retailers commonly call men wallet carriers. Or why the conventional wisdom is, sell to the woman, close to the man. Because while the man may not love the experience of shopping, he gets a definite thrill from the experience of paying. It allows him to feel in charge even when he isn't. Stores that sell prom gowns depend on this. Generally, when Dad's along, the girl will get a pricier frock than if just Mom was there with her.

In some categories, men shoppers put women to shame. We ran a study for a store where 17 percent of the male customers we interviewed said they visited the place more than once a week! Almost one-quarter of the men there said they had left the house that day with no intention of visiting the store—they just found themselves wandering in out of curiosity. The fact that it was a computer store may have had something to do with it, of course. Computer hardware and software have taken the place of cars and stereo equipment as the focus of male love of technology and gadgetry. Clearly, most of the visits to the store were information-gathering forays. On the videotape, we watched the men reading intently the software packaging and any other literature or signage available. The store was where men bought software, but it was also where they did most of their learning about it. This underscores another male shopping trait—just as they hate to ask directions, they like to get their information firsthand, preferably from written materials, instructional videos or computer screens.

A few years back we ran a study for a wireless phone provider that was developing a prototype retail store. And we found that men and women used the place in very different ways. Women would invariably walk right up to the sales desk and ask staffers questions about the phones and the various deals being offered. Men, however, went directly to the phone displays and the signs that explained the agreements. They then took brochures and application forms and left the store—all without ever speaking to an employee. When these men returned to the store, it was to sign up. The women, though, on average required a third visit to the store, and more consultation, before they were ready to close.

For the most part, men are still the ones who take the lead when shopping for cars (though women have a big say in most new-car purchases), and men and women perform the division of labor you'd expect when buying for the home: She buys anything that goes inside, and he buys everything that goes outside—mower and other gardening and lawn-care equipment, barbecue grill, water hose and so on. This is changing as the percentage of female-headed households rises, but it still holds.

Even when men aren't shopping, they figure prominently in the experience. We know that across the board, how much customers buy is a direct result of how much time they spend in a store. And our research has shown over and over that when a woman is in a store with a man, she'll spend less time there than when she's alone, with another woman or even with children. Here's the actual breakdown of average shopping time from a study we performed at one branch of a national housewares chain:

woman shopping with a female companion: 8 minutes, 15 seconds
woman with children: 7 minutes, 19 seconds
woman alone: 5 minutes, 2 seconds
woman with man: 4 minutes, 41 seconds

In each case, what's happening seems clear: When two women shop together, they talk, advise, suggest and consult to their hearts' content, hence the long time in the store; with the kids, she's partly consumed with herding them along and keeping them entertained; alone, she makes efficient use of her time. But with him—well, he makes it plain that he's bored and antsy and likely at any moment to go off and sit in the car and listen to the radio or stand outside and watch girls. So the woman's comfort level plummets when he's by her side; she spends the entire trip feeling anxious and rushed. If he can somehow be occupied, though, she'll be a happier, more relaxed shopper. And she'll spend more time and money. There are two main strategies for coping with the presence of men in places where serious shopping is being done.

The first one is passive restraint, which is not to say handcuffs. Stores that sell mainly to women should all be figuring out some way to engage the interest of men. If I owned The Limited or Victoria's Secret, I'd have a place where a woman could check her husband—like a coat. There already exists a traditional space where men have always felt comfortable waiting around. It's called the barbershop. Instead of some ratty old chairs and back issues of *Playboy* and *Boxing Illustrated,* maybe there could be comfortable seats facing a big-screen TV tuned to ESPN or the cable channel that runs the bass-fishing program. Even something that simple would go a long way toward relieving wifely anxiety, but it's possible to imagine more: *Sports Illustrated* in-store programming, for instance—a documentary on the making of the swimsuit issue, perhaps, or highlights of last weekend's NFL action.

If I were opening a brand-new store where women could shop comfortably, I'd find a location right next to an emporium devoted to male desire—a computer store, for instance, somewhere he could happily kill half an hour. Likewise, if I were opening a computer software store, I'd put it next to a women's clothing shop and guarantee myself hordes of grateful male browsers.

But you could also try to sell to your captive audience. A women's clothing store could prepare a video catalog designed especially for men buying gifts—items like scarves or robes rather than shoes or trousers. Gift certificates would sell easily there; he already knows that she likes the store. Victoria's Secret could really go to town with a video catalog for men. They could even stage a little fashion show.

(The only precaution you'd need to take is in where to place such a section. You want customers to be able to find it easily, but you don't want it so near the entrance that the gaze of window shoppers falls on six lumpy guys in windbreakers slumped in BarcaLoungers watching TV.)

The second, and ultimately more satisfying, strategy would be to find a way to get the man involved in shopping. Not the easiest thing to do in certain categories, but not impossible either.

We were doing a study for Pfaltzgraff, the big stoneware dish manufacturer and retailer. Their typical customer will fall in love with one particular pattern and collect the entire set—many, many pieces, everything from dinner plate and coffee cup to mustard pot, serving platter and napkin ring. It is very time-consuming to shop the store, especially when you figure in how long it takes to ring the items up and wrap them so that they don't break. Just the kind of situation designed to drive most men nuts. A typical sale at Pfaltzgraff outlet stores can run into the hundreds of dollars—all the more reason to find a way to get men involved.

As we watched the videotape, we noticed that for some unknown reason men were tending to wander over toward the glassware section of the store. They were steering clear of the gravy boats and the spoon rests and drifting among the tumblers and wineglasses. At one point we saw two guys meander over to the beer glasses, where one of them picked one up and with the other hand grabbed an imaginary beer tap, pulled it and tilted the glass as if to fill it. And I thought, well, of course—when company's over for dinner and the woman's cooking in the kitchen, what does the man do? He makes drinks. That's his socially acceptable role. And so he's interested in all the accoutrements, all the tools of the bartender trade—every different type of glass and what it's for, and the corkscrew and ice tongs and knives and shakers. They're being guys about it.

My first thought was that the stores should put in fake beer taps, like props, for men to play with. We ended up advising them to pull together all the glassware into a barware section—to put up on the wall some big graphic, like a photo of a man pulling a beer, or making some martinis in a nice chrome shaker. Something so that men would walk in and see that there was a section meant for them, somewhere they could shop. All the bottle openers in the different patterns, say, would be stocked there, too. And because men prefer to get their information from reading, the store could put up a chart showing what type of glass is used for what—the big balloons and the long stems and the flutes and the rocks glass and steins.

And by doing all that you could take the man—who had been seen as a drag on business and an inconvenience to the primary shopper—and turn him into a customer himself. Or at least an interested bystander.

We did a study for Thomasville, the furniture maker, and thought that there, too, getting the man more involved would make it easier to sell such big-ticket items. The solution was simple: Create graphic devices, like displays and posters, showing the steps that go into making the furniture, and use visuals, like cross sections and exploded views, to prove that in addition to looking good, the pieces were well made. Emphasizing construction would do a lot toward overcoming male resistance to the cost of new furniture, but the graphics would also give men something to study while their wives examined upholstery and styling.

One product where men consistently outshop women is beer. And that's in every type of setting—supermarket or convenience store, men buy the beer. (They also buy the junk food, the chips and pretzels and nuts and other entertainment food.) So we advised a supermarket client to hold a beer-tasting every Saturday at 3 p.m., right there in the beer aisle. They could feature some microbrew or a new beer from one of the major brewers, it didn't matter. The tastings would probably help sell beer, but even that wasn't the point. It would be worth it just because it would bring more men into the store. And it would help transform the supermarket into a more male-oriented place.

That should be the goal of every retailer today. All aspects of business are going to have to anticipate how men's social roles change, and the future is going to belong to whoever gets there first. A good general rule: Take any category where women now predominate, and figure out how to make it appealing to men.

Look, for instance, at what's happened to the American kitchen over the past decade or so. Once upon a time Mom did all the grocery shopping and all the cooking. Now Mom works. As a result, men have to know how to cook, clean and do laundry—it's gone from being cute to being necessary. Spenser, Robert Parker's tough detective hero, cooks. A man in the kitchen is sexy.

Is it a coincidence that as that change took place, kitchen appliances have become so butch? Once upon a time you chose from avocado and golden harvest when selecting a refrigerator or a stove. Now the trendiest stoves are industrial-strength six-burner numbers with open gas grills, and the refrigerators are huge, featureless boxes of stainless steel, aluminum and glass. If you go into a fancy kitchenware store like Williams-Sonoma you'll see that a popular gadget is the little blowtorch used for crystallizing the top of crème brûlée. Have Americans just now fallen in love with preparing elaborate, fatty French desserts? Or does cooking just seem more appealing to men when it involves firing up your own personal flamethrower?

(Similarly, as women stay single longer and sometimes become single more than once, the old-fashioned, boys-only hardware store is being killed off by Home Depot, where female homeowners can become tool-happy do-it-yourselfers in a nurturing, gender-nonspecific environment.)

Look at how microwave ovens are sold—the most prominent feature on the description sheet is the wattage. Likewise, when we interviewed men shopping for vacuum cleaners and asked which feature was most important, their (predictable) answer: "Suck." Read: *Power.* As a result, vacuum makers now boast amperage. In both cases, home appliances have gotten more macho as men have gotten less so. They seem determined to meet somewhere in the middle.

Even washday miracles and other household products are being reimagined with men in mind. I can't say for sure how Procter & Gamble or Lever Brothers came to their decisions, but why else would paper towels be called Bounty or laundry detergents be called Bold, except to make themselves respectable items for men to bring to the checkout? How many women wish they had Hefty Bags? Now: How many men?

The manliest monikers used to go on cars; now they go on suds. A very successful soap introduction in the '90s wasn't anything frilly or lavender. It was Lever 2000, a name that would also sound right on a computer or a new line of power tools. I'd drive a Lever 2000 any day.

Look beyond shopping to the most elemental expressions of contemporary male desire—just think of the difference between Marilyn Monroe and Elle Macpherson. Elle's biceps are probably bigger than Frank Sinatra's and Bobby Kennedy's combined. She's downright muscle-bound and hipless compared with the pinups of three decades ago.

Men have always bought their own suits and shoes, but women, traditionally, shopped for everything in between. Especially they bought men's socks and underwear. Now, though, that's changing—men are more involved in their clothing, and women have enough to do without buying boxer shorts. In Kmart menswear departments, you'll still sometimes find a female-male ratio of 2 to 1 or even 3 to 1. But in expensive apparel stores, among more affluent men, males shopping for menswear now—finally—outnumber females. We caught a signal moment in the life of the modern American male on videotape. A man was browsing thoughtfully at an underwear display when he suddenly reached around, grabbed a handful of his waistband, pulled it out and craned his neck so he could learn—finally!—what size shorts he wears. Try to imagine a woman who doesn't know her underwear size. Impossible. Someday soon, we can all hope, every man will know his.

(Conversely, I am told that women frequently won't buy lingerie without trying it on—over their own, I am assured. I don't know if I'll live long enough to ever see a man take a package of Fruit of the Looms into a fitting room.)

As women stop buying men's underwear, will men begin buying women's? I met a jeweler who told me, "A lot of my business is with men trying to buy their way back inside the house." Many a husband or beau would choose fancy lingerie or jewelry as gift items, but the stores that sell them, and the merchandise itself, make it daunting. If he can't remember his own size, how can he remember hers, especially when she has bra and underpants to think about, not to mention robe, nightgown, etcetera? And how can he be sure he's buying the ring or neck-

lace she wants, in a color that suits her? We frequently see men tenta-
tively enter these lairs of femininity, cast anxious glances around,
maybe study an item or two, and then flee in fear and uncertainty. Salesclerks have to be trained to lure these men in like the skittish beasts they
are. Making a personal shopper available for heavy-duty hand-holding
isn't a bad idea, especially considering the costliness of jewelry or even
lingerie.

There also must be a way to simplify apparel sizes to make such cross-
buying possible. Perhaps the simplest solution would be for women to
register their sizes at clothing stores of their liking, then just point their
men in the right direction. The first store that tries this is going to benefit from lots of latent desire among men to buy frilly underthings.

Another gender-related problem that clothing retailers have to solve
is this: How do you subtly tell shoppers where the men's and women's
apparel is in a store that sells both? Not so long ago it was unthinkable
that men's and women's clothing would be sold side by side, from the
same site. That wall was knocked down in the '60s, but some of the
bugs still need to be worked out. The cueing now being used, for instance, even in dual-gender pioneers such as The Gap and J. Crew,
doesn't always work, as you can tell when you suddenly realize that you
spent ten minutes browsing through shoes, sweaters or jeans meant for
the other sex.

Remember when the only men who saw babies being born were ob-
stetricians? Today the presence of Dad in the delivery room is almost as
required as Mom's. Men are going to have to be accommodated as they
redefine their role as fathers. It's a seismic change that's being felt on
the shopping floor just like everywhere else.

For example, almost no man of my father's generation had the habit
of loading Junior, a bottle or two and some diapers into the stroller and
going out for a Saturday morning jaunt. Today it's almost a cliché.
That's why progressive men's rooms now feature baby changing stations, and it's why the McDonald's commercials invariably show Dad
and the kids piling in—sans Mom, who's probably spending Saturday at
the office. (Mom won't let them order Big Macs anyway.) This isn't just
an American phenomenon, either—my informal Saturday observation

of Milan's most fashionable districts detected that roughly half of all baby strollers were being pushed by Papa.

We tested a prototype jeans section at a department store in Boston, part of an effort to improve the store's appeal to men in their twenties and thirties. We caught video of a young man walking down the aisle toward the section, accompanied by his wife and baby, whose stroller he pushed. They reached the jeans, and he clearly wanted to shop the shelves on the wall. But there were racks of clothing standing between him and the jeans, positioned so close together that he couldn't nudge the stroller past. You can see him thinking through his choice—do I leave my wife and child in the aisle just to buy jeans? He did what most people would do in that situation. He skipped the pants. You'd be amazed at how much of America's aggregate selling floor is still off-limits to anyone pushing a stroller. This is the equivalent of barring a large percentage of all shoppers in their twenties and thirties.

Two decades ago it was the rare father who ever bought clothing for the little ones; today it's more common to see men shopping the toddler section. Clothing manufacturers haven't caught up with this yet, however, as evidenced by the fact that children's sizes are the most confusing in all of apparel—guaranteed to frustrate all but the most parental of shoppers. The day that size corresponds directly to the age of the child is when men will be able to pull even more of the weight for outfitting the kids. It'll be Dad who springs for the outrageous indulgences here, too—the velvet smoking jacket for his son or the miniature prom gown for his daughter.

And when Saturday morning rolls around and Pop goes to pack the bottles and zwieback and diapers and baby powder and ointment and wipes and all the rest of that stuff, what does he put it in? Not the big pink nylon bag his wife lugs. In fact, he's probably disposed against any of the available options—even a plain black diaper bag says Mommy. But what if he could choose a Swiss Army diaper bag? How about a nylon Nike one that looks just like his gym bag? Even better, what if he could push a studly Harley-Davidson–brand baby stroller that came with a built-in black leather diaper bag? The whole baby category needs to be reinvented.

Other traditional female strongholds can also accommodate men, but it's got to be on masculine terms. You've got to be aware of the wimp factor. There are many stores where the floors and the walls and everything hanging on them whisper loudly to the foolhardy male trespasser, "Get the hell out of here—you don't belong!" Near my office there's a store that sells dishes and glasses and such, and it's remarkable because I can walk in and not feel like a bull in a china shop. Whereas in Bloomingdale's Royal Doulton section, I feel as though I'm back in my grandmother's dining room, and it's the grandmother who scared me.

There are other such places that men would gladly shop—actually want and even need to shop—if only they felt just a little bit wanted. For example, there are more health and grooming products for men than ever. But if you look at how they're sold, you see that most men will never become avid buyers.

In the chain drugstores and supermarket sections where these products are sold, the atmosphere is overwhelmingly feminine. Shampoo, soap and other products that can be used by either sex are invariably packaged and named with the assumption that women will be doing all the buying. It becomes a self-fulfilling prophecy. The products made especially for men, like shaving cream, hair ointment and deodorant, are stocked in a dinky little section sandwiched in among all the fragrant female goods. No-man's-land, in other words, so how's a guy to shop it?

I can think of one item in particular where men suffer as a result of female-oriented packaging and merchandising. There is an untapped market for moisturizing creams and sunblock among men who work outdoors—police, construction workers, cable TV and telephone line installers, road crews. Given all we know about skin cancer, these guys truly need access to these products. But they're not going to traipse through the blushers and concealers to find them. And they're not going to buy a product that presents itself as intended for women and children. If you went through your typical health and beauty section, you'd think that men don't have skin. But they do, and it needs help.

Clinique makes a complete line of shaving and skin products for men. But at the very sophisticated Bergdorf Goodman department store in New York City, a man has to visit the all-female cosmetics bazaar on the ground floor to find the stuff. It's not even available at the men's store across Fifth Avenue. Who would guess that the shaving cream is right next to the lipstick? I've no doubt that many women buy shaving products for their men, but that's the old-fashioned approach, not the way of the future. Gillette makes shaving creams for a variety of skin types, and there's no doubt that it's for men. But how is a man supposed to know which type of skin he has? A simple wall chart display would do the trick, but I've yet to see one. I recently visited a national chain's drugstore in Manhattan's Chelsea section, the epicenter of gay life here. Even this store shortchanges men—their section (which consisted only of deodorant, a few hair-grooming products, some Old Spice, a tube of Brylcreem) was jammed into a corner shelf between the film-processing booth and the disposable razors. This store would be a perfect place to create a prototype men's section. Instead, it was the same old dreariness.

Giving men their own products, and a place to buy them, would be a good start. But that still smacks of the health, beauty and cosmetics section designed for women. Someone needs to start from scratch in designing a "men's health" department, where you'd find skin products, grooming aids, shaving equipment, shampoo and conditioner, fragrance, condoms, muscle-pain treatments, over-the-counter drugs and the vitamins, supplements and herbal remedies for ailments that afflict men as well as women. There might also be some athletic wear, like socks, T-shirts, supporters, elastic bandages and so on. There should also be a display of books and magazines on health, fitness and appearance. The section itself would have a masculine feeling, from the fixtures to the package designs. And it would be merchandised with men in mind—the signs would be big and prominent, and everything would be easy to find. The number-one magazine success story of the past decade has been the amazing growth of a periodical called *Men's Health*, which sells over 1.5 million copies a month, more than *GQ, Esquire, Men's Journal* and all the others. If the magazine can thrive, why not the store section, too?

What Women Want

NINE

Before this chapter begins, may I take a moment to mark the passing of a great American institution and one of the last true bastions (if not actual hideouts) of postwar masculinity?

I'm speaking, of course, of Joe's Hardware. Or was it Jim's? Doesn't matter—you know the place. Creaky planks on the floor. Weird smell of rubber and 3-In-One oil in the air. Big wooden bin of tenpenny nails. Twine. Elbow joints. Mystic tape. Spools of copper wire. Drums of waterproof sealant. Brads. *Brads?* Hell, brads, tacks, staples, washers, nuts, bolts (Molly and otherwise), pins, sleeves, brackets, housings, flanges, hinges, gaskets, shims, wood screws, sheet metal screws, a calendar featuring Miss Snap-On Tools in a belly shirt, brandishing killer cleavage and a power router, and over there—atop the rickety ladder, chewing a bad cheroot, rummaging blindly in an ancient box of two-prong plugs, cursing genially under his stogie breath—Joe himself. I mean Jim.

Whatever happened to him? Dead. How about his store? Dead.

Who killed them? Who do you think?

Oh, those . . . women! Too fancy to shop at Joe's, am I right? Poor guy stocked everything you could want, but *it just wasn't enough.* Not the right *color.* Not enough *styles.* The place stinks like *cigars.*

Bye, Joe.

It's no surprise that women are capable of causing such tectonic shifts in the world of shopping. Shopping is still and always will be meant mostly for females. Shopping *is* female. When men shop, they are engaging in what is inherently a female activity. And so women are capable of consigning entire species of retailer or product to Darwin's dustbin if that retailer or product is unable to adapt to what women need and want. It's like watching dinosaurs die out.

Need more evidence? Two words: sewing machine.

In the '50s, I am told, more than 75 percent of American households owned sewing machines. Today it's under 5 percent. So roll over, Joe—here comes Mr. Singer. (In fact, the sewing machine giant has gone into the military weaponry business.) Women once made entire wardrobes for themselves and their families, and kept repairing garments until they had truly earned their rest. Then the past three decades of socio-economic upheaval happened and women stopped sewing anything more ambitious than a loose button.

One last illustration?

Paper grocery store coupons?

Gone. Whoosh! Today less than 3 percent of all manufacturers' coupons are ever redeemed. Women's lives changed, and the thought of sitting hunched over the kitchen table scissoring away at the *Daily Bugle* suddenly seemed as cost-effective as churning your own butter. Oh, there are some major pockets of coupon-clipping resistance—senior citizens, the highly budget-conscious and motivated, mostly women who aren't working at jobs all day. But otherwise—outtahere!

Of course, we're all familiar with how men have become better, more caring, more sensitive shoppers, willing to shoulder some of the burden even of mundane household purchasing and provisioning. But let's not forget that this reformation came about in large part because of gentle prompting (if not actual violent pushing and shoving) by women. And let's keep in mind also that while the future of retailing will undoubtedly show the effects of more male energy in the marketplace, for the most part the big shifts will continue to reflect changes in the lives and tastes of women.

But what, as marketing genius Sigmund Freud was moved to ask, do women want from shopping? We speak a great deal of the distinct differences in how men and women behave in stores, but rather than dish out generalizations, let me start with a good example. It's from a study we recently did for an Italian supermarket chain, and it comes directly from a video camera we trained on the meat counter.

There, we watched a middle-aged woman approach and begin picking up and examining packages of ground meat. She did so methodically, carefully, one by one. As she shopped a man strode up and, with his hands behind his back, stood gazing over the selection. After a brief moment he chose a package, dropped it into his cart and sped away. The woman continued going through meat. Then came a couple with a baby. The wife hung back by the stroller while her husband picked up a package, gave it a quick once-over and brought it back to their cart. His wife inspected it and shook her head. He returned it, chose another and brought it back to their cart. His wife inspected it and shook her head. He chose again. She shook again. Exasperated, she left him by the stroller and got the meat herself. As they walked off, the first woman was making her way through the final package of meat on display. Satisfied with her research, she took the first one she had examined, placed it in her cart and moved on.

What makes women such heroic shoppers? The nature-over-nurture types posit that the prehistoric role of women as homebound gatherers of roots, nuts and berries rather than roaming hunters of woolly mammoths proves a biological inclination toward skillful shopping. The nurture-over-nature fans argue that for centuries, the all-powerful patriarchy kept women in the house and out of the world of commerce, except as consumers at the retail level.

This much is certain: Shopping was what got the housewife out of the house. Under the old division of labor, the job of acquiring fell mainly to women, who did it willingly, ably, systematically. It was (and, in many parts of the world, remains) women's main realm of public life. If, as individuals, they had little influence in the world of business, in the marketplace they collectively called the shots. Shopping gave women a good excuse to sally forth, sometimes even in blissful solitude, beyond the clutches of family. It was the first form of women's liberation, affording an activity that lent itself to socializing with other adults, clerks and store owners and fellow shoppers.

As women's lives change, though, their relationship to shopping must evolve. Today most American women hold jobs, so they get all the impersonal, businesslike contact with other adults they want (and then some). They also get plenty of time away from the comforts of home. And so the routine shopping trip is no longer the great escape. It's now something that must be crammed into the tight spaces between job and commute and home life and sleep. It's something to be rushed through over a lunch hour, on the way home or at night. The convenience store industry is a direct beneficiary of how women's lives have changed—instead of a highly organized weekly trip to the supermarket, with detailed list in hand, women now discover at 9 p.m. that they're out of milk, or bread for tomorrow's lunches, prompting a moonlit run to the 7-Eleven. Catalogs, TV shopping channels and Web shopping all have flourished thanks mainly to the changes in women's responsibilities. And the less time women spend in stores, the less they buy there, plain and simple. As they hand over some of their traditional duties (cooking, cleaning, laundry, child care) to men, they also relinquish control over the shopping for food, soap and kiddie clothes. Women may even become more male in their shopping habits—hurried hit-and-run artists instead of dedicated browsers and searchers. Right off the bat, the advantages of the post-feminist world to retailers (women have more money) are offset by some disadvantages (women have less time and inclination to spend it in stores).

The use of shopping as a social activity seems unchanged, however. Women still like to shop with friends, egging each other on and rescuing each other from ill-advised purchases. I don't think we'll ever see two men set off on a day of hunting for the perfect bathing suit. As we've seen, studies show that when two women shop together, they often spend more time and money than women alone. They certainly can outshop and outspend women saddled with male companions. Two women in a store can be a shopping machine, and wise retailers do whatever they can to encourage this behavior—promotions such as "bring-a-friend-get-a-discount," or seating areas just outside dressing rooms, to allow for more relaxed try-ons and assessments. Stores with cafes on the premises allow women to shop, then take a break, without ever leaving sight of the selling floor. ABC Carpet, in New York, takes it a step farther—everything in the cafe, from the furniture and light fixtures to the salt and pepper shakers, is for sale.

When you've observed as many shoppers as I have, you realize that for many women there are psychological and emotional aspects to shopping that are just plain absent in most men. Women can go into a kind of reverie when they shop—they become absorbed in the ritual of seeking and comparing, of imagining and envisioning merchandise in use. They then coolly tally up the pros and cons of this purchase over that, and once they've found what they want at the proper price, they buy it. Women generally care that they do well in even the smallest act of purchasing, and take pride in their ability to select the perfect thing, whether it's a cantaloupe or a house or a husband. In fact, watch men and women in the produce section—the man breezes through, picks up the head of lettuce on top of the pile and wheels away, failing to notice the brown spots and limpid leaves, while the woman palpates, examines and sniffs her way past the garbage, looking for lettuce perfection. He'll even fail to notice how much the lettuce costs, something almost unthinkable among women. Men do take pride in their proficiency with certain durable goods—cars, tools, boats, barbecue grills, computers. Women, though, have traditionally understood the importance of the impermanent world—cooking a meal, decorating a cake, fixing hair and makeup.

Not that there's anything superficial about the female relationship with consumption. In fact, it's women, not men, who plumb the metaphysics of shopping—they illuminate how we human beings go through life searching, examining, questioning, and then acquiring and assuming and absorbing the best of what we see. At that exalted level, shopping is a transforming experience, a method of becoming a newer, perhaps even slightly improved person. The products you buy turn you into that other, idealized version of yourself: That dress makes you beautiful, this lipstick makes you kissable, that lamp turns your house into an elegant showplace.

In practical terms, this all means one potently obvious, overarching thing: Women demand more of shopping environments than men do. Males just want places that allow them to find what they need with a minimum of looking and then get out *fast*. If a male is made to wander and seek—in other words, to *shop*—he's likely to give up in frustration and exit. Men take less pleasure in the journey. Women are generally more patient and inquisitive, completely at ease in a space that gradually reveals itself. Therefore, they need environments where they can spend time and move about comfortably at their own speed in what sometimes resembles a semi-trance state. Consider the implications of what we call the butt-brush factor, the discomfort women feel when they are jostled from the rear while shopping. It indicates that women have an aversion to examining merchandise that's displayed below waist level, which takes in quite a bit of American retailing's selling space. You can't ask a woman to bend over and expect that she's going to feel comfortable for more than a moment or two. (This isn't limited to women, either—nobody likes to bend in a store. In fact, older women are probably more limber than their male counterparts.) You can't crowd a woman and think that she's going to linger. Watch shoppers' faces in busy aisles—as you'll recall, once they've been bumped a few times, they begin to look annoyed. And irritated shoppers do not tarry; in fact, they frequently leave before buying what they came for. Retailers must keep all this in mind when deciding where to sell what.

For instance, department store cosmetics sections require women to sit or stand in one spot while makeup is demonstrated, which can be a problem during busy times. Our research shows that women standing at the corner of a counter, where they can wrap themselves around the angle and nestle in a little bit, are more likely to buy something than women standing just a few feet away, along the main stretch of the counter. Some cosmetics departments use counters to create cul-de-sacs, recessed areas that allow shoppers to stand clear of passing foot traffic and browse without fear. We call them catchment basins, and they are successful at inducing women to shop a little longer. As discussed in Chapter 1, drugstores sometimes stock unglamorous cosmetics such as concealer cream at the very bottom of a wall display—meaning that older women, the shoppers least appreciative of having to stoop, are forced to bend low and stick their butts out where they'd rather not go. As a result of such disrespect, less concealer will be sold than if it was positioned higher.

Women's spatial requirements can be seen everywhere in retailing. Airport gift shops, for instance, are typically divided into the "grab and go" zone—near the register, where you dart in for a paper or gum, pay and run—and the "dwell" zone, farther into the store, where gift items are usually displayed. Our research shows that women in these stores gravitate away from the hubbub around the counter and toward the dwell zone, where they feel protected from foot traffic. Many of these stores' architecture features little nooks and crannies created by shelving and racks—perfect cul-de-sacs for uninterrupted shopping. That's how women prefer to shop: within view of the main flow of traffic, but sheltered in sectioned-off areas.

The butt sensitivity of women also establishes a relationship between store design and typeface: The narrower the quarters, the less time a woman will spend there, so the clearer and more direct signs and other merchandising materials must be. All print must be big and high-contrast; designers of shampoo bottles, for instance, or any products sold in the close quarters of a modern drugstore, have to heed this reality. We've studied many drugstore health and beauty departments and the result is always the same—women like to study products before they buy, especially if the product is new on the market. In one study, we saw that 91 percent of all drugstore buyers read the front of a package, 42 percent read the back and 8 percent read the sides. Sixty-three percent of women who bought something read at least one product package. So there's a clear connection between reading and buying. And reading takes time. And time requires space. Here's the breakdown from our compiled data base; times are for how long women who made purchases read the packaging first:

facial cleaners: 13 seconds
moisturizers: 16 seconds
hand and body soap: 11 seconds
shower gel: 5 seconds
sun care: 11 seconds
acne medications: 13 seconds

But if women don't feel comfortable, they won't pause for two seconds, and they certainly won't buy any of the products that require a little study. Retailers should walk every foot of selling space asking this question: Can I stand here and shop without being jostled from behind? Anyplace where the answer is "no" is no place for merchandise requiring a careful look.

Even in fast-food restaurants, males and females have different spatial requirements. Without much consideration, men choose tables up front, where they have a good view of the busiest part of the room. Women will often take a moment or two to shop for where they'll down their Big Macs, and then they gravitate toward the rear, to tables that afford a little privacy. In fact, women aren't all that crazy about going into fast-food restaurants alone. They make up a large percentage of fast-food diners who go through the drive-thru and eat in their cars in the restaurant parking lot.

You can really see the female shopping approach in stores where women dominate—for instance, at the greeting card shop. There, women aren't merely fulfilling obligations, they're searching for authentic emotional expression. Women will devote quite a bit of time to studying card after card to find the one that speaks their hearts. Card stores should therefore feel like places where the emotional life reigns. A few years ago Hallmark hired a designer with a lot of experience designing department stores to redo its retail spaces. She created a very stylish look, using lots of marble and other expensive materials, but the overall feeling was cooler and more elegant than Hallmark customers had been used to. They must have missed their familiar warm and fuzzy environments; in response to the redesign, shopping time dropped.

Card stores must be designed to allow quiet, unhurried contemplation, meaning that aisles should be wide enough to allow room for readers and for those just passing by. Aisles must also be wide enough for baby strollers. Adjacencies should be planned rather than accidental: You don't want to be trying to find the perfect message of condolence and have your concentration broken by the women next to you laughing at the dirty fortieth-birthday cards. Other important display issues also come to the fore in card stores. Women buy cards only after picking up, opening and reading a great many of them. But the merchandise is fragile—easily folded, torn or soiled. It amazes me that there is still no widely used display system that would allow shoppers to read sample cards but not touch the merchandise. Also, in card stores the displays usually start at about a foot or so off the floor and rise to about six feet high. There are two problems with that: One, the low cards are too far down to be seen without stooping; and two, the low cards are too easily touched by grubby-fingered small children accompanying their mothers. If the whole display were raised by a foot, the problems would be solved. Even if the highest cards were six and a half feet off the floor, they would be within reach of anyone taller than five feet.

The other great arena where female shopping behaviors are on display is in cosmetics. Whether it's in a department store's impossibly glamorous cosmetics bazaar or a chain drugstore's wall display of lipsticks and eyeshadow, this is where a woman in jeans and a sweater can be transformed into a princess just by testing a few items and gazing into a mirror. This is as public as a private art form ever gets. There's a good reason cosmetics are usually stocked along a wall or in their own sheltered area—this is where women let their hair down, literally and figuratively. They need a little privacy if they're going to cut loose.

Typically, women start as adolescents buying the cheaper brands down at the drugstore. Then they'll trade up to the fancy, high-priced stuff sold in department stores by the glam representatives of the various manufacturers—the dolls in the official white lab coats (but Saturday-night-out makeup) brandishing brushes loaded with rouge and base and the rest. This is the high-pressure school of cosmetics selling. You sit on the stool, she turns you into a slightly toned-down version of herself, and you buy what she urges on you (in theory, at least). The prices are intentionally obscure, figuring that you'll be too intimidated to ask.

That's still the standard setup, but it's quickly changing now thanks to the "open sell" concept finally having come to the cosmetics counter. It's a form of women's liberation—the makeup is being freed from the clutches of the demonstrator-saleswoman and is out on its own for shoppers to test, ponder, try and then buy—or not. Some of the old game of let's pretend is gone, but so are some of the old high-pressure tactics. This open sell also allows women to check the price of makeup without having to endure the humiliation of asking that imperious clerk. By lessening the sticker shock, stores should end up selling more cosmetics.

These are the immutables of how women shop, the fundamentals that still (and may always) apply. Which is well and good and necessary if anyone is going to sell anything. But it's not where the action is today.

We've seen what gender revolt means where male shoppers are concerned: All the contemporary effort lies in taking stores and products intended mainly for women and making them safe for guys. For women, it's just the opposite—the challenge is in making traditionally "male" products and environments appealing to female shoppers.

For example, the old-fashioned emporium of nuts and bolts still lingers here and there, but for the most part, one category killer has done away with it. How did Home Depot manage that? Mainly by reflecting the socioeconomic reality that women no longer depend on men in the old-fashioned way. What does that have to do with wing nuts and duct tape? Well, were the females who spent all day at the barricades of social and political enlightenment going to come home at night and beg hubby (for the fifteenth time) to paint the window trim or install the dimmers? Unlikely. Not to mention the rise over the past three decades of the single female homeowner—women with the money and the desire to feather their own nests. Can we have female cops and firepersons and CEOs and cyberentrepreneurs and vice presidential candidates and not have confident, ambitious, fully empowered handywomen, too? I don't think so.

And where would these women go to begin their careers as tool guys? To Joe's Hardware? No—the typical hardware store was exclusively, unapologetically masculine, and maybe even a little unfriendly to female ways. It was a tree house with a cash register. So something had to give. Enter the do-it-yourself chains. (And, from the other end of the retailing spectrum, the hardware boutiques.) They stripped hardware of its arcane side, rendering it unintimidating, even friendly, to the greenest tyro. Doing that required a major shift in mission as well as merchandising: Stores that sold nuts and bolts gave way to stores that sold lifestyles. Under that vast umbrella, nuts and bolts and lumber and Sheetrock could be sold alongside lighting fixtures and kitchen cabinets and Jacuzzis and frilly (and nonfrilly) curtains and everything else. These stores sold not hardware but homes. The retail hardware industry has gone from an "Erector set" mentality to a "let's play house" approach, from boys only to boys and girls playing together.

This has also been done by hiring salesclerks who were knowledgeable and able to instruct and inspire confidence. The new wave of home stores hires women for sales and managerial jobs traditionally held only by guys named Joe (or Jim). There's at least one Home Depot TV spot in which only females appear. The stores also make enthusiastic use of any opportunity for education, whether with how-to videos or free in-store handyman lessons. These stores realize that the woman who is taught to hang a picture today will spackle tomorrow and install crown molding next month. Who do you think is watching Bob Vila and Norm Abrams and all the other fix-it shows on TV? The manly men are watching the bass-fishing channel, while the women are watching the handymen, who resemble nothing more than Julia Child in a tool belt.

This infusion of female energy changes even how the stores display their goods. No longer can lighting fixtures simply be hung on a rack or stood on a shelf. Retailers have to show exactly how the lights will look in a room. Instead of displaying a box of bathroom faucets, stores now show the whole tub, complete with shower curtain and towels. Here's the indisputable proof of how Home Depot vanquished the old-fashioned nuts-and-bolts emporium: Before, you went to a hardware store only when you needed something. Now, you go just to browse, to see what's new and what's on display. You can now *shop* hardware—which means, by definition, that women have won and Joe (and Jim) have lost.

It's no accident that the most successful recent paint launches sell under the names of lifestyle gurus Martha Stewart and Ralph Lauren. In fact, at Kmart Martha's paint is often displayed way up front instead of where paint used to be (in the rear, behind the bags of peat moss). Paint has gone from being hardware to fashion, all because women got involved. Men don't paint until the walls are peeling and cracking; women will do it when they, not the walls, need a change. Of course, painting has always been within the abilities of your average man *or* woman. But only now has paint itself—the way it is packaged, marketed and sold—gone unisex.

There's another beneficiary of how hardware has changed—all we baby-boomer men who somehow made it to adulthood without ever learning how to be handy around the house. As women became more handy, men became less so; we, too, had begun to feel a little intimidated by the old-fashioned hardware store. But even this has come at some cost to men. In the days since feminism's rise, we've seen the decline not only of hardware stores but also of the guys-only barbershop, the shoeshine stand and the men's clothing and shoe store. First the barriers to female admission to universities, the military, private clubs and all the rest fell. Then unisex hair salons, and stores like The Gap, Banana Republic and J. Crew came along to desegregate clothing stores and even styles. The overall thrust of the second half of the century has been to flush men out of our dens, and for better or worse, or maybe both, it's worked. (Is the pendulum ready to swing back? Have you been to a cigar bar lately?)

A second great arena for gender upheaval is the computer store and other places where consumer electronics are sold. Stereotypically, we think of males as being the ones at the personal technology frontier—building stereo components from kits, or shelling out five-figure sums for speakers. More recently, personal computers and cell phones all began life as toys for boys. But the fact is that often, women are the earli-est adopters of new technology. When business began using comput-ers, the female office workers had to learn first about operating systems and software. The women, crunched for time on their lunch breaks, were the earliest enthusiasts of the automated teller machine.

How did we not notice? Because men and women use technology in very different ways. Men are in love with the technology itself, with the gee-whiz factor, with the horsepower and the bang for the buck. Back before cars had computerized innards, the commonest sight in America was three or four guys assembled around the raised hood of a car, watching its owner adjust a carburetor or install a generator, and offer-ing copious advice on how it could be done better. Today those men are gathered around the barbecue comparing the size of their hard drives and the speed of their modems. As they say, it's a dude thing.

Women generally take a completely different approach to the world of high tech. They take technologies and turn them into appliances. They strip even the fanciest gizmo of all that is mysterious and jargony in order to determine its usefulness. Women look at technology and see its purpose, its reason—what it can *do*. The promise of technology is al-ways that it will make our lives easier and more efficient. Women are the ones who demand that it fulfill its promise.

Therefore, while wireless phones started out as rather big and clunky toys fit only for the briefcase, they have become small, sleek and far more commonplace in handbags. Even the difference in how they are sold to men and to women is telling: The TV spot starring a male shows him on the golf course, calling business associates but otherwise whooping it up with the guys—the eternal child with his toy. In the fe-male commercial, the small daughters of an executive mom make her feel guilty, so she takes them to the beach, where she uses her cell phone to keep up with her job—the responsible adult with her imple-ment. There's also a difference in how men and women gather infor-mation about technology, as we reviewed in the previous chapter. In a study we performed in a wireless-phone store, male shoppers would walk in, read the wall displays, pick up the literature and then leave without ever talking to a clerk. Females would check out the phones, too, but they were much more likely to bring their questions to the sales desk to have them answered by a human being instead of a brochure. While both men and women required multiple store visits before purchasing, women usually required one more store visit than men before they bought, which may also reflect the fact that male customers had begun using cell phones earlier than women. By now, women have caught up.

As noted in Chapter 8, technology almost sells itself to men, but smart retailers do all they can to figure out how to sell it to women. RadioShack's customer base is overwhelmingly male. So when the chain decided it wanted to become America's favorite phone store, it wisely displayed telephones up front, the first thing inside the door. As a result, women window shoppers saw the phones, and the percentage of female shoppers rose dramatically. They bought phones, but they stayed to make other purchases, too—batteries, audio equipment, computer peripherals, toys and other items they normally found elsewhere.

That gets at the problem with all consumer electronics today—it's overwhelmingly aimed at male shoppers. From product design, packaging and marketing to the stores and their employees, computer hardware and software are made for men. Computers are now where hardware was years ago—a boys' club. It can't last much longer. Many of the emerging class of cyberentrepreneurs are female. More than 40 percent of all Web users are women. Soon, some computer maker is going to wake up and do what it takes to make female shoppers feel at ease.

What will that look like? Well, someday there will be a computer hardware company with a highly visible woman at (or very near) the helm, somebody to hold forth on the business page of the *Times* and on CNBC—kind of like a female Bill Gates (but with a better haircut). Its products will emphasize not the size of the RAM or the speed of the microprocessor but rather ease of use, versatility and convenience. It will focus on results, not process. Its computers will be sold like refrigerators instead of like scientific instruments. The most heavily promoted feature will be a toll-free number for plainspoken technical help when a program freezes or a printer malfunctions. Then, some agency will begin using images of women in its TV and print ads, maybe even in a campaign that lampoons how men relate to technology. A retail chain will make a point of hiring female staff, and human beings, not spec sheets, will be responsible for educating customers and answering their questions. Finally, designers will provide ergonomically improved keyboards. Computers will be easy to clean (they're almost impossible now). They'll even come in colors other than putty or black!

Need evidence that men and women see technology differently? At a computer software store we studied, the shoppers were overwhelmingly male, but the conversion rate, the percentage of shoppers who bought something, was highest among women. That's because they were in the store with some practical mission to carry out, not just to daydream over a new Zip drive or a scanner. Most women would rather just learn what they need to know to use the damn thing. Everywhere in the world of hardware and software, the sexes swap places: Men love to browse and wander while women are purposeful, impossible to distract while they look for what they need.

Similarly, men and women switch sides when shopping the Web: Men spend lots of time surfing from site to site while women go directly to their destination, click only enough to buy what they want and then log off. It's pretty much the same way men and women behave with the TV remote control—he restlessly jumps from channel to channel, which leads her to fantasize about strangling him so she can watch just one program all the way through.

The car industry, perhaps the most backward and anti-shopper business in America, has realized for a few years now that women buy cars. Saturn in particular acknowledges the presence of females in cars, by taking most of the sleazy wheeler-dealer out of the transaction. The TV spots almost always include women on both sides of the transaction. They make the cars seem as honest and wholesome as an oatmeal cookie. In our dealership interviews, we hear lots of female customers wish there were more females selling and servicing the cars. It's a matter of trusting that the salesperson isn't going to condescend or gouge just because he's a man and you're not.

Considering what a male-dominated world car sales has always been, dealers should be hiring lots of women to sell and service auto-mobiles. Hiring women to sell cars isn't just political correctness, ei-ther—most women surveyed say they'd feel more comfortable buying cars from other females. They're not male-haters so much as they are feeling a little condescended to and maybe even ripped off by male car salesmen.

Car salesmen live by the conventional wisdom that the male half of a couple makes the decision, not realizing that in many cases she's the one who's pushing for the new wheels, or that her objections are what must be overcome. So the pitch is directed at the male while the woman silently burns. After the sale is closed the buyers will usually be brought back to the service department to meet the manager. Back there it's usually 100 percent guy-land, starting even with the choice of magazines in the waiting area (*Car and Driver* and *Sports Illustrated* but not *Vanity Fair* and *People*). Someday soon we may see Ms. Good-wrench or the Pep Girls—Mary, Jo and Jill—but they're not here yet. Women report a distinct distaste for all their dealings with auto deal-ers, mechanics and auto parts stores. They feel patronized, scorned and ripped off, but they also realize there's not much of a choice so far. They deserve better.

Again, the smart first move would be to hire females to fix cars and sell parts. Using actresses in TV spots also goes a long way toward repo-sitioning this all-male world. A few years ago we did a study for a mass merchandiser's auto parts department. Ninety percent of the shoppers were male, but 25 percent of those who used the computerized infor-mation fixtures were female. Clearly, those women had questions and weren't getting answers from the salesclerks. Maybe the clerks didn't know the answers, or maybe the women just didn't enjoy asking those guys. Either way, it shows that women are eager to learn how to handle the basic maintenance and easy repairs of their cars.

If I bought a gas station tomorrow, the first thing I'd do is put up a huge sign saying "Cleanest Bathrooms of Any Gas Station Anywhere." Gas stations persist in displaying most prominently the price per gallon, down to the tenth of a cent, as though we even think that small. Gas is gas, and prices are fairly uniform, too. But clean bathrooms would draw female drivers, who make more use of facilities and so have more bitter complaints about horrible, filthy conditions. The fact is that while gas has become a self-serve item, we need assistance on the road now more than ever. We're going greater distances and so need directions, and decent places to eat and drink, and clean bathrooms. Maybe even someplace with a clean baby-changing table and a working sink and a trash can that isn't spilling all over the floor. No woman is going to sweat a few pennies in gas price if she is cared for otherwise. Don't men gas station owners realize that? Mostly they don't—why would they? But if there were more women involved in the car business, from dealerships to parts and repair to gasoline, the whole industry would look different. It would look like—hardware! Which may mean that even the car business isn't quite hopeless.

If You Can Read This
You're Too Young

TEN

No doubt you already know this statistic: By 2025, nearly one-fifth of the American people will be sixty-five or older. You also realize what that means: Old baby boomers. A lot of old baby boomers.

But what will *that* mean? Well, right off the bat, it means it'll be good to be old. How could it be otherwise? When boomers were young, youth was good. When they were middle-aged, a certain seasoned maturity was good. And old people of the twenty-first century won't be like the current sober crop of senior citizens. Future oldsters didn't grow up in the Depression, they came of age during the fat, self-indulgent '50s, '60s and '70s. They weren't force-fed the virtues of sacrifice, self-denial and delayed gratification, nor did they absorb the quaint notion that to be old is to accept infirmity and inability stoically, as one's lot in life. The little old lady of 2025 won't have a spotless Ford Fairlane (that she drives once a week, to church) sitting in her garage. She'll be buzzing around town in an Alfa-Romeo (standard equipment including seats with hydraulic lifts), dressed head to toe in the Nike "Silver" line, parking in the plentiful spaces reserved for people who are old but not

impaired (as mandated by the 2009 Perky Aging Americans Act).
Thanks to improved health care, nutrition, fitness and cosmetic surgery,
at seventy she'll look and feel like her mother did at fifty. The kids will
be grown and gone, working like ants to keep Social Security afloat,
while we geezers squander the fruits of our 401(k)s along with what we
inherited from our departed parents, whose demise is even now beginning to trigger the largest transfer of wealth in the history of money.

For the world of shopping, it's going to be a party! That's obvious.
All of retailing—stores, restaurants and banks—is going to have to cater
to us because we'll have the numbers and the dollars. But we're going
to need a whole new world. This one's not going to work. And we're
not gonna take it!

What's wrong with this world? For starters, all the words are too
damn small. See this sentence? How could you? Too damn small. How
about the morning paper? Forget it. Too damn small. The directions on
your jar of organic herbal laxative? Too. Damn. Small. And you're not
even going to try squinting. (It causes wrinkles.) If you can't read it, by
gum, you just won't buy it. And if *you* don't buy organic herbal laxative,
nobody will. And if nobody buys it . . . well, you see where this is going.

Human eyes begin to falter at about age forty, and even healthy ones
are usually impaired by their sixties. With age, three main ocular events
take place: The lens becomes more rigid and the muscles holding it
weaken, meaning you can't focus on small type; the cornea yellows,
which changes how you perceive color, and less light reaches your
retina, meaning the world looks a little dimmer than it once did. The issue of visual acuity, already a major one in the marketplace, will become even more critical—not just in some far-off future, but from this
moment on.

For example, every current study of newspaper readership comes
back with the same result: Readers want bigger text. Most papers now
use body text of roughly 9-point type. (This book is set in 11.75-point
type.) Readers want 12 point or larger. For the most part, they're still
not getting it. The fact that newspapers persist in using too-small type is
proof of how profoundly businesspeople misunderstand their customers and underestimate their dissatisfactions.

But typeface problems aren't limited to the publishing business. A large customer base for today's drugstore is older people, and that dependence will only increase. Certainly, of all the words we are required to read in the course of our lives, few are more important than the labels, directions and warnings on drugs, both prescription and over-the-counter. For instance, we have found that 91 percent of all skin-care customers buy only after they've read the front label of the box, bottle or jar. Forty-two percent of buyers also read the back of the package. Clearly, reading is crucial to selling skin-care and other health and beauty items.

But our studies of drugstore packaging also reveal some interesting comparisons. For instance, the directions, ingredients and/or warning information is 10 point or larger on the packaging for famous brands of hair dye, skin cream, acne medicine and toothpaste. But it's between 6 point and 9 point on aspirin and a host of other common analgesics. It is also between 6 point and 9 point on cold capsules and other sneezy-stuffy-drippy products, as well as on vitamins. In other words, the packaging designers make it much easier for teenagers to read their pimple cream than for seniors to read their headache or cold remedies. The only concession to age we found was on a box of Polident, which uses 11-point type for directions and 8-point for ingredients.

This is obviously a failing on the part of the wizards in drug companies' packaging divisions. (I do not accept the rationale that government regulations force manufacturers to use tiny type. Packaging should be about solutions.) But when you realize that most designers sitting at the CAD/CAM screens, including those who create labels, are in their twenties, it's easy to see why there has been such a gargantuan miscalculation. The people who make and commission the packaging seem to have no idea how it looks to the people who must read it or the retail environment where it is going to end up. Take a gander at publications intended for youthful readers—I mean magazines like *Wired*, *SPIN* or *Raygun*. In all, the type is tiny and frequently printed on backgrounds that provide little contrast. The message is clear: This magazine is meant for the young and will make no concessions to decrepitude. It's equivalent to when Mick Jagger, a well-born college graduate, slurred and swallowed his lyrics, rendering his music inaccessible to ears that had grown up on Bing Crosby and Patti Page. In the next century, the disparity of age between designers of drugstore products and their most frequent readers will only broaden.

At Eckerd's stores in Florida, magnifying glasses on chains have been attached to the shelves. This is a clever makeshift solution, but it's not going to be enough. Drugstores report that overall, about one shopper in five seeks employee assistance, but almost double that percentage of senior citizen customers ask for help. Invariably, what they require is the aid of younger eyes to find a product or read a label. You can go through *any* kind of store and find commercial type that's a challenge for aging eyes to read. The nutritional information on the side of a cereal box. The laundering instructions on a silk shirt. The directions on hair dye, a self-test for cholesterol, the manual for a camera or software or a VCR. The specifications on a computer printer ink-jet cartridge. The song titles on a CD. The size on a pair of golf shoes. The label on a bottle of wine. The price on a paperback. And how are future customers going to find your business—by reading the telephone directory? I can't read it *now*. And let's not forget restaurant menus, train schedules, government forms, birthday cards, postage stamps, thermometers, speedometers, odometers, the radio dial, the buttons on your washer and dryer and air conditioner and refrigerator, your humidifier, your hot-water heater. . . . Did I mention those little stickers that tell you the pear you just bought is, in fact, *a pear?* How will you ever know? In every instance, the object makes itself forbidding and even hostile to older shoppers by dint of typeface size alone. Today's senior citizens endure this minor form of discrimination without complaint, as their lot in life. But old boomers, accustomed to having existence itself tailored to their specifications, surely will rebel. By 2025, anything smaller than 13-point type will be a form of commercial suicide. Even today, as our vision begins to fuzz, using 9-point type qualifies as a self-destructive tendency.

But did you notice the dilemma here? The better educated (and therefore better off) the shopper, the more he or she makes decisions based on what's written on labels, boxes and jars. In fact, all retailing depends on the written word now more than ever before. That would seem to suggest putting as much information on products, packaging and merchandising materials as possible. But when designers are told to squeeze in more type, they usually do so by making it smaller. Maybe bigger packages are a solution (although that would cause their own difficulties when it's time to allocate shelf space, not to mention the waste of more good trees). Maybe labels should make greater use of graphic images. Maybe it's time for bigger and better signs, or talking display fixtures. Maybe we should try all of these ideas because we're going to need a culture-wide jump in type size before long.

And size isn't the only optical consideration. The yellowing of the aging cornea means that certain subtle gradations of color will become invisible to a large part of the population. So, for instance, more people than ever will trip up (or fall down) stairs as the clear distinction between step and riser disappears. The difference between blue and green will become more difficult for many shoppers to perceive, and yellow will become much trickier for designers to use—*everything* will look a little yellow. As a result, packaging, signs and advertising will have to be designed for contrast, not just for the nuanced interplay of colors. We're going to have to see a lot more black, white and red and a lot less of any other hue.

For instance, we tested merchandising materials for a large southern California savings bank, and while interviewing departing customers we found that a large poster on the wall behind the tellers had low recall among older patrons. The poster, which promoted the bank's Visa Gold, showed an oversized credit card sitting atop a gold brick. To us, the image was clear. To older eyes, though, the distinction between the card and the gold was invisible, so it looked like a single, large, mysterious yellow shape—a meaningless poster to many people over sixty-five. We studied signage at a major New York hotel and realized that the color scheme for the room numbers, gold lettering on an off-white background, was making the place difficult to navigate for old eyes.

Finally, the typical fifty-year-old's retinas receive about one-quarter less light than the average twenty-year-old's. That means lots of stores, restaurants and banks should be brighter than they are now. There can't be pockets of dim light, not if shoppers are going to see what they're shopping for or even where they're walking. Illumination must be bright, especially during those times of day when older shoppers tend to arrive. And again, all print will have to be bold and high-contrast—dark colors on white (or light) backgrounds. One of our fast-food clients realized that diners over fifty-five were their fastest-growing demographic, despite the fact that the menu boards used type that was almost impossible for older people to see well. The company redesigned the menus using large photos of the food, and even though it meant listing fewer items, sales rose.

Changing the visual world to accommodate aging eyes will be easy compared to the structural alterations that are going to be required. Even in the twenty-first century, old people will be creaky. And keep in mind that senior citizenship is going to last longer than anyone ever imagined—many of us will be old for decades, longer in some cases than we were young. The same world will have to be navigable by robust sixty-five-year-olds and rickety eighty-five-year-olds. Twenty years ago many of the newly retired bought retirement condos in seaside areas, and some of those apartments were two- or three-story walk-ups with ocean-view porches—perfect aeries to while away one's golden years, it seemed. Now, however, two decades later, many of those springy-gaited sixtysomethings are wheelchair-bound or otherwise unable to climb, rendering those getaways obsolete. How will our stores and streets and malls fare when today's swarms of baby carriages are replaced by motorized wheelchairs? Doorways, elevators, aisles, cash register areas, restaurant tables, bathrooms, airplanes, trains, buses and private cars will all have to be considerably wider than they are now. Ramps will be required by commercial considerations if not by government fiat. Stairs will be relics. Escalators will be anachronisms. Think of all the multilevel malls that in twenty-five years will seem inconvenient, if not downright impossible, to one-fifth of the population. Remember, older shoppers will be everywhere then, at the drugstore but also at The Gap and Ralph Lauren and Toys "R" Us and Starbucks and Borders, the brand names on which tomorrow's codgers—we—came of age. Once manufacturers start making stylish, sporty motorized wheelchairs (they'll be more like street-ready one-person golf carts) and sleek, European-styled walkers, we'll really see the difference. We'll need cops to direct pedestrian traffic.

It won't just be for the immobile that the retail landscape will have to change, either. Even ambulatory older shoppers can't bend or stretch the way they used to. And they don't really want to—bending and stretching make them feel their age, which is the last thing they want to feel. At RadioShack, the slowest-selling batteries were for use in hearing aids, so the conventional wisdom dictated they should be stocked at the bottom of the freestanding "spinner" fixtures. Of course, who buys hearing-aid batteries but old people, the shoppers least able to stoop? When the batteries were moved higher on the spinners, sales went up, and sales of the batteries that were moved to the bottom didn't drop at all. We looked at the women's couture floor of a New York department store and found a similar issue. Not surprisingly, many of the women who can afford these clothes are older, and therefore tend to be of generous proportions. The designers, however, in order to keep up their image, stock sizes 4 and 6 on the racks and keep sizes 14 and 16 in a back room somewhere, forcing the humiliated shopper to ask one of the painfully thin salesclerks to go fetch her something a little roomier. Elsewhere in apparel a similar situation obtains: Racks and shelves of underwear or trousers are organized in size order, the smallest up top and the largest way down at the bottom—forcing the fattest and oldest customers to strain themselves, while making it easy on the young and the supple.

(Personally, I'd like to lead a revolt of tall shoppers, those of us who are forced to bend low at every pay phone and water fountain in existence. We're getting taller as a populace, and older, too, meaning that bending will truly hurt in two or three decades.)

In supermarkets, products stocked too low or too high are virtually off-limits to the older shopper: It's just not worth the trouble, they sigh. I'll find it elsewhere. This is especially so with heavy items like cases of soft drinks or large boxes of detergent—if you can't just slide it off the shelf and into your cart, you won't buy it there. (In fact, for the sake of shoppers of all ages, bulky packages should be shelved at shopping-cart-top height.) In Chapter 1 I describe how older people (along with children) are the prime purchasers of pet treats, which means that they and other such products must also be stocked with extra care, no higher than waist level (and no lower, either). Making life easy on older shoppers not only sells goods, it also engenders warm feelings among a group that is often badly served by retailers. The geezer who comes in for hearing-aid batteries and doesn't have to exert himself to get them will probably return when he needs to buy a telephone or a computer.

One of the ongoing challenges in contemporary banking is getting older customers to use ATMs. The automated tellers can be intimidating if you're not already comfortable with interactive touch screens and machine-speak. Senior citizens can be taught, though, but it shouldn't be by youngsters or by officious junior v-p wannabes: Older customers prefer to be instructed by their contemporaries. One older bank employee stationed by the teller lines can escort multitudes of senior customers to ATMs. It also helps to have ATMs within sight of the teller lines; if seniors can watch people use the machines, the ATMs lose some of their fearsomeness. Owing to failing eyes and arthritic fingers, those ATMs will have to adapt, too—the buttons will have to become larger, as will the screens *and* the words on them. If the gains in economy made by self-serve are to be maintained, lots of machines will have to be redesigned for older hands and vision. The written directions and buttons on the stamp vending machines and do-it-yourself scales at the post office, for instance, are too small for the aged to manage easily. The same is true of the credit card reader and pump at the self-service gas station line, or the commuter train ticket machine.

Tiny buttons and hooks on clothing, especially the inconvenient back closures on women's garments, will have to be replaced with simpler fasteners, on beyond Velcro. Mobile phone makers currently compete to see who can go smallest, but at some point the phone with the largest buttons and liquid crystal display will be most desirable, at least among older users. (That'll be at about the same time that mobile phones go from being yuppie toys to senior citizen lifelines.) Remote controls for TV, VCR and CD player, the buttons on the camcorder, the notebook computer keyboard—at the current rate, all will essentially miniaturize themselves out of the running for senior citizen dollars. I keep speaking as though all this is going to take place in the future, but that's wrong; it's already begun to happen. The world of retailing is having an interesting response.

Where are all the energy and innovation and capital expenditure in retail environments going today? To serve the coming tsunami of ancient shoppers, of course, am I right? No, I'm wrong—they're all devoted to the big entertainment-retail emporiums, to the brand-name chains with major kiddie merchandising tie-ins, like Disney and Nickelodeon, to the stores aimed at youthful dollars, like MTV and Nike, Hard Rock Cafe and Planet Hollywood. The new interactive fixtures and displays coming out of the design labs are dazzling—you're never sure if you're in a store or a theme park, which is the whole point, I guess. It must be a lot of fun to dream up such gizmos and the stores that contain them. And so it's no wonder that's where all the action is.

Unfortunately, these stores are catering to a market that's already on the decline. In the year 2025, based on U.S. census data, the number of Americans over 65 will increase by almost 80 percent over today's figures, by far the fastest-growing segment of our population. There's plenty of work ahead in making the world of retail better serve senior citizens. For our own sakes, let's hope some of that labor, too, is carried out with imagination and verve.

In fact, the time to begin that work is now. Let's start small—by demanding better elevator music! I want to make my supermarket sojourns to the sounds of the Doors themselves, not 1,001 Syrupy Strings' version of "Light My Fire." In fact, I can't wait to join a senior citizen social center, where we'll all prop ourselves up on our walkers and careen around the dance floor as the DJ spins the special fiftieth anniversary edition of the *Saturday Night Fever* soundtrack.

I mentioned the brave new world of wheelchairs earlier, virgin territory that no one, to my knowledge, has staked out yet. These personal vehicles will surely receive a makeover, including souped-up engines, cruise control, lots of upholstery choices (will black leather be too hot in summer?), big tires like the ones we had on our jeeps back in the '90s, phone chargers, cup holders, CD players and the appropriate bumper stickers (If this wheelchair's a-rockin' don't come a-knockin'). There will be plenty of licensing opportunities, bringing brand names like Harley, BMW and John Deere (or Louis Vuitton, Chanel and Prada) to the marketplace. They won't even be called wheelchairs—and, in fact, they'll more closely resemble tractor mowers or three-wheeled motor-cycles. These babies won't even necessarily connote a handicap. They'll just be cool conveniences, something for the geezer who has every-thing.

At the other end of the spectrum, it's no secret that next to kids, old people are the biggest market for sneakers. Who else has a lifestyle that doesn't ever require serious grown-up footwear? In fact, athletic gear—soft, rubber-soled shoes, baggy, open-necked shirts, loose pants with elastic waistbands—is tailor-made for the needs of aging fashion plates. Senior citizens have a lot more money to spend on sneakers than kids do, and would gladly pay for features designed to bring extra comfort. Still, no self-respecting teenager wants to wear the same athletic shoes as Grandmom, which is probably why all those ads for Nike and Reebok feature youngsters rather than oldsters. Is there no way for a major ath-letic wear maker to target aged customers? I bet we'll see it before long—it'll just be too lucrative to miss. (Maybe the commercials will star the sixty-five-year-old Michael Jordan playing one-on-one with the twenty-first century's premier eight-foot center.)

There's a similar question brewing over how *the* baby-boomer fash-ion staple will age. Will kids buy the brand of jeans preferred by their grandparents? I'm assuming that we boomers will wear blue denim right up to the tomb (and why stop there?). But if it's the uniform of the senility set, will anybody else dare touch it? Or will jeans go the way of fedoras?

The world of health and beauty aids now doesn't pay enough atten-tion to the older consumer, but it will have to in the future. There should be entire brands devoted to the needs of people over sixty-five, including special formulations of products for hair, skin, teeth, male grooming and cosmetics. Somebody is also going to have to figure out how to sell incontinence products to aging boomers. The current category—a few low-key brands of adult diapers sold sheepishly in the feminine hygiene aisle—isn't going to cut it. Will it be Fruit of the Loom, Calvin Klein or Johnson & Johnson? Or will incontinence products be sold next to the extra-hold sports bras and athletic supporters?

The mattress store of the future will do well to specialize in selling to seniors. They'll shop long and hard for bedding that's ergonomically sound, and they'll pay for it, too. Mattresses will become more quasi-medical products than home furnishings. They'll be part of the entire spinal health category, which will no doubt be huge by then.

When there aren't so many kids afoot in America, the fast-food trade will have to redouble its efforts to keep senior citizen diners interested. They already make up a large part of the fast-food audience, without even being acknowledged beneath the golden arches. Someday, it won't be the latest Disney animation flick that gets the Burger King tie-in, it'll be *Grumpy Old Men 4*. And instead of a Beanie Baby, the Happy Meal will come with a Hummel figurine.

When parents shop for clothing, toys, books and videos for their children, they usually know what size to get, or which favored plaything, or at what level the little one is reading. Thirty years from now, though, today's parents will be buying for their grandchildren, and they'll need a little guidance. Will clothing makers have wised up by then and created a sensible, standardized system of sizes? It's chaos out there now, as anyone who shops for kiddie clothes knows. If such a system isn't in place, stores will have to do whatever's necessary—big, easy-to-read size charts, mannequins of different heights, lots of attentive salesclerks, all of the above—to ensure that the grandparents can buy clothing with confidence.

If they can't buy clothing, they'll opt for toys or books or videos instead. But again, manufacturers and retailers have to make it easier than it is now. The appropriate reader's age should be marked prominently on all kiddie and adolescent books. Same for videos and video games, too. Grandmom doesn't want to accidentally buy Mortal Kombat for her dear little five-year-old grandson, and she needs a hand to make sure she doesn't.

And in the future retailers will have to figure out how to avoid scenes like this one: A woman in her seventies goes into a video store and asks the young clerk, "Do you have anything with Roy Rogers?"

"Hmm," he says. "Well, there's no Roy Rogers around here, but there's a McDonald's right up the block."

We heard that during a video rental study we conducted. During the same project we heard an elderly man ask a clerk, "Will this color video-tape work in my black-and-white TV?" Makers and sellers of technology do a fairly dismal job of reaching older customers today. Of course, we boomers are born technocrats, but who knows what new marvels will exist to intimidate us three decades from now? New technologies usually bring benefits that are perfectly suited to the older shopper: Internet shopping and e-mail make it easy if you can't get around the way you used to, and the pocket PCs of the future (like today's palm-size organizers, only better) will have plenty of memory for the times when yours fails, such as when you need a phone number, or you're standing in the middle of the supermarket and can't remember why.

But look at how technology is marketed and sold—you'll never see anybody over thirty in an ad or behind the counter of a store. And the product itself is unfriendly to older users, from the miniature keyboards to the type design on Web sites to the frequency with which printer and computer on-off switches are located in the back. Maybe some of high tech's appeal is lost when it's easy enough for your grandmother to use. But a couple of decades down the road, when *we're* the grandmothers, there's going to be hell to pay.

Kids

ELEVEN

With gender revolt (or reconfiguration, at the very least) having changed so much about our lives, and men and women off boldly shopping new terrain, the effect on children today is quite simple: Kids go everywhere.

Where did they ever go? To school, of course, which left their mothers free to perform the myriad tasks of the domestic superintendent, high among them the acquisition of food, groceries, clothing, and other supplies and services as needed. Dad bought booze, tires, cigars, lawn mowers, groceries (maybe once or twice a year) and Mom's birthday gift. Banking was done either by Mother or Father, depending on the household's particular division of labor. Only major purchases required the presence of the entire family, but how often did anyone get a car or a sofa? Not so often that the children who came along for the ride required very much in the way of accommodation.

Today both parents are almost certainly working at jobs, which means buying that cannot be done over lunch hours must take place during times the family might happily spend together. Shopping then becomes an acceptable leisure outing—less pleasurable, perhaps, than a week at Disney World, but not entirely without potential for fun, as we'll see. Also, divorce is common enough that the single parent (either one) in the company of the brood is a common sight in movie theaters, restaurants and stores. On any given Saturday afternoon, is there a video store or game arcade in America that goes unvisited by divorced dads with their weekend-custody kids? Kids go everywhere because we take them, but once there, they alter the shopping landscape in obvious and subtle ways.

There is also the fact that our children consume even more mass media than we adults do, much of it vying to sell them things. The marketplace wants kids, needs kids, and they're flattered by the invitation and happy to oblige. They idolize licensed TV characters the way children once were taught to worship patron saints, and manage to suss out the connection between brand name and status at a very early age. It's just one more example of how capitalism brings about democratization—you no longer need to stay clear of the global marketplace just because you're three and a half feet tall, have no income to speak of and are not permitted to cross the street without Mom. You're an economic force, now and in the future, and that's what counts.

All this, like every major upheaval, is both boon and burden. In practical terms, it means three things:

1. That if a store is somehow unwelcoming to children, parent-shoppers will get the message and stay away. I can't tell you how many stores that depend on female customers fail to ensure that all aisles and paths between racks and fixtures are wide enough for a baby stroller to pass. If they're not, at least half of all women in their twenties and thirties will be shut out at least some of the time. (A great many men shoppers will be, too.) This country's shops are dotted with "dead zones" created by stroller inaccessibility. We did a job for a department store and determined, using a tape measure, that the baby and children's clothing section was more crowded with racks and fixtures than any other part of the store. As a result, it was the most difficult part of the store to navigate if you were pushing a stroller; it was also the least visited section of the store, which was no coincidence. Every year Hallmark spends a small fortune on TV commercials for its Christmas orna-ment section. In one prototype store we studied, the fixture sat on a narrow aisle. Every time a shopper with a stroller ventured there, the section was totally blocked off. As a result, our research showed, only 10 percent of a store's shoppers ever saw the ornaments. By store design and fixturing alone you determine whether you will be kid-friendly or kid-avoidant: Automatic doors, wide aisles and no steps make it easy on parents pushing prams or dragging (or chasing) toddlers.

2. That children can be counted on to be enthusiastic consumers (or co-consumers) as long as their needs have been considered. In other words, if you want to sell something to kids, you've got to put it where they can see it and reach it. That goes for obvious items, like bubble bath in a Barney-shaped container, but also for things like dog treats, as I explained in an earlier chapter, since children (along with old people) are the main market for liver-flavored cookies. Conversely, if you don't childproof the store the way you would your home, you'll be in for many unhappy surprises.

3. That if the parent's sustained close attention is required (by, say, a car salesman or a bank loan officer), then someone must first find a way to divert the attention of a restless, bored child.

The first time I paid practical attention to the effect of children on the "adult" world was not in any retail emporium but in a temple of cul-ture, the Rodin Museum in Philadelphia. I was wandering among the great one's larger-than-life bronzes, lost in aesthetic reverie, when I heard a young voice exclaim, "Look, Mom—a bottom!" I turned to see an angelic tyke gripping with both little hands the buttocks of Balzac.

I then gazed around the room and noticed that there were touch marks on all the statues, roughly at the height where this adorable child had grabbed poor old Honoré. Clearly, this little fellow was not the only touch-oriented art connoisseur in America.

That moment illustrated several truths about children. First, they are exuberant participants in the world of objects. If it is within their reach and it offers even the slightest inducement, they will touch it. A child's creative impulse is expressed in his or her search for the essential toy-ness in everything, from the most mundane objects to the loftiest ones. An ironing board? That's a toy. Balzac's butt cheeks? They're a toy, too. I realized that if you want children to touch something, you must only put it low enough, and they will find it. In fact, objects placed below a certain point will be touched by children *only*.

Supermarkets have been at the forefront of exploiting the hands-on shopping style of children. We have countless videotape moments showing kids in grocery stores—begging, coaxing, whining, imploring Mom or Dad to choose some item (and when that fails, simply grabbing it and tossing it into the cart). If it's within their reach, they will touch it, and if they touch it there's at least a chance that Mom or Dad will relent and buy it (Dad especially). Even this must be done with care, though—we once studied a market that had placed products with kid appeal on the bottom shelf, not realizing that for children riding in shopping carts, the shelf just below the middle one is ideal.

Supermarkets have gotten so good at appealing to children that parents are in semi-revolt. In response to complaints about the candy and gum racks by the cashiers, some markets have begun to offer candy-free checkouts. (Now the confectioners are complaining.) We found an alarming trend in a study a few years back: a growing number of parents who assiduously steer clear of the cookie and cracker aisle in order to spare themselves the predictable youthful hue and cry. To counter that maneuver, our cookie manufacturer client began securing strategic adjacencies—with appropriate aisle partners (cookies on one side of the aisle and baby food on the other, for example) and better freestanding and endcap displays.

In the '80s, General Mills devised a new product for callow palates, a microwave popcorn that came in different colors. They advertised the stuff heavily on kiddie TV, but then—in a classic example of the merchandising hand not knowing what the marketing hand's doing—failed to make sure it was being displayed within reach of its intended consumers. In fact, assuming that parents would do the buying, the firm's typical supermarket planogram had positioned it on the high side, and this, we felt sure, was to blame for the product's disappointing sales. We still show clients the video of a boy of six or so making repeated flying leaps at the shelf where the popcorn was kept, trying to knock one to the floor so he could show it to Mom. He finally got it down, but his mother refused to allow it in the cart. Dejectedly, he put it back on the shelf—not where it had been, but down at *his* eye level. And sure enough, the next kid who came by saw it, grabbed it and tossed it into Dad's cart, where it remained. A classic moment in the wisdom of watching the shopper.

It would be almost impossible for families to shop together if not for the advent of kid-friendly dining, and McDonald's, more than anyone else, has prospered from this—the restaurants are part convenience, part bribery for the little citizens if only they'll behave through a morning at the mall. McDonald's realized early on that if it could appeal to children—not only through its menu but also with the toys and licensed character cups and playlands—it would get the parents as well. It's no coincidence that America's dominant fast food is also the favorite among kids. But even McDonald's doesn't get everything right. One glaring omission: The counters are all too high for children to use. A seven- or eight-year-old is certainly capable of going alone from table to counter to order more fries or another soda. But the design of the restaurants forbids it. Even the menu boards are so high that only an adult can comfortably see them. There should be kid-level menus that employ large photos of the food and as few words as possible.

What with boomers having put off childbearing as long as possible, and Gen Xers marrying young, there are more kids in bookstores today than ever before. Once, the children's books section consisted of a few shelves stuck way in back, behind the dictionaries. Today it may be the best-looking, most inviting part of the store.

Here's how smart booksellers stock the shelves: They place the books featuring characters from popular TV shows down low, so the little ones can grab Barney or Teletubbies unimpeded by Mom or Dad, who possibly take a dim view of hypercommercialized critters. Children's classics—*Grimm's Fairy Tales, The Little Prince* or anything that seems old and wordy—are displayed high, at eye level for adults, since that's who'll be choosing those worthies. In the middle go the books whose appeal spans generations—*Babar*, for example, or *Curious George*, or Dr. Seuss. (Video store planograms should work the same way bookstores' do: The venerables that parents might choose—*Old Yeller* or *The Wizard of Oz*—displayed high, and contemporary favorites like *Rugrats* or *Sesame Street* down where children can grab them and commence their noisy yet still somehow charming pleas.)

We always advise our bookstore clients to group sections by gender, acknowledging the tendency of men to cluster in sports, business, do-it-yourself and computers while women troll psychology, self-help, health, food, diet, home and garden. Place the children's books within sight of those women's sections, we counsel—and use low shelving for the kids, so that mothers can browse their books and look over from time to time to keep an eye on the children.

At the Barnes & Noble superstore near my office, there's a kiddie section with lots of miniature seating, which is good, but it ignores the fact that most children are accustomed to being read to while sitting in a parental lap. I'm always tempted to grab one or two of the large armchairs from elsewhere in the store and drag them into the kiddie section.

The publishers of children's books do a fairly lame job of making their product appealing for its main audience—adults. If you're buying books for your own child, whose tastes and reading level you know well, you probably don't require much direction. But what about all those grandparents and aunts and uncles and friends of the family who wish to buy books for the kiddies? They need some clear indication on the books (and maybe on the bookshelves and other displays) about for whom each book is intended—which grade (or age) reading level, mainly. But few children's books or book displays carry this important information. This is a classic example of a product's designers and marketers having no clue about what shoppers require. You'll see potential buyers standing in the stores reading, as though they'll find a clue there, and then, fatally uncertain about their choice, they put it back and decide to get Junior something else instead. It may also be important to find a way to let shoppers know about the focus of a particular book—whether it's meant to teach relationship-building, or imaginative play—as a way to signal a book's appropriateness as a gift.

Here's another way publishers fail shoppers at gift time: Kids' books tend to be relatively inexpensive, meaning that if you're buying, you may buy more than one. But even in the successful children's series, such as *Goosebumps,* you'll find few boxed sets, even though collections of four or five books would make a perfect present.

Though technically adults are the ones who select and buy toys, the kids are the real decision-makers. Even if Junior is still pre-verbal, you'll see his parents take a toy from the shelf, consider it and then dangle it in the little one's face to get the opinion that counts. If he bites, they'll buy—it's why most toy packaging now allows you to push the buttons or pull the string without opening the box. But I like the way the Zany Brainy stores acknowledge how kids prefer to operate: Toys and games are simply taken from their boxes and placed on the floor.

The principle, then, is simple: If adults are highly tactile shoppers, kids are uninhibitedly so. They'll touch anything. You've just got to watch them in action and plan accordingly. But there are at least two troublesome aspects there, both of which require common sense on the part of the retailer.

First, you've got to realize that the degree to which you are successful at getting children to see and touch and pick up and then desire items is also the degree to which you will frustrate and annoy their parents—the ones who brought the children in the first place. Like those adults who avoid the cookie aisle or the checkout piled with candy and gum and Sesame Street toys, for instance. Shopping is much more difficult when you're chasing after a child who believes he or she is the one doing the shopping. After a time the experience of a store with too much kid appeal becomes one the adult wishes only to avoid. There's a balance there, one worth striking.

Second, if you're going to merchandise your store for kids, you've got to protect them from it as well. In other words, babyproof it the way you do your home—wander it with your eyes trained on the area from the floor to about three feet off it, seeing exactly what kind of mischief can be created by an energetic four-year-old. The obvious dangers like electrical outlets and sharp-edged shelves should be easy enough to spot and address. But you've also got to make sure that heavy items can't be too easily yanked or toppled. We spent a day at a Burger King that controlled the line at the counter with a "hard maze"—a waist-high running ledge. In eight hours we counted a total of fifty-two boys and girls who climbed, clambered over, walked or jungle gymed on that hazard, and I have no doubt that some kids have taken nasty spills there.

A few years back we studied three AT&T phone stores in different parts of the country. All were attractively designed. All had the same number of employees to handle roughly the same number of customers. One store, though, had a much lower shopper interception rate—the percentage of potential customers who were spoken to by a salesperson—and a much lower average time spent with customers. There was just one other difference: That store was the only one to employ a "waterfall" display system—a row of pedestals of descending height on which the equipment was shown. We watched various videotaped angles of the sales floor, and after a while a pattern emerged: In the underperforming store, staffers were constantly having to run to the rescue of phones and fax machines that were within easy reach of children in the store with their folks. The salespeople would be involved in a conversation with a shopper, but with one eye always out to see what the little darlings were about to grab from that waterfall display. It wasn't just for the sake of neatness, either; the store had only one or two of each model in stock, so, for instance, if an expensive fax machine fell off its pedestal and broke, there were no replacements to sell. It seemed as if the poor clerks spent more time rescuing expensive telecommunications equipment than talking to shoppers. It was smart to place phone equipment within reach of curious shoppers, but not so smart to put them within striking distance of children.

One Envirosell staff person reports that he sat one afternoon with a highly regarded designer of interactive video fixtures as he unveiled his latest prototype, a video game station to go in the play area of a fast-food restaurant. The first two kids sat in the contraption and played it without incident. The third boy took off his shoes, leaned far back in the seat and worked the touch screen with his toes. The next child took the hard plastic toy that came with his lunch and began pounding the video screen with it.

"My God," the designer gasped, "look what he's doing!"

"He's interacting."

That interaction was also a reminder of a mild contradiction in the world of shopping today. Everyone knows that in the future, the demographic group that all retail will have to accommodate is senior citizens. Still, all the exciting innovations in stores today are inspired by young shoppers—the entertainment stores like Disney, Nickelodeon and Warner, and restaurants like Planet Hollywood, Hard Rock Cafe and Rainforest Cafe. From a child's perspective, these places are like amusement parks that just happen to sell merchandise. Everything cool in video, interactive, digital and computerized whatever, is happening in the stores favored by eight-year-olds. The ways of children are even gaining supremacy, as we discovered recently while visiting the Nickelodeon stores. There, signs indicating where to find merchandise featuring the various characters showed the image only—no words. Which was fine for the kids looking for their favorites. But it left the adults in the dark.

You don't have to be Barney himself to keep kids relatively entertained. But especially in businesses where customers have to remain in one spot and pay attention, providing child diversion is a must.

That thought will seem painfully obvious to any parent. So it's amazing how few businesspeople make any allowance for it. I recently watched a two-year-old run wild while her mother tried to shop in an establishment that really should be aware of the presence of children in the lives of its customers: a maternity clothing store. Diverting a child can mean simply setting up a TV and some Disney videos in a little alcove, as is done in French hypermarkets. (I'm always amazed to see that of all places, video stores frequently fail to run kiddie programming on at least one monitor, leaving parents free to browse a few minutes longer.) Placing some plastic toys in a five-foot-square area where Mom and Dad can glance from time to time can suffice in a small store. Ikea is famous for its kiddie pen, the avalanche of colorful plastic balls having become a friendly icon. No surprise that a Swedish chain would be at the forefront here; Europeans are less paranoid about the safety of their children and will leave them in the custody of store personnel while they shop. A few years ago there was a ruckus in New York when a young Danish woman parked her sleeping baby in a stroller just outside a restaurant's window, then went inside (to a window table) to enjoy lunch. Police were called, child welfare workers descended and the woman very nearly had a custody battle on her hands.

For whatever reason, American parents *are* paranoid where their kids are concerned. Here, Ikea has had to institute a rigorous ID check for adults trying to retrieve their children from the play area. Many parents simply refuse to leave their children in play areas that can't be seen from the rest of the store at all times. A few years ago Blockbuster built a clever little drive-in theater for kids, complete with big-screen videos and tiny cars where the tykes could sit and watch. Unfortunately, it was positioned in a corner just inside the exit, giving some parents the willies. We don't really have much experience with public day care here. So it's no surprise that children end up traipsing throughout our stores and banks and other retail businesses.

We did a study for Wells Fargo a few years ago showing that 15 percent of all those entering its branches are under seven years old.

"What's your most effective selling tool?" we asked a loan officer there. She reached into her desk drawer and pulled out a lollipop. She said it could usually be counted on to buy her two minutes of uninterrupted face time with a parent, all she needed. The bank also offers a coloring book starring a puppy who lives in a Wells Fargo branch. That and a handful of crayons can add up to a brand-new home equity loan, no question. In New York, Citibank produces an activity book for children. In both cases, the banks are buying quiet today and—given how we like to fetishize our happy childhood experiences—loyal customers of tomorrow.

There are just a few principles of designing a good area (as opposed to a holding pen) for children. The sight lines must allow parents to see their children at any time, so it must be in an open area, unshielded by walls or obstacles. It must be safe. It must be large enough. And ideally, it would allow children of different ages to be segregated. Otherwise, the older kids will always dominate, making it an unhappy experience for the small ones who get in their way.

Car dealers tend to do a lousy job of diverting children. Which is disappointing, when you think about it, because kids are already disposed to liking cars—toy ones, at least. A lot could be done, but the car business is far behind most selling. As a result, shopping for a car is more difficult for families than it needs to be. If no car dealer addresses this, then all are safe. But the minute Ford or Chrysler starts acknowledging the reality of kids in dealerships, the rest will be forced to respond.

Another place where children must be amused is in the pharmacy waiting area. There, among sickly adults waiting for prescriptions to be filled, the charm of youthful exuberance wears thin. Many of those children are likely to be ill themselves, which doesn't do much for their dispositions. Drugstores can easily stock toys or coloring books and crayons near the waiting area, creating an efficient adjacency. That's another great way of amusing children—give them something to shop while their parents do the same thing just a few feet away. Especially given how many parents resort to bribery as a way to quiet their progeny, this could be a smart strategy all around. Since women still do most of the shopping, it makes sense to place products for children near sections being shopped by their mothers. Is this child exploitation, or is it doing a mother a favor? Maybe it can be both.

A few years ago I read a news report on a convenience store that was having problems with teenagers loitering in the parking lot at night. Hiring a security guard to stand out there and scowl was an expensive solution. So here's what the store did: It began piping the smooth, suave sounds of Mantovani through the loudspeakers. No more loiterers.

Teenagers are still young enough to be total suckers for image, for all the blandishments of advertising, identity marketing, media messages, trends and labels. They still believe in a brand name's power to confer status, cool, charisma, knowledge. They construct their identities by the shopping choices they make—they're a lot like adults were back in the '50s, before we all became so wise in the ways of image hucksters.

Kids also have fewer media choices than adults, so messages come through to them in concentrated form. They love to scour the world for icons or any other clues that something—some product, some store—is intended for them. They'll flee easy listening music as if it were anthrax, while we can tolerate just about anything.

Which should make them fairly easy marks in the marketplace. But they have some built-in limitations, too. During a study of how jeans are sold, we noticed an odd pattern to adolescent shopping: Teenagers in groups spent a relatively long time in the jeans section (3 minutes, 52 seconds) compared to teens with parents (2 minutes, 32 seconds). And teens in groups examined one-third more product. But the percentage of teenagers with parents who bought jeans was nearly double the number of teens in groups who bought, 25 percent to 13 percent. Then we realized: They come with their friends to browse—to pre-shop, as it were. Having made their choices and gained the approval of a jury of their peers, they return with Mom or Dad—the wallet bearer—and make quick work of the transaction, wishing not to risk the humiliation of being seen in public buying clothes with their ancient caretakers.

Does this not suggest that commerce in general and banking in particular can do a better job of serving young shoppers? How about inaugurating direct deposit of allowance, accessible by ATM/debit cards? Does any retailer still offer layaway, and should it become common again, but aimed at young shoppers? I've done some consulting for Crédit Agricole, the French financial institution, which is experimenting with a branch design for students—a smart idea in banking, where the key to long-term success is customer acquisition. The branch won't look like a bank or sound like one—the design, graphics, operating hours, staffing, music and so on will all reflect its Gen X target. There will be on-site seminars on how to rent a first apartment, how to finance a motorcycle, etcetera.

That's a wise approach, for it acknowledges the fact that a product or service meant for youthful shoppers thereby declares itself off-limits to the rest of us. Clarion no longer exists, but it was for a while a heavily promoted cosmetics brand. It was an early user of interactive computer fixtures—women would type in some information about their coloring and skin type, and the computer would tell them which Clarion products to buy. For some reason, though, the fixtures gradually migrated downward to low shelves, positioned perfectly for adolescent girls. They returned the favor by making use of the computers. Once adult women saw this, naturally, they assumed that Clarion was meant for beginners, and steered clear. Thus was Clarion's reputation sealed, and before long it was withdrawn from the market.

IV

See Me, Feel Me, Touch Me, Buy Me:
The Dynamics of Shopping

So far we've seen all that must be done simply to make retail environments user-friendly. The demands of anatomy must be obeyed just for shopping to be practical. The behavioral differences based on gender and age must be accommodated or else stores, restaurants and banks will be best suited to a generic—sexless, ageless—human being who does not exist. Once all that is seen to, of course, things really get challenging. This third aspect of the science of shopping is where we find most of the art—the presentation, the romance, even the seduction, if you will. Shopping, for all we know about it, remains a mystery. Why does someone who walks into a store thinking IBM walk out lugging Compaq, or vice versa? What makes a shopper who decides to kill a few minutes in a boutique walk out $1,000 lighter but feeling more fashionable—more beautiful—than ever before? Yes, the simple answer is that he found something he wanted, but there's no easy explanation for why and how *that* happened. Good stores perform a kind of retailing judo—they use the shopper's own momentum, her largely unspoken inclinations and desires, to get her to move in a direction perhaps unplanned, and often unaware. In the end, it's not enough that goods be within reach of the shopper—she must want to reach them. And having reached them, she must then wish to own them, or all this effort goes for naught. Amid so much science, we discover in the end it's love that makes the world of retailing go round. What do shoppers love? A few important things, we've learned, such as:

Touch. We live in a tactile-deprived society, and shopping is one of our few chances to freely experience the material world firsthand. Almost all unplanned buying is a result of touching, hearing, smelling or tasting something on the premises of a store—which is why merchandising can be more powerful than marketing, and why the Internet, catalogs and home shopping on TV will complement but never seriously challenge real live stores.

Mirrors. Stand and watch what happens at any reflective surface—we preen like chimps, men and women alike. As we've said, mirrors slow shoppers in their tracks, a very good thing for whatever merchandise happens to be in the vicinity. But even around wearable items such as clothing, jewelry and cosmetics, where mirrors are crucial sales tools, stores fail to provide enough of them, much less put them in the right place.

Discovery. There's little more satisfying than walking into a store, picking up the (metaphorical) scent of something we've been hunting for and then tracking it to its lair. Too much signage and point-of-purchase display take all the adventure out of a shopping trip; stores shouldn't be willfully confusing or obscure, but they should seduce shoppers through the aisles with suggestions and hints of what's to come. The aroma of warm bread can be enough to lead supermarket shoppers to the bakery aisle; a big, beautiful photograph of a James Bondian stud in a creamy dinner jacket carries more levels of information than the clearest "Formalwear" sign can ever convey.

Talking. Stores that attract lots of couples, friends or groups of shoppers usually do very well. If you can create an atmosphere that fosters discussion of an outfit, say, or a telephone, the merchandise begins to sell itself.

Recognition. As they sang in the *Cheers* theme, you want to go where everybody knows your name. This is a battlefield where the small, locally owned store can compete with the national chains. Given a choice, people will shop where they feel wanted, and generally they'll even pay a little more for the privilege. Even the smallest stores can build customer loyalty by making their customers feel special. Our studies show that *any* contact initiated by a store employee increases the likelihood that a shopper will buy something. If the salesperson suggests a few things or offers information, the chances rise even higher. Of course, shoppers don't love pushy salespeople, so there's a line here.

Bargains. This seems obvious, but it goes beyond simply cutting prices. At Victoria's Secret, for example, underwear is frequently piled on a table and marked four pair for $20, which sounds like a much better deal than the $5 a pair normally charged. At even the poshest stores, the clearance racks get shopped avidly. Still, while shoppers expect a certain amount of elbow-to-elbow crowding around the discount table, they won't bite if the physical discomfort becomes too noticeable. They'll extricate a blouse from a jammed sale rack, for example, but if there's no room to back up and examine it as closely as the full-price merchandise, they won't buy.

On the other hand, shoppers tend to hate:

Too many mirrors. A store shouldn't feel like a fun house. At a certain point, all that glass becomes disorienting.

Lines. Not only do they also hate to wait, they also hate to feel negative emotions while they do it—like frustration at watching inefficiency, or anxiety wondering if they're in the fastest line, or boredom because there's nothing for them to read, watch or shop while they wait. The memory of a good shopping trip can be wiped out by a bad experience in the checkout line.

Asking dumb questions. New products especially should be out where shoppers can examine them, not behind glass. And there should be enough signs, brochures, instructional videos, newspaper articles, talking displays and whatever else is necessary for browsers to bring themselves up to speed before they ask a question. When stores work at making new or complicated products accessible, sales always increase.

Goods out of stock. Self-explanatory.

Obscure price tags. Ditto.

Intimidating service. Also rude service, slow service, uninformed service, unintelligent service, distracted service, lazy service, surly service. Probably the single best word of mouth for a store is this: "They're so nice down at that shop!" When service is poor, shoppers will find another store; bad service undoes good merchandise, prices and location almost every time. Regardless of how practical an activity shopping seems to be, feelings always come first, and good is always better than bad.

In the chapters that follow we'll discuss what is perhaps the most powerful inducement to shopping—the opportunity to touch, try, taste, smell and otherwise explore the world of desirable objects, and how the artful juxtaposition of those objects can sometimes make all the difference in the world. We'll see how not just the merchandise but the displays, too, determine what gets noticed or ignored. We'll discuss how retailers can manipulate even our perception of time in order to control the shopping experience. We'll also take a look at what might seem to be the antithesis of sensual shopping—the future world of retailing via the Internet.

The Sensual Shopper

TWELVE

This might seem like an odd question coming from anyone at any time but especially coming here and now, at this late stage of an inquiry such as the one we're conducting. But I need to ask it anyway: What *is* shopping?

I don't mean what is buying. I don't mean what is entering a public place where goods are kept until they can be exchanged for money. I definitely do not mean what is retailing, or what is commerce, or what is trade.

I mean what is shopping? Who does it, and how? How does one go about this shopping activity?

For the purposes of this discussion, let's stipulate that shopping is more than the simple, dutiful acquisition of whatever is absolutely necessary to one's life. It's more than what we call the "grab and go"—you need cornflakes, you go to the cornflakes, you grab the cornflakes, you pay for the cornflakes, and *haveaniceday.* The kind of activity I mean involves experiencing that portion of the world that has been deemed for sale, using our senses—sight, touch, smell, taste, hearing—as the basis

for choosing this or rejecting that. It's the sensory aspect of the decision-making process that's most intriguing because how else do we experience anything? But it's especially crucial in this context because
virtually all unplanned purchases—and many planned ones, too—come
as a result of the shopper seeing, touching, smelling or tasting something that promises pleasure, if not total fulfillment.

I want to repeat this because I think it's key: We buy things today
more than ever based on trial and touch.

Now, why might somebody wish to touch something before buying
it? There are plenty of very practical reasons, the most obvious being
that if a product's tactile qualities are what's most important, we must
know how it will feel. For instance, we like to touch towels before we
buy them—in a study we did, towels were touched on average by six
different shoppers before they were purchased. (Which is why you really ought to wash them before you use them.) Bed linens, too—how
sheets feel is pretty much the whole ball game. And clothing—we need
to pet, stroke and fondle sweaters and shirts especially, but most apparel
falls into this category. I think men's underwear makers are missing a
bet by sealing the goods inside plastic bags. No women's underwear is
sold that way, for good reason—women want to test anything that will
go against their skin. Today's men would, too, if only someone gave
them the chance.

There are also nontextile products that come into contact with our
bodies and are therefore touch-worthy—lotions and moisturizers, lipstick, makeup, deodorant, powder, just to pick a few items from the
health and beauty aisles. You need to touch something if it will be held
or carried or wielded in some way. A hammer, for instance—you've got
to heft it before you know it's right for you. Same goes for a handbag,
briefcase or suitcase. An umbrella. A knife, a spatula, tongs. Anything
you're going to carry around all day, like a wallet. Looking gives you a
pretty good idea of how it's going to feel, but nothing takes the place of
your own hand.

What don't you need to touch? Lightbulbs—*nobody* touches lightbulbs. But even they cry out to be experienced. You can buy them in a
box in the supermarket, or hanging from a rack in a hardware store. Or

you can go to a big home center and see those lightbulbs in action, glowing cozily inside lampshades. Which method sells more bulbs, do you think, especially expensive bulbs?

The rule of thumb in these matters is usually that shoppers want to spend time investigating and considering those products in which they have a high level of "involvement," meaning products that offer possibilities or invite comparison. In the supermarket, for instance, you might want to try a new brand of ketchup, or cheese, or a pricey variety of apple or peach, before you buy. Salsa makers, for some reason, always seem to be conducting taste tests of new variations. Nobody needs to taste-test Budweiser, but if you're going to buy that expensive new lambent ale or that Armenian beer, you'll want to try a little first. How about sugar? Waste of time—sugar's sugar. Ditto vegetable oil, although people taste olive oil as though it's vintage wine. Twenty-year-old balsamic vinegar is always going to be a specialty item, but if stores let you try a little you might spring for it. Milk? As long as it's cold and the expiration date hasn't come and gone, you're convinced.

Close to 90 percent of all new grocery products fail, but it isn't because people didn't like them—it's because people never tried them. In my opinion, a new product introduction that doesn't include a well-funded, fully supported (with marketing and ads) effort to give shoppers samples is not a serious attempt. Cigarettes may be bad, but the tobacco companies had a great method for getting samples out there—pretty boys and girls standing on street corners handing out freebies. Even nonsmokers took them, not wanting to reject such pleasant entreaties. Maybe we need to retrain those kids to hand out stuff on the supermarket floor.

Of course, a combined marketing-sampling effort still must properly decide on its target audience. In the earliest days of microwave popcorn, we were hired by General Mills to help expand the market for its product. "Who buys it now?" we asked. "Sixty-four percent of our purchasers are females," came the reply. That was partly because back then men had yet to discover the ease of microwave cuisine, and partly because most of the marketing effort—the TV commercials and print ads—was placed in women's programming and media.

"Whom do you want to reach with the sampling campaign?" we asked. "Well, women, of course," came the reply. Which was the wrong answer—they had already reached a substantial female market. And when you think about microwave popcorn, you realize that it's perfect for men. It's the easiest thing in the world to make, it's a salty snack food and men are suggestible, impulsive shoppers who can be convinced to try almost anything. The product was being sold in six packs for around $4. To gear it toward men, we advised, required less of a commitment—sell a two-pack for a buck and advertise it on the bass-fishing program or during hockey games.

Once you get beyond food, grocery involvement drops. I'm convinced there's room in the marketplace for high-end toilet paper. People would spend more if only it were possible to show them the difference on the floor of the supermarket, and there's the rub. Makers of brand-name plastic food wrap, aluminum foil and trash bags experience a great deal of frustration over this issue. Most shoppers will buy whatever's cheapest, and it's almost impossible to convince them that there's any point to buying a better (and more costly) trash bag. Why spend more when only your trash will know the difference?

Supermarkets are wisely trying to become more conducive to sensual shopping. Most good ones now feature on-premises bakeries, which fill the air with warm, homey scents. You may be in the vitamin section when that aroma hits you, and before you know it you've followed the olfactory trail right up to the counter. Suddenly you're thinking, I need bread! Stores have taken a tip from Starbucks and begun brewing and selling by the cup the expensive coffee beans they sell loose, another way of putting a product's sensory assets to work. In a perfect world we'd enjoy lots more scents in stores. The laundry aisle would smell of soap and fabric softener. In the meat section there'd be steak on the grill or bacon on the griddle. More meat would certainly be sold, but it would also add something to the overall shopping experience—it would become a sensualist's journey, not just a trip to the supermarket. In England, some infant apparel stores now pipe in baby powder through the air ducts, to put shoppers in mind of the sweet-sour smell of newborns, which is perhaps the most powerfully evocative scent of all. When we suggested to American baby powder makers that they add smell to their packaging, they recoiled, fearful that store managers would banish any product that threatened to contaminate the supermarket's sterile, odorless confines. And it's true that with the exception of the produce aisles, supermarkets have no tradition of feeding our desire for sensory stimulation, for scent or taste or touch or even sight. They're still stuck in the early '60s, the time of frozen food, canned food, processed food, powdered food, packaged food and the germless ideal of blinding white cleanliness. As a result, supermarkets have become dangerously dull (dangerous to the markets, I mean). I wish one would install a big open kitchen, like something you'd see on a TV cooking show, where the store chef can whip up snacks and pass them (and their recipes) out to shoppers. How about if the manager announced over the loudspeaker, "Attention all shoppers! For the next fifteen minutes, in the frozen foods section . . . free passion fruit sorbet for everyone!" How about a DJ and a dance floor in produce, a puppet show in the cereal aisle, a jazz trio or the high school glee club at the checkout? It's possible to bring a little more life to a store that is the epitome of shopping puritanism.

Touch and trial are also more important than ever to the world of shopping because of changes in how stores function. Once upon a time store owners and salespeople were our guides to the merchandise they sold. They were knowledgeable enough, and there were enough of them, to act as the shopper's intermediary to the world of things. We could take a clerk's word for something because he or she had been right so many times before. That was, not coincidently, back in the day of grand wooden cabinets with glass fronts behind which goods were displayed, the heyday of the hardware store and the haberdasher and the general store, when space was clearly divided between shoppers and staff.

Today the "open sell" school of display puts almost everything out there where we can touch or smell or try it, unmediated by salesclerks. In 1960, 35 percent of the average Sears store was given over to storage. Today it's less than 15 percent. Today it's almost pointless to ask a clerk if an item you want is in the back room. In some stores there *is* no back room to speak of. Everything is either on the shelves or in the little storage cupboards above or below. It's a brilliant innovation—what good is anything when it's in storage? You can't buy it unless you can find a clerk, and what do you do when there are too few clerks, or too few knowledgeable ones, or too few clerks who are actively trying to help you buy anything? It makes perfect sense to just put it all out there as invitingly and enticingly and conveniently as possible, and then let the shoppers and their good senses discover the stuff on their own.

Another reason touch and trial have become so important is the waning power of product brand name. When consumers believed in the companies behind the big brands, that belief went a long way toward selling things. Now we're all individualists. This is an extreme example, but revealing: In a study we did for a national brand of skin and hair products, we found that of all ethnic groups, Asian-American shoppers were most aggressive about opening the packaging and touching the lotions, soaps and shampoos. In fact, 23 percent of those shoppers tore into the boxes or opened the bottles to test the viscosity and scent of the products. Clearly this was due to the fact that the brand, despite having spent many millions on ads and media, still had not gained instant recognition and loyalty among an important and growing ethnic segment.

For that matter, we are all post-Nader shoppers—we'll believe it when we see/smell/touch/hear/taste/try it. Depending on what we're buying and what it costs, there's a healthy skepticism (or is it a nagging doubt?) in our heads that must be put to rest before we can buy at ease. We need to feel a certain level of confidence in a product and its value, which comes only from hard evidence, not from TV commercials or word of mouth. It's shocking how little stores seem to understand something so simple. We've done lots of research in computer retailing, and we've come upon this over and over: big sections of printers on display, but only some of them are actually plugged in and working and stocked with paper, despite the fact that most printers make it easy to run tests.

And it's not just for big-ticket items like cars, stereo speakers or designer suits that we need to build our confidence. We performed a study of a newsstand design meant to accommodate a refrigerated soft drink case. One plan hid the cooler discreetly under a counter, then allowed for a display of empty cans to show customers what was available. A very unconvincing scheme, we soon learned—people don't believe the sodas are cold unless they can see the frost on them. The need for proof here (as elsewhere) seems almost instinctual. Once the cases were placed where customers could see inside, lots of very cold sodas were sold. Convenience stores excel at this—they taught supermarkets that shoppers prefer to buy their soda or beer cold, even if they're not planning to down it on the spot. Warm beer just *feels* unnatural.

A great deal of our firsthand (ha!) experience of the world comes to us via shopping. Where else do we go with the specific intention of examining objects? To museums, of course, but don't try touching anything that's not in the gift shop—a retail environment. Stores alone are abundant with chances for tactile and sensory exploration. Even if we didn't need to buy things, we'd need to get out and touch and taste them once in a while.

The purest example of human shopping I know of can be seen by watching a child go through life touching absolutely *everything*. You're watching that child shop for information, for understanding, for knowledge, for experience, for sensation. Especially for sensation, otherwise why would he have to touch or smell or taste or hear anything twice? Keep looking: Watch a dog. Watch a bird. Watch a bug. You might say that ant is searching for suitable food. I say he is shopping.

If you still don't believe all this, go to the home of a product fairly unconcerned with matters of smell, touch or any other sensual experience—a bookstore. There you'll be treated to the sight of shoppers stroking, rubbing, hefting and otherwise experiencing the physical nature of a product where no physical attribute (aside maybe from typeface size) has anything to do with enjoyment. Still, helplessly, we touch. We are beasts like any other, and despite all our powers of imagination and conceptualization and intellectualization and cerebration and visualization, we physical creatures experience the world only via our five senses (and maybe, if you're so inclined, our sixth sense—the *über*-sense, the meta-sense, the sense that senses that which cannot be sensed). The world and everything in it reaches out to us and stimulates us through our senses, and we react. So fundamental is our ability to sense and our need to do so that even when we come upon something we can't know via our senses, we speak of it as though we can.

Do you see what I mean? Does this sound right? Do you feel that I'm making sense? Or does my reasoning stink?

Here's a final reason touch is so important. When does a shopper actually possess something? Technically, of course, it happens at the instant that the item is exchanged for money—at the register. But the register is the least pleasing part of the store; nobody is savoring the joy of possession at that moment. In fact, all that is experienced is loss (of money) and pain (of waiting in line, of waiting for the credit card approval, of waiting for the clerk to get the thing into the bag so you can leave). Clearly, possession is an emotional and spiritual process, not a technical one. Possession begins when the shopper's senses start to latch onto the object. It begins in the eyes and then in the touch. Once the thing is in your hand, or on your back, or in your mouth, you can be said to have begun the process of taking it. Paying for it is a mere technicality, so the sooner a thing is placed in the shopper's hand, or the easier it is for the shopper to try it or sip it or drive it around the block, the more easily it will change ownership, from the seller to the buyer.

That's shopping.

So, then, the principle seems simple enough: Shoppers want to experience merchandise before buying it. Therefore, the main function of a store is to foster shopper-merchandise contact. Stores should be begging shoppers to touch or try things, though frequently they make it as difficult as possible. I don't care if we're talking about computer keyboards, shower massagers or a new flavor of Jell-O. If a product does something, it should do it in the store. If it has a taste, shoppers should be able to taste it. If it has a smell, shoppers should be able to smell it. In fact, even if its smell has nothing to do with its purpose, we should be permitted to smell it, for there are times when a product's primary use has absolutely nothing to do with how it will be experienced.

For instance, what do air conditioners promise to do? Make rooms cool. How do we know they can keep that promise? Oh, ask your friends, or read *Consumer Reports,* or rely on the salesclerk's opinion. You can't tell by looking, or even by turning it on in the air-conditioned store. So, in the absence of hard evidence, you buy the brand you always bought or the brand that's on sale. But there's another issue here: How does that air conditioner sound? Precisely because cool air *is* cool air, does this matter. In the final analysis, it's one of the few things that distinguish one air conditioner from another. The unit is going to be humming (or clattering) away in your house for a number of years, after all. In a typical summer, I'll bet I have three or four conversations about air conditioner decibel levels. That's what actual human beings care about when it comes to air conditioners, but you'd never know it when you're shopping for one. The manufacturers and retailers are missing an opportunity here: Maybe, if the salesperson was encouraged to flip a few switches to show you how they sound—this one like a prop airplane, that one like a busted blender, this other, more expensive one like a very small kitten purring in its sleep—you'd have some new basis for choosing one over another.

The same holds true, to some extent, for all major appliances—refrigerators, dishwashers, vacuum cleaners, washers and dryers—and even some minor ones, like coffee grinders, food processors or can openers. We can stare at the box and see at a glance if it's the thing we want. We can read the spec sheet to know more or less what it will do. But then we can at least *hear* it in action.

Here's another way that stores miss the point about how we wish to experience products. Judging by how bed linens are packaged, you'd think the most important issue is something called thread count. What is thread count? Damned if most people know, but it is posted on nearly every sheet and pillowcase package you see. Bed connoisseurs know thread count. Normal human beings, however, judge a sheet mainly by this measure: How does it feel? The problem is that most sheets are sold in plastic bags, which allow you to look but not touch. So you tear open the bag with your nail and furtively rub the fabric. Now if you decide to buy, you'll choose another package, because who wants one that's been damaged (even if *you* did the damaging)? And either way, you still don't know how that sheet will feel, owing to what is known as the sizing. What exactly is sizing? Damned if I know, but you have to wash it out of new sheets or they'll be stiff and scratchy. So why, then, are shoppers made to touch sheets at their absolute worst? There's a huge bed and bath emporium near my office where display sheets have all been laundered once to pillowy perfection, then hung from hooks so shoppers can know what the linens will feel like once you get them home. Which is all that anybody cares about.

Perhaps the most obvious arena for touch and trial is in clothing. Today it's a rare clothes store where shoppers can't touch and fondle and stroke all the goods, whether it's $3 sweat socks or $1,500 designer suits. You still can't go into the Museum of Modern Art and rub a Picasso, but you can walk over to the Calvin Klein or Giorgio Armani stores and have your way with masterpieces of ready-to-wear apparel. For the most part, the men and women who design clothing stores do everything possible to allow us to touch all that's for sale. But then, when it's time to design the dressing rooms, they show how completely they misunderstand what happens inside that store.

Where do they go wrong? They think of dressing rooms as bathrooms without the plumbing. They see them as booths where shoppers can strip, don the garment in question, emerge for a quick, dutiful glance into a mirror and then switch clothes again. They design dressing rooms with all the romance and glamour of changing stalls at public pools. It's the most misguided aspect of store architecture and design, a trade that at best isn't terribly responsive to retailers or shoppers. The store designers skimp on dressing rooms, I believe, because they don't want to "waste" space by making these rooms too large. They don't want to blow too much of the budget on rooms that will never be photographed by the design magazines.

In fact, the dressing room may be more important than the floor of the store. It's a truism that improving the quality of dressing rooms increases sales. It never fails. A dressing room isn't just a convenience—it's a selling tool, like a display or a window or advertising. It sells more effectively than all of those combined, if it's properly used. I am an incurable dressing-room visitor—I'll make a special trip into a store's dressing room if I'm anywhere in the vicinity. If the coast is clear, I'll even ask if I can look in on women's dressing rooms. The truth is that I could write an entire book about dressing rooms—there's that much to say. Here's a formula we've recognized after studying a great many clothing stores: Shopper conversion rate increases by half when there is a staff-initiated contact, and it jumps by 100 percent when there is staff-initiated contact *and* use of the dressing room. In other words, a shopper who talks to a salesperson and tries something on is twice as likely to buy as a shopper who does neither.

Still, we did a study for a major apparel chain, one that has been extremely successful, where the dressing rooms were just dismal. Stark, cheesy little cubicles, a long corridor of them, with a single, badly illuminated mirror down at the end of the row. In this store we measured, people who buy spend between one-quarter and one-third of their total shopping time inside the dressing rooms. In other words, they are captives in a very small space with nothing on their minds but the desire to buy something that will make them beautiful. In any other business, such a time would be avariciously thought of as "the close"—the critical moment when the buyer is vulnerable and ready to take the plunge. In a car dealership, which is itself no great shakes at the art of retailing, there are rooms set aside just to orchestrate this critical juncture. Here, however, there was absolutely no effort to make the rooms even minimally pleasant, or to make the area conducive to seeing the clothes in their best possible light. Neither was anyone viewing this as the moment for bringing all the charm and service of the sales force to bear on the situation. I mean simple things, too, such as the clerk escorting the customer to the dressing room, then going out to find a few belts that might go nicely with the trousers, or a shirt, or a vest, knowing that many times the right accessory sells the garment. When the customer is in the dressing room, he or she is in a total buying mode. But instead of taking advantage of that moment, most stores squander it.

In fact, I visited the couture floor of a major department store in New York and saw what may have been the most horrible dressing rooms I've ever seen. Dirty, shabby, worn rugs. Harsh, unflattering lighting. The same wall hooks and seats you'd find in a low-rent discounter. Mirrors that distort the viewer's body, and not for the better. When I pointed this out a saleslady sardonically asked, "Doesn't *every* woman want bigger hips?" The furnishings should be what you'd want in your dream boudoir. The lighting should make everybody look like a million bucks. In fact, the illumination should have several settings, so you could see what a color would look like in daylight, or under fluorescent lighting, or by candlelight. The mirrors should be large, plentiful and first-rate—they should be like the frame for a flattering portrait, not just a slab of glass hung by clips on a Sheetrock wall. If there's space for a little ante-room outside the dressing rooms, so much the better. A shopper and his or her companion can really look the goods over out there. A shopper could see what it feels like to sit down wearing the garment, an impor-tant issue if it's to be worn at a special dinner, for instance. And there should be fresh flowers. Fresh flowers say that someone has paid atten-tion to the room today, not yesterday, and that's the proper message.

Even outside the dressing rooms, apparel stores often mishandle something as simple as mirrors. Most commonly, there are too few of them or they're placed badly. There should be a mirror anywhere there's merchandise that can be tried on or even just held up for inspec-tion. If you pick up an item and can see in an instant how it looks on you, you might buy it. If you've got to search for a mirror, at least some of the time you'll decide it's not worth the trouble. If the hats are here, the hat mirror should be here, too—not five feet away. And I've seen more than one self-serve shoe department with no mirrors down at floor level. I've seen self-serve shoe sections with no chairs! This all seems so simple. Why is it ever wrong?

There must be enough dressing rooms, and they must be clearly marked so they're easy to find, even from a distance. The farther they are from the clothes, the fewer shoppers will bother to make the trip. A truly determined shopper will always find a dressing room, but no store can survive only on the stouthearted. We've seen stores where you had to cross the entire selling floor and then go up or down a few steps to try something on. That's fatal. We did a study for a department store where our video cameras caught shoppers wandering uncertainly, garments in hand, searching (and searching) for the dressing rooms. There were enough of them, but they were hidden in corners, bare little doorways marked by inconspicuous signs. Finding a dressing room shouldn't be a challenge.

Okay, what have we here? A guy, in an office supply store, one of the big chains. He's standing at the pencil sharpener shelf, where he finds a few manual ones, some battery-powered and some big plug-in jobs. He turns the handles on the manual ones to get their feel. Then he lifts a battery model and pries open the compartment to find . . . nothing. He moves on to the plug-in models and lifts them, too, then looks around to see if there's an outlet. Nothing. Even had he found a battery or an outlet, there's the small matter of pencils, none of which are anywhere in sight. He grabs a sharpener, then wheels away, out of the aisle, in search of an electrical outlet, I presume, and maybe a pencil, too.

Does this seem like a serious effort to sell pencil sharpeners? Clearly, there must be a difference in sharpeners, else why would there be so many choices? But how can this poor guy choose one over another—or any one at all—without a test grind? It seems like the simplest matter in the world to anticipate what shoppers will want to do and where they'll want to do it. In the absence of a pencil-sharpener clerk, please allow me to figure it out myself. But bad stores get it wrong all the time, even large, sophisticated, profitable national chains of bad stores. In that same store, there is a ten-foot-high wall rack of paper sold in reams, which themselves are encased in paper wrappers. Some of the paper is cheap, some of it more expensive—but there is not a single chance to see or touch the paper being sold. As a result, every fifth or sixth package has been torn open for some frustrated shopper's furtive inspection. This is a classic example of how a decision to be cheap (not allowing shoppers to touch even one sheet of paper) ends up costing money (lots of packages are torn and unsalable).

Making goods inaccessible hurts in other ways, too. We studied a jewelry store whose owner had recently scored a coup by hiring a designer well known for creating museum exhibitions to design some jewelry display cases. The result was beautiful, but distancing—the guy was accustomed to making displays that allowed the public to see but kept them at arm's length, exactly what you don't want in a store where people are encouraged to take the goods home. The displays performed poorly compared to less exalted fixtures.

Here's how good stores do it. We were performing a study for RadioShack just when the chain had decided to try to become America's favorite phone store. We watched countless shoppers approach the wall of telephones on display, look them all over, check out the prices and then, almost without exception, pick up a phone and hold it up to an ear. What were they hoping for? Nothing, probably—it's just a reflex action, I think. What else do you *do* with a phone? On what other basis do you compare phones but by how they feel in your hand and against your ear? Well, we reasoned, if the first principle of trial is to make it as lifelike as possible, you can complete the experience by putting a voice in that phone. We advised RadioShack to connect the phones to a recorded message that would be activated when a receiver was lifted. Once that happened, the stores were alive with shoppers picking up display phones, listening a moment and then holding the receivers out for their companions to hear—which was a bonus, because that would provide some basis for discussing the purchase, which greatly increases the chance that something will be bought. (People in stores love to talk about whatever it is they're shopping for.) This was also a good way for RadioShack to sneak in a commercial message. In another phone store study, the store used a counter display so that you could see and heft the various models, but each phone was also activated, which is the only way to do it—customers picked up the phones and dialed a spouse or friend to discuss the very gadget they were considering. The phones sold themselves, which is the whole point.

Other stores, like The Sharper Image, Brookstone or the French beauty retailer Sephora, which recently opened stores in New York and Chicago, all understand the value of putting merchandise out there for shoppers to experience, damage be damned. If The Sharper Image displays a vibrating chair and after a few months it's shabby from shopper use, that's okay—they've no doubt sold enough to cover the loss. Stores that strive to make everything accessible to browsers will lose a little to shopper abuse but gain more in sales.

Store displays can be remade to allow shoppers to touch and try the merchandise. But if product packaging doesn't change as well, a great many opportunities will continue to be lost. In the health and beauty aisles, for instance, smell and touch are vitally important. What is skin lotion's first responsibility if not to feel good when applied to skin? Why does anyone buy deodorant except for its scent? And while shampoo's main job is to clean hair—something you can't really test in a store—it also must leave that hair smelling like the rain forest on a good day, and that's something you *can* investigate in the aisle, if only the manufacturer will permit it. Unfortunately, today's tamper-proof packaging thwarts every respectful attempt to experience the product.

Gillette made quite a splash with its clear gel deodorants for men— they come in a variety of scents, each with an evocative (yet manly) name. Somebody at Gillette was thinking right when they decided to give men more of a choice than Right Guard menthol or regular. But then the boys in packaging got their mitts on the idea. In the store you are faced with several varieties of deodorant, differing only in scent, so naturally you wish to learn, how do they smell? You remove the lid from one and are confronted by a formidable strip of heavy-duty foil tape sealing the applicator. (Why? Can terrorists kill people through their armpits?) Now, if no one's watching, you might peel that tape back some and give it a sniff. But that would be wrong. So what's a shopper to do? If he's not terribly motivated, he'll put it back and walk away. If he is persistent, he'll glance up and down the aisle, and if the coast is clear, rip back that tape and take a whiff. Of course, if he then decides against buying the Alpine Dawn underarm experience—maybe he feels like more of an Arizona Twilight kind of guy—how will the next shopper who comes along feel when he discovers that the tamper-proof strip has been tampered with? A lot of perfectly good deodorant is going to be ruined that way, by package designers who refuse to acknowledge how human beings shop.

One solution for this and all the rest would be for drugstores to create a sampling bar, a counter where new items can be freely auditioned.

The tactile issues of body products are so important that resolving them would surely result in increased sales.

The biggest struggle in this area has to do with how cosmetics are sold. Manufacturers and retailers want to sell the products in as clean and orderly a way as possible. Women don't object to that but, understandably, they want to try before they buy, which is not always a clean and orderly impulse.

In days of old, most cosmetics were sold by the same kindly druggist who doled out prescriptions and fountain sodas. You'd ask for foundation, say, and he'd go behind the counter, open a drawer and begin pulling out boxes until he found your brand. It was kind of arm's length, and no one would stand for that today, but it was efficient and neat. The world of cosmetics was liberated in large part by Cover Girl, which was the first brand to make wide use of the peg wall, allowing shoppers to touch makeup without an intermediary getting in the way. This was what moved cosmetics toward its future as a self-serve category. That also put a serious crimp in the future prospects of another cosmetics tradition, the department store bazaar. There, even to this day, shoppers perch on stools at counters while Kabuki-faced representatives of makeup purveyors paint and daub them into perfection, the result of which is a small but costly shopping bag of makeup on the departing shopper's arm.

But even that method of selling cosmetics is passing from the scene—women are fed up, I think—and is being replaced by the open sell layout. So you have each manufacturer trying a different display system that allows shoppers to look at cosmetics, and even, under controlled conditions, to try them. But not too much. And you have women who wish to undo those controls so that they can test products as they please. The interests of seller and buyer shouldn't be at odds, but often they are. Designers of cosmetics fixtures are sometimes culprits, too—they build displays without considering that shoppers need simple amenities like tissues, for instance, which would improve the overall neatness of cosmetics sections. Or they don't put enough mirrors, so women have to scramble around the store as they try out makeup. The designers of these sections never visit them at 5 p.m. on a

Saturday afternoon, I can assure you, because if they did they'd design them differently, with more accommodation for the women who use them. Shopper-unfriendly packaging intended to prevent cosmetics trial is almost always a bad idea—bad because it discourages buying, and because it encourages women to damage merchandise. In any product category, the best way to limit package destruction is to offer shoppers a way to try things without doing any damage.

The advent of shrink wrap has made it difficult to experience a great many products firsthand. In fact, many products seem to be overly packaged, which is a pain if you're a hands-on shopper. We've come a long way from the simple listening booths once found in record stores. Today there are several rather complex electronic systems that try to make samples of recordings available to shoppers. Typically, these involve listening stations—headphones plugged into a board, and then a menu of CDs that can be dialed up. One problem is that you may be unfamiliar with these gizmos, so you push the button for the disk you want, but then . . . nothing. In fact, there's a wait while the song cues up, but no indicator on the machine tells you so. You give it a moment and either shrug and give up, or you assume you've chosen a nonworking channel and push another button, and then more buttons, ultimately sending the machine into meltdown.

The best system is always the simplest and most direct one, like what's in use at some Blockbuster Music stores. There, a shopper selects any CD from any rack and brings it to a listening bar, where a clerk opens the package and plays the disk. That's it—no gizmos, no buttons, no menus, no waiting. Instead of spending money on complicated, unreliable song sample-playing machines, the store buys one shrink-wrapping device to repackage whatever's not purchased, and that's that. Such systems must also allow shoppers to listen to music as human nature intended—meaning, nobody listens to music standing still and staring at the floor. In a store we researched in Alabama, listening station headphones were equipped with twenty-foot-long cords, so music fans could move around and even shop nearby racks. With that, the stores go from being places to buy records to places where one can listen to them, find out what's out there, what's new, who's playing what.

It turns the store into an interactive radio station and makes shopping a fun experience. Best of all, from the store's point of view, it lessens the retailer's dependence on the record companies to market their merchandise properly. When a store allows access to merchandise, it is in essence doing its own marketing—one-on-one, to an interested consumer who is in a position to act on his or her desires on the spot.

Packaging often suffers when the shopper's desire for information is thwarted. We see this with electronics—the shopper for stereo headphones, for instance, finds a stack of them, boxed, in a store. There's no display model in sight. If the box were properly designed—with a large, clear photo of the headphones, and all the features and specifications listed in readable type—maybe seeing the headphones would be less crucial. But when the packaging forces shoppers to guess, it becomes easier to just rip the box open, pull out the headphones and see for yourself. If the shopper doesn't buy, you're left with unsalable goods. No one's going to buy anything being sold in a shredded box.

Packaging need not always be such an impermeable barrier to touch, however. Manufacturers realized that adults wanted to try toys before they bought them. Maybe this was because so much toy advertising is deceptive, giving gullible kiddies the impression that this cheap plastic airplane would be capable of zooming around the kitchen like a miniature bomber on an air strike. At any rate, the trend is now to design packaging that allows toys to be tried without having to molest the box or the plastic wrap. You can push the button or pull the string and Cookie Monster sings from inside his cardboard prison. This suddenly made it a lot easier to know what you were buying in the toy store, and this was one of those instances where shopper confidence led to increased sales. I recently saw maybe the smartest toy packaging yet—a kiddie plastic tricycle that was boxed in a way that left exposed the seat, pedals, handlebars and wheels, thereby allowing a child to test-drive it without disturbing the box. If that principle were applied to all product packaging, shopping would be a lot more fun than it is now.

Security considerations are behind some reasons for placing merchandise off-limits. Personal stereos—those little tape or CD players with headphones—are one such product. I guess any pricey item with lots of appeal for teenagers is heisted frequently. But the decision to sell these behind a locked counter should be enough; instead, they're also packaged inside bulky, clear plastic "clamshell" containers, which makes it impossible to hear the player before buying it. I'm sure that shoppers would trade up to more expensive models if only they could comparison-shop a few models.

Costume jewelry is another category that's often guilty of this sin. You've got items that cost maybe $20 or $30 padlocked behind glass and steel, depriving shoppers of the chance to see how the chains and pendants would look and feel on a neck or a wrist. In the same store you'll see plenty of other merchandise of equal or greater value on open display. It's reflexive but makes no business sense. We see the same thinking about one of the hottest items to grow out of the computerization of America—printer ink-jet cartridges. Frequently they're displayed inside locked cabinets, owing to their small size and high price. But when you've seen as many frustrated shoppers prowling store aisles searching vainly for a clerk with a key as we have, you wonder if there isn't something self-defeating about all that security.

Clothing retailers have learned a trick or two about placing goods on display without allowing them to be abused in the process. Let's go back to that beautiful Armani store on Madison Avenue. You've got shoppers whose hands have been who-knows-where, and they're groping costly Italian adornments as though they already own them. Would you feel at ease knowing how many fingers have already had their way with your suit sleeve? Here's one strategy: If a suit comes in several colors, the store will place the dark shades down where they can be reached easily, and display the beiges and pale grays and off-whites up high, where they can be seen but not touched. If a sweater displayed on a table comes in several shades, you'll always find the lighter ones on the bottom and the dark on top, where they'll be rubbed and grubbed, but who will know?

Selling is the main reason for making merchandise as available as possible to shoppers. But it's not the only one—there's also selling up. If you have no real basis for comparing one product to another, the normal instinct is to buy what's cheaper. But if a store sets itself up to educate shoppers, even just a little, a certain number of them will spend more than what is absolutely necessary. If given a choice of three brands, or three models, and given the chance to pit one against the others, the shopper will at least have a sensible reason for choosing the better item.

This is an issue for just about every product we've mentioned so far—men's underwear and coffee and stereo headphones and sweaters and skin cream, etcetera. In mattress stores, too, typically, you find a whole field of undressed beds awaiting inspection. Some are cheaper than others, but it's just as expensive to stock and maintain the $400 mattress as it is the $2,000 one. So if you can get just one customer in five to start out trying the cheap number and work up to a better one, you're doing pretty well.

And how, aside from trial, can that be made to happen? Clearly, no other way. And the beds are all out there, ready for you to recline, isn't that right? Well, kind of. You really need to feel comfortable to try out a mattress. It's a vulnerable position to take in such a public space, in front of strangers. You may even wish you didn't have to lie down while the salesman stands there, looming over you. (He, of course, is afraid that if he backs off five feet and stops sending you telepathic "Buy this mattress now!" messages, you won't purchase anything.) And you're on a mattress that has been helpfully positioned in the front of the store, where your supine form can be seen easily through the front window, and where, if you are a woman in a dress or skirt, your modesty will be severely tested. How much worse can this experience be made? How about no sheets on the bed, so you never even see how it will feel if and when you get it home, and no pillow either, so you get no idea of the comfort this baby will (or will not) provide?

It seems that if the better mattresses were positioned away from public view, maybe even partly partitioned, to give the experience a little of the feel of a dressing room, maybe shoppers would be encouraged to upgrade their bedding desires. More thought is given to the trial experience when you're buying a pair of $40 jeans than when you're buying a $2,000 mattress. We did a study of mattress retailing, during which we asked a manager whether pillows of various thicknesses and firmness could be provided, along with freshly laundered pillowcases, for mattress tryouts.

"But we don't *sell* pillows," was his flat rejection of the idea. Never mind that pillows have a much higher margin than mattresses even, or that selling pillows was a way of adding on accessories to a product that had few opportunities for such novelties.

Similarly, at AT&T Phone Stores, the focus was on selling the main product; almost as an afterthought, they sold a dopey little item called the Soft Talk phone holder. It was a soft plastic cradle to make it more comfortable to keep your phone jammed between your neck and shoulder. The thing didn't look like much of anything, but once you tried it you learned that it was ingenious and truly effective. Without trying it, however, it looked pointless, and because none were on display there was no easy way to try it, and thanks to the sales staff's lack of effort nobody ever did. Sure, it was only a $5 or so item, but the margin on it, as with most accessories, was obscenely high—the most profitable thing in the joint. We computed that if every third customer bought one, the profit would cover a store's monthly rent.

A similar issue was uncovered in another phone store study ten years later. Again, it had to do with placing too much of the focus on selling wireless service contracts and not enough of it on just making money. In this store, the phone automatically came with a standard, no-frills leatherette carrying case, free of charge. But if you wanted something a little sportier—say, a faux leopard skin case or something in red suede—you were out of luck. None were for sale. The store was so intent on selling the contracts that it never occurred to anyone to show a little more ambition. Even today, if you sign up for AT&T wireless service and decide that you want to add on a fancy phone case, or a spare battery or a charger, you are stymied and out of luck. The operator who just spent twenty minutes selling you can't do accessories. He or she can only direct you to call another number, setting you up for what will probably be an endless wait for another live human being to pick up. Faced with that obstacle, you'll probably find your accessories elsewhere.

There's one final issue regarding the sensory and tactile nature of shopping. Oddly, it involves letting shoppers know that it's *all right* for them to touch. At Hallmark stores we studied, some front-end Christmas ornament displays were so artfully designed and painstakingly constructed that shoppers didn't know if they were supposed to take or just gaze adoringly. Bookstores, too, sometimes run into the same problem when tabletop displays show a little too much effort. People know how hard it is to get anything looking nice, so they can be reluctant to undo somebody's hard work. We ran into this while helping Einstein Bagels test-drive a prototype restaurant in Utah, of all places. A brilliantly anomalous decision, by the way, inventing a new way to sell bagels in a place where there is no bagel culture to speak of—if you can get it working there, it'll work anywhere. At this store, a wall rack holding bags of variously flavored bagel chips was positioned so that customers standing in line to pay would be able to reach out and grab something on impulse. The problem was that the bags were stocked so neatly, and with such an orderly eye, that customers were never quite sure if they were meant to touch the thing. The solution was to have an employee come out every so often and mess the shelves up, pulling a few bags out so there would be obvious gaps. *Then* the customers touched. (People are awfully polite in Utah, aren't they?) Actually, the clerks would create a total sensory experience by grabbing a bag, ripping it open and proffering it to those waiting in line, as a way to introduce the locals to the wonders of jalapeño-cheddar–whole-wheat bagel chips. Which may sound like a joke, but don't laugh until you've tried them.

The Big Three

THIRTEEN

I've got a brilliant idea: Let's save money! We're in charge of merchandising and display for a chain of video stores here, so let's make an executive decision to replace our expensive old wooden shelving with a cheaper new wire grid system. The difference in cost goes directly to the bottom line. There. Done. Next?

What? Oh. Well look at that. Yikes. Who knew? The wire shelving seemed perfectly beautiful and functional—until actual video boxes were placed on it. At that point (or minutes after, I should say) the main drawback to the wire grid became clear: Every time a customer touches a box, it tilts. Sometimes, to be honest, nobody touches a box and it tilts. I think the damn boxes may be tilting each other. And you look down the long expanse of wire grids and every fourth or fifth video box has tipped, and it looks like hell, I'll be the first to agree, so somebody needs to go straighten it. The boys over in operations are screaming like wet chimps: We're now paying people $6.50 an hour to straighten video boxes. On a busy Saturday night, as the lines grow long, we're talking an hour or more per store of wasted labor. How many stores? How many hours? How much did we save? Uh-oh.

And that's not a hypothetical scenario, either—it's verbatim from the Envirosell playbook. It illustrates one of the most important principles of shopping. Retailing 101 starts with the notion that a store has three distinct aspects: design (meaning the premises), merchandising (whatever you put in them) and operations (whatever employees do). These Big Three, while seemingly separate, are in fact completely and totally intertwined, interrelated and interdependent, meaning that when somebody makes a decision regarding one, a decision has been made about the other two as well. In this particular instance, the mistake was one that's made all the time: Display designers apparently never go into stores to see their creations in action, so they don't have a firm grip on what happens in the real world. The larger lesson here is that if one of the Big Three is strengthened, it takes some of the pressure off the others. If one is weakened, it shifts more burden onto the remaining two. This is not a good thing or a bad thing—it just is. It's the *geometry* that rules the shopping universe.

Here's an example. The trademark of The Gap and many other clothing stores is that you can easily touch, stroke, unfold and otherwise examine at close range everything on the selling floor. A lot of sweaters and shirts are sold thanks to the decision to foster intimate contact between shopper and goods. That merchandising policy dictates the display scheme (wide, flat tabletops, which are easier to shop than racks or shelves). It also determines how and where employees will spend their time; all that touching means that sweaters and shirts constantly need to be refolded and straightened and neatened. That translates into the need for lots of clerks roaming the floor rather than standing behind the counter ringing up sales. Which is a big expense, but for The Gap and others, it's a sound investment—the cost of doing business. The main thing here is that it was a conscious decision.

Sometimes it's not a decision so much as a response to a fact of life. Revlon's merchandising must work in a variety of settings—mass merchandisers, specialty stores, drugstores. In the latter, typically, the aisles are narrow and jammed with stuff. Because of that design reality, the dreaded butt-brush factor—the fact that women don't like to be bumped from behind while shopping—comes into play. Revlon's drugstore merchandising must be clear, bold and direct, so that women can spot the brand name, find what they're looking for and be on their way as quickly as possible. If the signage and displays were more subtle or oblique, those women would have been butt-brushed out of the aisle before they chose a single thing. This issue comes up all the time because the people who design packaging and merchandising materials don't spend enough time in stores, visiting their creations where they live. For instance, college-educated shoppers tend to read what's printed on a package. That's how they prefer to info-load before deciding whether to buy. So a company selling herbal remedies should instruct its package designers to incorporate a fair amount of text on those bottles. The designer follows orders. But small type is hard to read for older shoppers, who are a prime market for vitamins and herbal supplements. And these products tend to sell well in drugstores, where aisles typically are narrow, which discourages shoppers from reading any package for very long. That's how a good decision (adding more information to a package) leads to a not so good result (no one can read it).

The point here is that whenever a decision is made, it should be examined closely for its farthest-reaching implications. In real life, that doesn't often happen. It doesn't happen in small firms, where a few people are run ragged making all the decisions. And it especially doesn't happen in big firms. Frequently, we'll go into some company's conference room to deliver our findings, and chiefs of store design, merchandising and operations will be present. Sometimes it's clear that they barely know one another. In some extreme cases, they may even be based in different cities. The suspicion, hostility and turf-warring can seem palpable. The executives either don't know what the others are doing or don't care to know. A lot of shortsighted decisions get made.

Here's a good example. In a big, famous department store, the boss of ladies' shoes decided that he needed more display space, and that he'd get it by shrinking the register area. As a result, the clerks who once used the counter for bagging had to start placing bags on the floor and lowering the shoes in. This added several steps to the process and made ringing up sales more arduous for the clerks, who usually wore pretty fancy shoes themselves. By the end of a day these women were hurting and dragging—and, understandably, a little bitter. As part of our research we trained video cameras on the register and then, back at the office, we timed transactions with a stopwatch; at 4:30 p.m., it took almost twice as long to ring up a sale as it did at 11 a.m. Shrinking the counter space also added to the general clutter, making transactions less crisp than they had been. The overall result was that a mild improvement in merchandising required a change in design, which hurt operations quite a bit. In order to show a few more shoes (maybe a dozen pair), transaction time grew longer, customer patience grew thin, and employee energy and morale grew short. Considering that employees sell shoes better than any display, this was a very bad decision—all because someone who should have known better forgot that when you change one thing, everything changes.

Another client, a video chain (not the same one in the opening example), made some interesting decisions about how its stores would look. The dominant color would be a deep burgundy. And a lighting motif would be rows of lightbulbs, as movie marquees once employed. It all looked good on the drawing board, maybe, but then real life happened. The burgundy kept getting scuffed and dented and chipped and dinged, meaning the store got dingy-looking fast, and the painters were spending an awful lot of time on the premises doing touch-ups. That's usually the fate of any surface painted a rich, dark shade—every scuff shows. Also, the dark walls and display racks required more illumination than off-white would have needed. Which was expensive just for the electricity, forget about the fact that all those lightbulbs had the habit of burning out, which meant they had to be replaced at once or risk looking like something from Times Square—the old Times Square. In the end, bad design decisions added quite a bit to the chain's overhead and maintenance, which came right out of the bottom line.

Relations between the three aspects of retail are under a fair amount of stress today for one main reason: Most firms are constantly looking to save money on labor. From the businessperson's point of view, this falls under the heading of operations. From the shopper's perspective, it means service. Retailers try to maintain service while cutting labor, which is usually impossible to do. Back when stores were properly staffed, and employees were encouraged to stay in their jobs and learn their category, the demands on design and merchandising were few and simple. A store could even be cluttered and disorganized because there was always a clerk available to help, and he or she always knew where everything was kept.

Today, when many retailers underpay and undervalue their sales staff, the opposite is true. The burden falls on design and merchandising, which are sometimes up to the job, but not always. For example, retailers try to make up for staff cuts by using interactive computerized fixtures or kiosks to answer shoppers' questions. The only problem is that the fixtures are frequently badly designed—they're confusing, or don't answer questions fully, or are so slow that you'd think they stopped working. So what do shoppers do? We've seen lots of them give up and walk away grumbling. Some just grab a salesclerk and drag him or her over to figure out how to use the thing. That's some labor-saving device.

At a department store we studied, the beleaguered staff saved time by overstocking the fixtures—jamming more clothes onto the racks than they could handle comfortably. Some shoppers didn't even bother trying to extricate garments, it was such a struggle. Customers who did wrestle a hanger out invariably pulled other garments along with it, dragging them to the floor. And whose job was it to pick them up, dust them off and re-hang them? The time saved by overstocking was wasted in maintenance. Even worse, while the clothes lay on the floor no shopper would touch them. You should have seen the lingerie section—would you buy underwear off the floor?

But it is possible to use design and merchandising to save operations some work. One example comes from the United States Postal Service, which is testing a number of prototypes of the new and (vastly) improved post office. In one such "store," the self-serve section—you buy stamps and envelopes from an open display, weigh your own packages and apply your own postage—was positioned beyond the traditional counters staffed by postal workers. In another configuration, the self-serve was right inside the entrance, with the full-serve counters in the rear. The first store had a fairly low rate of self-serve; people who were

used to dealing with clerks just got in line and never even saw the machines in back. The second prototype had a much higher self-serve
use—customers would enter fully intending to stand in the teller lines,
then see people quickly taking care of things on their own. Banks find
the same pattern—if ATMs and automatic deposit machines are in view
of the teller lines, full-service customers "migrate" over to the automated side.

The second example comes from a giant drugstore chain. Pharma-
cies have changed a lot in the past two decades, but one thing remains
constant: the large burden on staff to stock all those little bottles, jars
and boxes in perfectly straight rows in aisle after aisle of shelving. Every
time a customer picks something up to read the label, you're guaranteed that the thing needs to be straightened, or turned so it faces front.
It's a lot of work. Not long ago Wal-Mart tried an experiment: It began
replacing traditional shelves with a system of bins. Instead of a shelf
facing of aspirin bottles, say, the shopper would see a blowup of the aspirin label. Under that blowup was the bin, into which the aspirin bottles had been dumped.

This made an enormous difference. First, it solved the problem of
stocking—a clerk could just roll a trolley of merchandise to the aisle,
open the bin, dump in the goods and move on. No more straight lines.
The shoppers liked it better, too—instead of facing a row of bottles
with tiny print, they saw a large, easy-to-read version of the label. It was
much easier on the eyes, especially for older shoppers. Wal-Mart's main
concern in making the change was whether shoppers would perceive
the bins as being somehow cheaper and lower in quality than the
shelves. In fact, just the opposite was true—shoppers interviewed said
they thought the bins were an upgraded display system. A very elegant
solution.

Time, Real and Perceived

FOURTEEN

In stores, as in life, there's good times and there's bad times. Good times—meaning anytime a customer is shopping—you want to stretch. Bad times you want to bend.

Bad times are whenever the customer is made to wait. Understandably, they don't like it, but as reasonable beings, they'll do it—up to a point. Beyond that, though, comes trouble. In study after study, we've seen that the single most important factor in determining a shopper's opinion of the service he or she receives is waiting time. If shoppers think the wait wasn't too bad, they feel as though they were treated capably and well. If the wait went on too long, they feel as though the service was poor and inept. Quite simply, a short wait enhances the entire shopping experience and a long one poisons it.

But it's possible to "bend" waiting time—to alter how shoppers perceive it. You can even turn bad times into good times.

First, a word about the whole issue of time and perception. There's the watch on your wrist, which is probably a highly accurate instrument, but there's an even more important clock inside your head. That mental timepiece is highly susceptible to outside influences, yet it counts more than any Rolex. We've interviewed lots of shoppers on the subject and have found this interesting result: When people wait up to about a minute and a half, their sense of how much time has elapsed is fairly accurate. Anything over ninety or so seconds, however, and their sense of time distorts—if you ask how long they've been waiting, their honest answer can often be a very exaggerated one. If they've waited two minutes, they'll say it's been three or four. In the shopper's mind, the waiting period goes from being a transitional pause in a larger enterprise (purchasing goods) to being a full-fledged activity of its own. That's when time becomes very bad. Time's a cruel master in the world of shopping: Taking care of a customer in two minutes is a success; doing it in three minutes is a failure.

The obvious appeal of drive-thru shopping (or banking, or dining) is in its convenience and efficiency—you save yourself the trouble of finding a parking spot, then parking, then getting out of your car and going inside and then having to do it all over again in reverse. One of our favorite pieces of videotape shows a bank drive-thru in Whittier, California, where the cars in line were joined by one time-stressed man on foot. But even if drive-thru didn't move things faster, the comfort of waiting in your own car, sitting in a comfortable seat with the CD player and heater or air conditioner on, would without question make it *feel* faster.

Most of this matter of time centers on the cashier area—when shoppers are standing in line to pay, see a teller or order a meal. And it's there that measures can be taken to bend waiting time. Such as:

Interaction, human or otherwise. Time a shopper spends waiting after an employee has initiated contact goes faster than time spent waiting before that interaction takes place, our studies show. Having an employee simply acknowledge that the shopper is waiting—and maybe offer some plausible explanation—automatically relieves time anxiety, especially when it comes early in the wait. I once visited a big chain drugstore where the manager clearly loved customer contact. When the checkout lines got a little too long he'd leave his office and work the front of the store like a combination expediter–standup comic. His presence seemed to make the cashiers move a little faster, and he was entertaining, too. If, during busy times, I had a choice of deploying three cashiers or two cashiers and a line manager, I'd go with the latter. The line manager serves as a pre-cashier—he or she can gently suggest to shoppers that they have their orders ready, or answer any questions the customers may have, thereby shortening both the perceived and the actual wait. This can be a great way to train even your customers to be more efficient.

Another, related way to bend time is to tell shoppers their wait will be finite and controlled rather than open-ended and subject to the vagaries of fate and chance. Some banks do this by posting an electronic sign that announces how many minutes the wait for a teller should last. These signs are never accurate, but that's okay—just being told that your patience must last only two minutes makes the four minutes you actually wait go faster. I recently called a computer manufacturer's telephone technical help hotline. A recorded voice informed me that my wait for a human being would last "an estimated one to five minutes." Which is a wide span, when you think about it, but they were placating my time anxiety while playing it safe, a smart move.

Orderliness. European shoppers don't seem to mind queueing up in a great, heaving mass of humanity, but Americans and Britons like their lines single file, crisp and fair. Making people guess about where to stand frustrates them. Allowing chaos to reign causes anxiety. If customers see that they're being helped in the exact order they arrived, they relax, and the time spent waiting seems shorter. This is the secret to bending time—get rid of the uncertainty and you cut the perceived wait.

The organization of cashier lines is still one of the great ongoing quandaries in the world of shopping. Without question, the fastest, fairest system places customers in a single checkout line. This way guarantees that shoppers are taken in the order they arrive, and there's no angst about whether they've chosen the swiftest line. There's just one problem: You will sometimes have one *very* long line—a worrisome sight for a shopper in a hurry. Somehow, three lines of five customers each promise less of an ordeal than a single line of fifteen people. It's irrational but true, and such is the difference between perception and reality.

Companionship. The wait seems shorter if you've got someone to talk to, no surprise. A store can't do much about that, except to recognize that the lone shoppers are the ones who need employee contact most.

Diversion. Almost anything will suffice. Video stores should play movies suitable for all audiences. (And the monitors should face the queue—we once did a job for a video store where the clerks had turned the monitors so that *they* would be entertained.) One bank we studied used a TV tuned to soap operas to entertain the line—a bad idea because to enjoy a soap you need to see the entire half hour. A much better solution was used by another bank, in California, where a big-screen TV played old Keystone Kops shorts during the afternoon, when most customers were retirees. Everybody's considering video systems these days, but some low-tech entertainments work just as well. Many food stores serve free samples, a good time killer that promotes new products. Positioning racks of impulse items so they can be shopped from the cashier line is smart merchandising, but it's also good time-bending. But placement is key—we studied a record store where the displays near the checkout were turned so that it was impossible (by about a foot) to grab a CD from the line. Also keep in mind that the first person in line doesn't require much diversion—he or she is in the on-deck circle, just waiting for the sign that they're up. Merchandising materials, signage, shoppable racks and anything else should be positioned for the second or third person in line.

The racks of sleazy tabloids at the supermarket checkout are a great use of diverting merchandise, allowing you to absorb all the trash you need without having to watch Jerry Springer. Another popular form of shopper diversion is, believe it or not, signage. Customers perceive waiting time as shorter if there are signs to read, our research shows. In fact, smart retailers view waiting time as a kind of intangible asset—it's one of the few opportunities when you have your customers standing in one spot, facing in one direction, with nothing much else to do. This is when bad times can be turned into good times: Waiting may be a necessary evil, but you can use it to communicate some message and, at the same time, shorten how shoppers perceive it.

Even away from the cashiers, waiting time is a problem in stores today. Retailers typically cut costs by cutting back on labor, which means that shoppers now spend more time than ever searching for a clerk who can answer a question. This is a particularly deadly form of waiting time; we've watched countless shoppers dart back and forth in stores looking for help or directions. After they've wandered in vain for a minute or so, you can see the steam coming out of their ears. Male shoppers are particularly vulnerable to this—if they can't get an answer fast, they give up and go home (or to another store). We studied a department store that had just made a change in staffing policy; instead of keeping cashiers stationed throughout the place, in the various departments, the registers were consolidated in front (*fewer* registers, naturally). As a result, waiting time in line instantly became quite a bit longer. Plus, it suddenly was very hard to find an employee on the sales floor. *Plus,* the mob of impatient-looking shoppers lined up to pay just inside the front door gave entering customers the impression that the store was packed. In all, saving on a few salaries created a lot of expensive new disadvantages to overcome.

This equation pops up all the time in retailing today: At what point does saving money on labor end up costing money in shopper frustration? Banks in particular are vulnerable. They tend to hire part-time tellers for not much more than minimum wage, meaning they're not getting workers with seasoned math or people skills. As a result, wait time increases. At some point, customer dread will take its toll. We studied two businesses—a European bank and an American electronics store—that, mainly for security reasons, used a single cash drawer. At the bank, tellers had to run back and forth from their windows to the drawer for even the simplest transactions. At the store, shoppers beheld the spectacle of salesclerks jostling each other out of the way to get at the register. Neither setup did much for consumer confidence, and the effect on waiting time was just what you'd expect.

We've studied quite a few stores where time-consuming anti-shoplifting policies ended up costing sales, we felt sure. In each exam-

ple, the merchandise was small in size but not inexpensive (prestige per-
fumes in one case; computer printer ink cartridges in another; video
game players in a third). All three stores decided to display the items in
locked glass cases, meaning that shoppers had to make their selection
without being able to touch their choice or see it up close. That alone
guarantees that purchasers are being discouraged. Shoppers then had to
track down an employee, praying they had found one who was permitted to carry the key in question. In all those instances we watched customers search in vain for help, then give up on the purchase altogether.
Did fewer thefts make up for the loss in sales? Probably not.

Cash/Wrap Blues

FIFTEEN

I t's a necessary evil. Maybe someday it won't even exist. Stores will all offer self-service aisles, as gas stations, toll booths and banks now do. Shoppers will feed their purchases into a computerized gizmo where a scanner will read the product code, total up the damage, add on the taxes, then swallow a credit or debit card, get the approval and emit a receipt, a bag of the appropriate size and a tinny "Thank-you-for-shopping-at-Paco's-beep-please-accept-this-coupon-for-10-percent-off-your-next-purchase-of-men's-accessories-beep-have-a-life-affirming-day-beep-Thank-you-for . . ."

Part of the technology is already in use—like the portable scanners used by FedEx and UPS drivers. Many supermarkets already depend on shoppers to perform the ritual debit card swipe. In Europe, some restaurants present the diner with a portable scanner instead of a check, so that the credit card transaction can be done privately.

And let's face it, for all the glamorization and glorification of the twentieth-century shopping experience, for all the art and science that have been brought to bear by geniuses of commerce, nobody has found a way to make the cash/wrap lovable. Retailers try to exploit it by stocking high-profit, high-impulse merchandise there. They create distractions to take shoppers' minds off the fact that they're waiting in line for the privilege of handing over money. That's ultimately what's so frustrating about the cash/wrap: In theory, since it's where the shopper is being separated from his or her dough, it should be where all the dazzle goes. Instead, it's the dreariest part of the process. It's also the source of most shopper anxiety. "Where do I stand? How long will this take?" The rest of the shop seems so well designed and user-friendly. Here, the illusions fall away and the true function of a store is revealed—it is a machine where goods are exchanged for money. If the machine is badly designed, or poorly built, or misunderstand by its operator, here is where it shows.

As we've noted, the biggest quandary in cash/wrap is where to put it. Up front, near the door, is the logical choice. You enter the store, make your way around, choose a few things, then return to the front, pay and leave. From the staffing perspective this also makes most sense. A small store can be run during off-peak times with one employee if the register is near the door. If it's not, then you need two employees, or a clerk and a guard at the very least. We once studied a shoe store where the misguided architect had placed the cash/wrap in the rear and the register itself facing the back wall. This guaranteed that during every transaction there was a moment when the clerk's back was to the entire store and all the shoppers in it—a setup that practically guarantees theft.

But it's a mistake to position the cash/wrap so that it's the first thing an incoming shopper sees. It's like entering a restaurant through the kitchen. It just doesn't do much to stoke your anticipation of the store. And if things are a little slow there, and shoppers are stacked up, it's the kiss of death for incoming customers. Countless times we've watched shoppers peer into a store, see a line at the registers and just walk away. A cash/wrap is just the promise of misery—it says that even if you do find something you want, you'll have to undergo a little bit of torture to get it.

When pondering its location, you must also consider the effect of cash/wrap on the rest of the store. You'll look at the blueprint for a new store, or the artist's rendering or the architect's model, and you'll see a beautifully ordered, serene space. That's how designers prefer to imagine their creations—devoid of human clutter. This is how every magazine devoted to architecture depicts stores: empty. But then the store opens, customers show up and suddenly you see that the lines at the register cut the space in two. The shoppers waiting to pay snake around in a direction the designer in his aerie never anticipated (his wife does all the shopping). And there you have it—a wall of shoppers that makes half the store difficult to see and inconvenient to reach. If those shoppers in line are pushing carts, you've really got an obstacle. Most incoming customers can't even see over the line, meaning that if what they want is back there, they may never even know it. We measure shopper movement patterns in several ways, among them by department density. Every hour on the hour, we tour the entire floor and count how many shoppers are in each area. During busy times in stores where the cash/wrap has been badly positioned, the number of shoppers to be found in the rear of a store is low. The line of people waiting to pay acts like a human barricade.

Ironically, crowding at the cash/wrap is often no indicator of the state of the rest of the store. A few time-consuming transactions can give the false impression that the store is crowded. So you've got a mob up front, behind which is total shopper paradise, if only someone was there to enjoy it.

Why do stores mishandle something as nuts and bolts as cash/wrap? Mainly because retailers fail to recognize how an efficient cashier system affects the overall shopping experience. That is a dangerous way for businesspeople to think, as you know if you've ever done a slow burn and vowed never to return to a store because the cash/wrap was so badly bungled. Retailers and the architects they hire stop trying to please shoppers when they design the cash/wrap area. They don't give it enough space, they cut corners whenever possible, and too few employees are stationed there most of the time. I can think of two instances where management tried too much piggybacking at the register, to the ultimate misfortune of the store.

One was at Hallmark, which does quite a bit of business at Christmas, you may be surprised to know. A large part of that business is in fancy, high-priced tree and other ornaments. Many of these are given as presents—so many that the stores end up gift-wrapping quite a few. The wrapping in many stores is done at the cash/wrap by the same clerks who ring up sales. Have you ever been in a card shop around the holidays? Can you imagine what happens when a clerk must stop ringing transactions for the two minutes required to wrap a box and tie a ribbon? It's worse than the airspace over O'Hare on the night before Thanksgiving. Meltdown. Gift-wrapping should be done from its own site, but every year fewer stores do it that logical, old-fashioned way. By trying to save on a clerk's wage, management creates gridlock at the register. One truly efficient way to handle gift-wrapping is to set up a do-it-yourself station, complete with paper, ribbons, tissue, scissors and tape, but no employees at all.

The second instance was at RadioShack. There, the cash/wrap shared a counter with repairs and returns. This meant, of course, that there would be lots of extraneous traffic slowing down shoppers who wanted only to buy something and be on their way. But it also meant that happy shoppers who were about to acquire a tape recorder, say, or a computer monitor, had to stand elbow to elbow with unhappy shoppers who had some complaint about tape recorders and computer monitors—the very same tape recorders and monitors, sometimes. This setup did not do wonders for consumer confidence. Put repairs and returns somewhere else, we counseled—somewhere in back, away from the main flow of shoppers.

I have a personal stake in at least one little corner of the world of cash/wrap—hotel check-in and checkout counters. Like lots of people these days, I spend roughly half my life on the road. The hospitality industry is booming as a result of the peripatetic nature of modern business. Yet the most problematic part of the hotel experience has remained more or less unchanged. The scenario is always the same—you arrive late, tired, jet-lagged and looking forward to the shortest possible transition from the road to your room, where you can begin e-mailing, reading, writing, phoning or just ordering room service and a movie. Instead, you spend eternity standing in a line when all you really need is your key, the rest of the transaction having been managed in advance over the phone or through a travel agent.

One hotel I visited had progressed to using small, circular check-in islands in the lobby, where guest and clerk can sit side by side at the computer terminal. That's a start, but some hotel is going to score huge points with business travelers by taking it further. Then, there will be a check-in section of the lobby consisting of some comfortable easy chairs. When a clerk sees you sit there, she or he will come over with a portable, palm-size computer, a credit card reader, a room key and your choice of beverage, and the paperwork will be handled in that civilized way.

Magic Acts

SIXTEEN

To the extent to which there is magic, to the degree to which there are tricks, it's mostly in what we call merchandising. The rest of this book concerns itself with sensible subjects such as ergonomics, anatomy, kinetics and demographics. This chapter is all about getting products to jump up and hit shoppers in the eye.

The world of merchandising breaks down into two distinct aspects. One is the effort to position products off the shelves, away from where they are forced to compete on equal footing with their competitors. Who wants to settle for that? So a great deal of effort and money are expended on getting products out on their own. Shelves are fine for libraries, everyone agrees, but elsewhere they are to be avoided if at all possible. And in fact, the Baltimore library system tried an experiment by displaying some books face out, and borrowing increased dramatically. There's a lesson in there for bookstores, which do a fairly uninspired job in the display department, at least for the majority of titles. The downside would be a big decrease in the number of books available, which would no doubt raise a cry from woebegone authors and publishers.

The other aspect of merchandising is the subtler art and science of adjacencies—placing one item next to another to create some spark and sell more of both. A big part of what adjacencies can deliver is add-on sales. Sometimes this is just the typical cash register impulse buy, like the Almond Joy or batteries or paperback thriller tossed into a shopping basket at the last second. But add-ons can happen anywhere in a store. Retailers pay too little attention to this, in my opinion, and their businesses suffer as a result. Because add-ons typically have a high profit margin, they can make the difference between a store that just gets by and one that prospers. They can make a failing store into a success. I once was part-owner of a bar in New York where the proceeds from the jukebox, cigarette machine and video games covered the rent. Retailers must accept the fact that there are no new customers—the population isn't booming, and we already have more stores than we need. The usual figure is that 80 percent of a store's sales will come from 20 percent of its clientele. So if stores are to grow, it will be by figuring out how to get more out of existing customers—more visits, more time in the store, more and bigger purchases.

And so The Gap now sells fragrance and candles. Club Monaco clothing stores sell cosmetics, thinking (wisely) that women will shop for makeup wherever they are, especially if they're already in a store designed to enhance their comeliness. The U.S. Post Office branch in the Mall of America sells toy mail trucks, leather jackets, teddy bears in mailman uniform and other related items. Someday that's what may keep the whole system afloat. Or, taking a tip from the video stores that sell microwave popcorn, jujubes, Coke and other movie food, the Barnes & Noble superstore near my office now has a display of Godiva chocolates, providing the bonbons to accompany the new Anne Rice. (Why not? You were gonna buy 'em somewhere!) Many bookstores seem seriously challenged in the creative add-ons department, in part, I think, because of the attitude among sellers that they purvey not mere merchandise but ideas. I have always thought bookstores should sell bookshelves—from plain-Jane Danish modern to antiques. The margin on shelving is high, the cost of fixturing becomes a movable asset and the bookstore becomes distinctly more interesting.

Let's say we have a clothing store where the typical sale is a $30 shirt. If you can convince that typical customer to also buy a $6 pair of socks, you've just increased sales by 20 percent. Not too shabby! If she takes a $20 belt, sales just rose by 66 percent. You're a genius! Now, you just have to figure out how to make that happen. One good way is to gently suggest to the shopper that she is not buying enough for your purposes, and doesn't she need a mousepad to go with that mouse? Another good way is just to place the mousepad next to the mouse so that the juxtaposition does the talking for you. A lot of this is as simple as can be. Where do belts go? Near trousers. How about socks? Near shoes. (But where do shoes go? On your feet.) Tomato sauce? Near the pasta. Department stores do well selling neckties on the ground floor, mainly to female shoppers. But ties also have to be near suits and sports jackets, and surprisingly, they often are not. That's a big mistake because sometimes you need to actually see and touch that amazing Technicolor tie to imagine yourself in that somber gray suit. And anyway, nobody wears just a suit—you need the shirt, tie, socks, shoes, cuff links and belt before you can leave the house. So why sell the most expensive part of the package in such unnatural isolation? Computer stores make an even bigger botch of this. Typically, they'll display the computers themselves in one section, the printers elsewhere, the furniture in a different spot and then the accessories from cables to wrist rests in yet other places. Could anyone devise a less sensible, less inviting display system? That organizing scheme is right for the warehouse, not the selling floor. It all needs to be shown as people use it—computer, monitor, printer and accessories, all hooked up, plugged in and turned on, on furniture so that a shopper can sit down and give it a test-drive.

There's a similar issue back in the supermarket, starting with this urgent question: Where do we put the taco shells? With the rest of the Mexican food? That's how it's usually done. Not near the ground beef? It might require the combination of tacos and meat to trigger fiesta in the mind of a shopper wondering what to make for dinner tonight. How about stocking taco shells both places? And while we're at it, how about just over the meat counter also being a good place for bread crumbs, steak sauce, tenderizer, peppercorns and sea salt and fresh herbs? In Italy, a supermarket is experimenting with grouping food displays by meals—breakfast ingredients here, dinner there.

What about something truly tricky—say, packaged cake-by-the-slice? You could decide to stock it in the cake section, but why would anyone looking for a whole cake buy just one piece, and vice versa, for that matter? It could go with other refrigerated desserts, such as pudding, in the cooler. But how about if a slice of cake could be found by the salad bar, as a reward for choosing an otherwise virtuous meal? Such placement alone would identify the cake as something other than the stuff for callow kiddie palates over in the cooler. In Chapter 12 I discussed how name-brand aluminum foil makers have a tough time convincing shoppers to spend the extra money on better quality. One way to get around this is by merchandising it better—in summer, for instance, supermarkets could sell charcoal, barbecue sauce, funny aprons and aluminum foil all from the same fixture, somewhere near the meat counter. Men especially would be likely to grab the whole kit at once rather than have to assemble it aisle by aisle. And in this context, the superior strength of the name-brand foil might seem relevant.

In a drugstore, where do the books about vitamins and dietary supplements go, with books or with vitamins? It's easy to say both, but at some point your store is going to run out of room. And all those multiple placements are pointless if they don't increase sales. Also in the drugstore, and on the subject of multiple placements, where do you stock the sample sizes of shampoo, conditioners and so on? Typically, they get their own display case, but they really should be sold from the same shelves as the full-size products. That may be all it takes to get you to try a new product, something you wouldn't attempt if you had to buy the big bottle or jar just to see if you like it. Common sense says that if I hit the shampoo shelf first and bought my usual brand, I'm less likely to pick up something new when I arrive at the sample shelf.

Adjacencies are also about order—coming up with a sensible, logical sequence of products. We once were hired to study how potato chips are sold in employee cafeterias. In one, the rack of chips and pretzels was positioned at the head of the line, right where you picked up your

tray. In another, the chips were down at the end of the line, just before
the cashier. Did it make much of a difference? When the chips were
near the end, sales were dramatically higher than at the head. How can
you decide what kind of chips you want before you've chosen your
sandwich? What goes with pimento loaf and Swiss on white, corn chips
or barbecue-style potato chips? Similarly, one December we studied a
department store where a Christmas wrapping paper fixture was positioned just inside the entrance, and it wasn't selling much because nobody buys the paper before they buy the gifts. It was moved so that it
was one of the last things shoppers came upon, and sales went up. Supermarket planograms are designed to make the most of adjacencies,
the thinking being that if a popular item like Corn Flakes is positioned
correctly, at the bull's-eye, it will help sales of other Kellogg's products
arranged around it. Because most shoppers are right-handed, the best
spot should be just to the right of the bull's-eye, to make it as easy as
possible for the quick grab.

Sometimes, though, it's the irrationality of combinations that provides their power to grab our attention. Consider how expensive chests
are sold in a furniture store as opposed to how they're sold in a newfangled home and hardware store. In the former there were dozens of
chests neatly lined up, nothing but chests, one after the other, chest
chest chest, with all the charm of a warehouse sale. In a Restoration
Hardware store, the chests were treated like furniture, placed next to a
chair, or in a corner, with a lace doily or a picture frame or a mirror on
top. Sitting on one chest was a big, old-fashioned glass jar containing
chrome-plated ball peen hammers, of all things. So maybe the jar or the
shiny hammers caught your eye, and you picked one up, and suddenly
you noticed the chest, really noticed it, and you realized it wasn't just
there to hold the hammer jar but it was actual merchandise, with a discreet price tag hanging from a drawer pull. You didn't feel overwhelmed
by forty similar pieces of furniture to study. You could actually see how
the chest would look in a home, as opposed to a showroom. And the
fact that you could start out looking at hammers and end up considering furniture satisfied your love of discovery—it kept you on your toes.
Anybody can sell furniture to people looking for furniture; it takes a lit-

tle ingenuity to sell it to people who aren't. I'd wager that more than one doily shopper has gone home with a new maple dresser.

You can figure out intelligent adjacencies just by standing near one thing and asking yourself, what else is on my mind here? In the paint section, there should be some cross-selling of power tools, even if it's only a poster or some literature or a chain saw just lying on a table—who could resist picking it up? In the bookstore, we advise clients to group sections by the gender of their likeliest readers, meaning that computers, sports and business books should flow from one to the other, as should self-help, diet and nutrition, health and home (and I'll leave it to you to guess who shops which). We were consulting on how to sell computer printers and advised the retailer that maybe they should be grouped by manufacturer—Hewlett-Packard here, Okidata there. Then we saw that shoppers don't buy that way; they're more interested in comparing all $300 printers than seeing what one manufacturer is offering. So we quickly changed our recommendation. Golden Books, the children's publisher, was organizing its sections by price point until we saw that with such inexpensive goods, price doesn't matter to anyone, and that the books should be grouped by character—little ponies here, teddy bears there.

How's this for a bright merchandising idea: We'll take pantyhose and sell it in plastic eggs! Pretty weird, I agree, except that this signature package turned L'eggs into the country's number-one brand in its category. In a series of well-documented blind tests a number of years ago, women preferred the No Nonsense brand, which is usually sold right next to L'eggs. Still, L'eggs rules, which makes it a true merchandising victory, since, in theory, any fool should be able to sell the superior brand.

If you're not involved in retailing, you might not be aware of the size and scope of the industry that provides all the in-store merchandising materials—signs and display cases and impulse goods fixtures and all the rest. From supermarkets and drugstores to home centers and auto showrooms, what's become known as the point-of-purchase business—

PoP for short—has come a long way in a short time. PoP materials have existed since forever, of course, going back to the first cigar-store Indian or red-and-white-striped barbershop pole. But since the early '80s, PoP has really become a player, and now commands a seat at the selling table right next to marketing's.

Until then, though, merchandising was the stepchild of the marketing trade. The marketing geniuses called all the shots for how a product would be presented to the world, and the boys in merchandising were left to work out the petty details of how it would work at the retail level—the in-store signage and displays. Then, the two sides began to change places. Suddenly, retailing realized that to a growing extent, shoppers were making their buying decisions on the floor of the store. As was noted elsewhere, surveys showed that more than half of all supermarket purchases were unplanned. And this all happened as marketing's influence was coming down from its peak—the monolithic TV networks gave way to many viewing options, and consumer devotion to brand name yielded to a more skeptical, independent-minded shopper. That all added up to more dependence on merchandising, which led the industry to grow from a $5-billion-a-year pushcart to a $25-billion-a-year roller coaster almost overnight. Traditionally, it's been a business of smallish (and now, some not-so-small) family-owned firms, meaning it's been short on sophistication and long on guts, verve and energy. It's a cowboy business, and I mean that in the best way. Owing to its youth, there are still lots of lessons its practitioners are learning, and they learn as they go. In fact, a great deal of our work in the past decade has been just in testing and measuring the effects of in-store signage, fixturing and display systems, trying to figure out what works and why.

Here's a good example of the terrible magic that smart merchandising can perform. I once heard a talk given by the vice president of merchandising from a national chain of young women's clothing stores in which she deconstructed a particular display of T-shirts. "We buy them in Sri Lanka for $3 each," she began. "Then we bring them over here and sew in washing instructions, which are in French and English. Notice we don't say the shirts are made in France. But you can infer that if you like. Then we merchandise the hell out of them—we fold them just right on a tasteful tabletop display, and on the wall behind it we hang a huge, gorgeous photograph of a beautiful woman in an exotic locale wearing the shirt. We shoot it so it looks like a million bucks. Then we call it an Expedition T-Shirt, and we sell it for $37. And we sell a lot of them, too." It was the most depressing valuable lesson I've ever had.

Car dealerships aren't anyone's idea of how merchandising is supposed to work, which makes them good lessons in what not to do. We studied a foreign-car dealership that was practically a college course in itself. The salespeople would load shoppers down with literature but fail to give them folders, so you ended up walking around that showroom burdened with pieces of paper. There were plenty of brochure racks but no brochures, which is a problem not because shoppers love pamphlets so much, but because empty literature racks give shoppers the (correct) impression that the details don't get taken care of in this place of business. One-sided posters were taped to exterior and interior windows, meaning that shoppers frequently found themselves staring at blank white rectangles. In one dealership, as noted in Chapter 5, we saw a sign heralding new cars—the previous year's new cars. The signs that did receive prominent placement were "awards" to the dealership from the car manufacturer—just the kind of thing to leave shoppers yawning. The display that showed buyers available colors was a real mess—a spiral-bound portfolio held together by duct tape. And instead of being able to see a picture of the car in each color, shoppers were shown a tiny swatch book more appropriate for choosing drapes. Signs meant to hang over cars were placed on tables instead. Favorable auto reviews were clipped from newspapers, but they were simply taped to walls rather than displayed properly. Some of the articles had begun to yellow and curl up. And this is meant to support the customer spending anywhere from $12,000 to $60,000!

Retailers aren't alone in screwing up the design and deployment of merchandising materials. Many times the firms that design and make them (and sell them to hapless retailers) screw them up before they get to the floor of the store—simple things, too, like using displays made from uncoated cardboard. We saw one such fixture, for sun products, arrive in a drugstore on a Friday night. It hit the floor immediately and sold well. Then the cleaning crew came in and, as cleaning crews will do, mopped the floor without moving all the fixtures and displays to one side. The base of the suntan lotion display got a little wet. By Saturday afternoon it was listing. After the floor was mopped that night, it had begun to tilt seriously. By Sunday night it was in the trash.

Or nobody will have devoted any thought to the question of what a display will look like when half the merchandise is gone. Will what remains look like a hot item, or will it look unattended and forlorn? Some of this has to do with what shoppers see after a ketchup bottle or whatever has been removed—will brown kraft paper be visible, or will there be some kind of message, or a photo of the bottle? It makes a difference.

And other questions: Can you read it from twenty feet away? If a display works only when you're on top of it, it seems to be doing only half a job. Is the back of it blank? The sides, too? Because the designer of that display has no idea how it will be positioned in a store, and so can't really be certain which surface shoppers will see first (if any).

Endcaps and freestanding displays are staples of American retailing. Some of them succeed and some fail, depending on how they work once they are placed in the store. As with signs, you can't say which are good and which are not until you see them in action. The latest trend in displays is the so-called activated fixture—one that uses movement, especially moving lights, to get the attention of shoppers. Our testing of types of fixtures has yielded some impressive results: In soft drink coolers, the activated version was noticed by 46 percent of shoppers, compared to 6 percent for the nonactivated one. An activated endcap got 37 percent notice, compared to 16 percent for the old-fashioned version. But at a certain point the displays begin to cancel each other out. There are so many fixtures screaming for the shoppers' attention that they become the visual equivalent of a dull roar, with nothing discernible among the clutter. Merchant prince John Wanamaker once said (and I paraphrase) that half his advertising was waste—but he couldn't figure out which half. Same goes today for merchandising materials and strategies.

We were hired to study a terrific idea for solving all confusion regarding over-the-counter cures for indigestion, heartburn, nausea, gas and other even more wretchedly human gastrointestinal maladies. The shameful nature of these conditions is what engenders such woeful ignorance of how to treat them, the patent medicine company's research showed: Shoppers were a little reluctant to approach the cashier or even the pharmacist with problems such as these. (Personally, it was an extremely illuminating job, since I, too, was never quite sure which product was for which form of gastrointestinal distress, and I had no great desire to ask. Perhaps like you, I was taking cures for burps when I had farts and confusing the relief for the runs with that for the pukes.) The cure for all this was a signage system: a horizontal cylinder with a dial on one end: You'd dial up your symptom—say, heartburn—and in the little window the name of the drug that cures it would appear. Can't miss, we all thought. Then a few prototypes were installed and we studied how shoppers interacted with them.

Actually, we saw how they *didn't* interact, for the fixture went all but unused. Maybe shoppers were less confused than the research showed. The fixtures were perhaps a little too tastefully rendered, so the gray tubes didn't stand out on the shelves as much as they might have. It was even a little unclear that the dial on the side was meant to be turned—a big red arrow would have helped a lot. In any event, gastric uncertainty is going to be with us awhile longer, for the idea was a bust.

Here's another example. The question wasn't whether one of America's leading marketers of spices was going to get a fancy, expensive new system of supermarket fixtures to display its wares. That part had already been decided, to the tune of more than a million dollars' worth of displays as proposed by a major PoP firm. The prototype was a beauty—it organized the company's products by whether they were spices, extracts, essences or flavorings, something that hadn't ever been done successfully before. Everything's a battleground in supermarkets; spices were becoming a two-horse race, and this was looking like a way for the leader to distinguish itself where it counts, on the floor of the store.

The fixture's prototype was brought into the firm's headquarters for all to see, and there, in the flesh (as it were), it got raves from all concerned. And so into the stores it went, where it had no positive effect on sales.

It had no negative effect either, which was a good thing, but for all that it cost, it did no better than the old displays it was meant to replace. What had gone wrong? Well, for one thing, the distinctions the display made—spice, extract, essence, flavoring—were more or less meaningless to the shopper. Who cares which it is? What it does to food, how it tastes and smells, is all that counts. What exactly do I do with turmeric? Where does the rosemary go in a chicken? There was a lot you could tell people about spices, and some of that might encourage them to buy more. What does saffron smell like? A fixture that could manage to answer that question would be a genuine advance, but this display was not that. And although the displays were a feast for the eyes when seen in the monochromatic gray (or was it beige?) headquarters of the firm, the swirling, heaving, dizzying cacophony of a supermarket was something else again. It is tough to get noticed in an environment where even Cap'n Crunch himself must shout to be heard.

So say goodbye to those nice new fixtures. Maybe some new display system for spices was warranted. But the process that yielded this one was flawed from the start. The major decisions about how a company's goods will be presented on the floor of a store are made by the firm itself and then by three outside entities—the ad agency, the package designer and then the PoP agency, which usually has no input into what the first two decree. Those three all have their own agendas, and their own priorities, none of which have any meaningful contact with what happens to displays once they reach the selling floor. Until the many agendas are settled into one sensible, practical-minded one, there will be plenty of flawed display systems.

Here's a final tale. A big-name soft drink maker had just spent a lot of money on new supermarket displays and hired us to test the prototype. When I arrived at a supermarket with the client, we looked in through a window and saw a giant pile of soda cases just sitting on the floor—a huge, bright, monochromatic mountain of pop.

"I wonder why they left it there like that," she said. "It sure looks a mess."

Before she could arrange to have the sodas stocked properly, I asked if we could video it as it was for a day. By our measure, 60 percent of the people who passed that mountain noticed it, a higher rate than most of the firm's in-store merchandising materials ever scored. Clearly, that big mass of color was all that was required to stop shoppers in their tracks. There's a lesson in there somewhere.

In Cyberspace, No One
Can Hear You Shop

SEVENTEEN

You can meet someone on-line. You can fall in love on-line. You can even consummate that love on-line.

So it was inevitable that someone would think you can shop on-line. As in love, the traditional shopping relationship involves two parties, the shopper and the shoppee, but this one becomes a triangle with the addition of the cyberjockey. The agendas of the first two remain more or less as they are in the physical world: The shopper still wants selection, convenience and price, all within the context of a satisfying shopping experience; the shoppee still wants sales, profits and a cost-effective way to reach new customers. The cyberjockey's game is a bit trickier to discern, if only because it is newest to our eyes. He (or she, though it's always he) is there to engineer and facilitate Web-based retailing, of course, but he's also on a bigger mission.

I could attempt to characterize the nature of that mission (and I will, in a minute), but let me start with an illustration. It has to do with a limitation of nearly every one of the thousands of transactional Web sites in existence, namely this: Few Web sites will permit you to see if a particular item is in stock in a store near you, order it, pay for it and then go in person to retrieve it. In other words, a hybrid cyberphysical transaction. You'd visit the site of, let's say, an apparel chain, a well-known one, with many stores from coast to coast. You'd type in your name and e-mail address and zip code, and then you'd type, "I want a pair of chinos, khaki color, 34 waist, 32 length, cuffed, and a black V-neck T-shirt, medium. Do you have these in a store near me?" You'd send that e-mail, and an hour or so later, a reply would come back saying, "Our store at Paco Street and Underhill Avenue has your selections in stock, and we'll charge the credit card number we have in your file, and everything will be rung up, bagged and ready for you to pick up in thirty minutes at the will-call desk just inside the entrance, thank you very much, and how about a brown leather belt to hold up those trousers?"

That sounds straightforward enough, doesn't it? It seems simple from the Web site designer end and the retailer end, and a genuine advance in the shopper convenience department, if only for sparing us the torture of the cash register line. You might not buy a designer suit that way, but certain standardized goods—books, records, office supplies, housewares, computer hardware, uniform-y clothing—are well suited to this method of selling.

That transaction should sound vaguely familiar, operationally speaking—your computer talks to their computer, and then at the store some task is completed on your behalf, hmm, wait, yes, of course . . . it's just like what human beings used to do on the telephone! Except that instead of computers talking back and forth (over the same telephone wires your grandmother used, let's not forget), in the olden days you yourself spoke, to . . . a salesclerk who checked to see if your choices were in stock and prepared them for your retrieval. In exactly this way, retailing was conducted in, oh, 1938—even earlier.

Similarly, today it would seem to be a great advance, almost Jetson-like in its futuristicality, to take a momentary break from your electronic spreadsheet and visit your supermarket's Web site, order everything you need for dinner tonight, and have it all boxed and bagged and charged and tagged and ready for you to breeze in, grab it and go on your way home from work. It sounds like the promise of the digital age being gloriously fulfilled, until you remember that people shopped that way in 1951—except that then, of course, you (or somebody) were at home during the day, so if shopping in the flesh was inconvenient, those groceries could also be delivered (free of charge) to your kitchen within an hour or so of ordering them over the phone. Progress has more or less done away with that ancient practice and any similar conveniences—try to imagine the milkmen, breadmen and fishmongers of old doing business today, tooling around in rattletrap home delivery trucks equipped with dashboard-mounted notebook computers and wireless modems (e-mail your order to jerry@joe'sfish-cart.com). But you see the similarities between what the Internet *could* make possible and what retail was already managing with modem-less telephones and human beings five decades ago.

Why, with a few exceptions, don't retailer Web sites offer such a simple, useful service? For a decidedly unbusinesslike reason, I submit: Because it's too easy. Because it barely challenges the technology that runs the show. Because it feels old-hat. Requiring shoppers to visit an actual store runs counter to the agenda of the cyberjockeys who are pulling the on-line shopping sled. There's something almost cultlike about these guys, and part of the cult's evangelical mission is to eradicate the physical world wherever they find it. To their minds, if you feel the need to move your carbon-based butt away from the computer screen, out the door and into a store, you ought to give your modem to somebody who deserves it. The wizards who start, design, oversee, maintain and run on-line retailing sites could easily make such transactions possible, but why bother? The fact that it's good retailing isn't good enough. Why do you think the on-line community is so in love with the idea of selling software, books, recordings and videos over the Internet? Because instead of physical goods being delivered, someday these may all simply be downloaded, permitting the entire consumer experience to be conducted in digital format.

And that'll be cool, right? Undeniably so. But on the strength of such selling the Internet is never going to seriously challenge reality-based retailing. The cyberjockeys and the futurists won't agree with that view. They don't remember that only a decade or so ago, catalogs were going to replace physical retailing. Thanks mainly to the fact that working women loved their convenience, catalog operations gave stores a genuine run for their money. But even catalogs maxed out at roughly a 10 percent share of total retailing, which was a staggering success by any measure. Web site shopping is an improvement on catalogs in some ways, but not every way. The Web is faster and more convenient, and can show more goods and provide more information; in catalogs the glitches are fewer, the pages turn faster, the pictures are better, and you can't shop a Web site on a commuter train or on the toilet. The Web won't even wipe out catalogs. Today it is estimated that roughly two-tenths of a percent of American retail sales are made on-line. Surely that will grow, though once transactional Web sites are forced to start charging sales tax—something that will put a serious dent in the price breaks shoppers now enjoy—growth will slow. Even if Web site shopping doubles the catalog's success rate, 80 percent of shopping will continue to be done in the real world.

Still, I have no doubt that the Internet will transform the world of shopping. Some estimates predict that by 2002, 61 million Americans will shop on-line, and they'll spend around $41 billion. Right now, Dell sells $5 million worth of computers on-line *each day*. The seller of another kind of software—Eddie Bauer—reports that its on-line sales are growing by 300 to 500 percent annually. (And speaking of catalogs, Spiegel's on-line business is soaring even as its catalog sales are plunging.) As Americans age, the convenience and ease of shopping on-line will become more important than ever, and unlike today's crop of codgers, tomorrow's oldsters will be completely Internet-fluent. So let's get used to the fact that the Internet will change how retailers and manufacturers do business. The companies that understand this tool and use it well will have an edge over the ones that misunderstand it, and in some cases, that edge may even be decisive.

Here's what cybershopping can provide that physical retailing cannot:

Limitless selection: In theory, you could create a retail Web site where every kind of merchandise known to man would be sold. In books, to take one example, a superstore can house 175,000 or so titles, while the on-line bookstores keep upping their boast—2 million titles, then 3 million, now 5 million titles "in stock," though the fact that there are no stockrooms, stockboys *or* stock (except in the abstract) is what makes the huge selection possible.

Convenience: You can shop at home, in the office, anywhere there's an electrical outlet and a phone jack. You can shop at any time of day, on any day. You can get to any store in minutes flat. You never have to look for parking. You never have to wear a coat. You never have to wear *anything.*

Speed: You can enter a Web site whenever you want (assuming that you can connect, which isn't always the case during busy times) and move through it at your own pace (assuming the pages load quickly, which isn't always the case at any time), then zip through the payment procedure like lightning—with a single click of the mouse, in some cases. No more friendly chats with the cashier, of course, but no more growing old in line, either.

Information: On-line, limitless amounts of product information and other reading materials can be summoned and then saved, all in an instant, far beyond anything possible in the real world of brochures, manuals and the memory and knowledgeability of salesclerks.

So far, the Web does best with merchandise that involves a certain amount of thought but not a lot of browsing, touching, prodding or stroking. Trading stock on-line is a perfect use, and is responsible for driving broker commissions down to rock bottom, another benefit to the buyer. Airline tickets on-line are also a great use. Books, records and videos are easy to buy on-line. Gifts are easy, too—food, wine and flowers, even clothing, since you probably weren't planning to try on your wife's Christmas bustier anyway. The most popular transactional Web site in America now is one where you can send electronic greeting cards via the Internet. Computer hardware and software are booming on-line categories, no surprise considering the profile of the average cybershopper (single, college-educated guy in his thirties earning around 60 K). Many buyers go to real-world stores, find what they want and then shop the Web for better prices. Lots of products will be bought that way someday, especially big-ticket standardized goods such as watches, mattresses and major appliances, where deep discounts will make a big difference. Motivated shoppers will visit stores all day long, make their choices, then go home, log on and buy from a retailer who keeps prices low by not having to pay rent, overhead, insurance or labor costs. This is going to be the real battlefield between all-cyber retailers—the so-called pure play companies—and the retailers of the physical world who establish Web sites as well. The latter won't even be able to compete on price—they'd be undercutting their own stores.

But can you smell a ripe peach on-line? Can you accidentally discover a shoe that feels so good you impulsively take three pair? While paying for groceries on-line, can a display rack suddenly remind you that you need breath mints? Can your best friend goad you into buying that red silk suit in an on-line apparel shop? There are three big things that stores alone can offer shoppers:

touch, trial or any other sensory stimuli
immediate gratification
social interaction

Notice how these have not much to do with the orderly, planned acquisition of goods and everything to do with the sensual, experiential aspects of shopping—the worldly pleasures that normal people love but cyberjockeys scorn. That's why they're cyberjockeys.

Of course, we shoppers and shoppees don't have to become full-fledged citizens of the brave new world in order to benefit from it. We should think of cyberjockeys the same way we think of vegans—we understand the good that comes from an all-plant diet, but we're not going to that extreme. Instead of eating meat ten times a week, however, we'll cut back to five and consider ourselves half-perfect.

Owing to the religious fervor of the cyberjockeys and our own love of technology, many retailers started Web sites without even knowing exactly why. Some were simply fearful that if they didn't go on-line they'd be missing the boat. (*Which* boat? Don't ask.) It may not even have occurred to them that you *need* a reason to start a Web site—that there has to be something you want the site to *do*. They knew only that everybody else had one, and that all the smart-sounding guys with big heads and skinny necks on CNBC talked as though everybody absolutely needed one. But having one for no reason, or having one and not knowing what to do with it, or having one and not having the time or the money or the staff to run it properly, is actually worse than not having one, for this simple reason: If Web surfers visit your site and find it confusing, unfocused or generally worthless, they'll never come back.

Some retailers resist establishing Web sites for this specious reason: They think that selling goods on-line will cannibalize their physical stores' sales. These guys have it backwards. Not because selling on-line won't take business away from their stores—it *will* do that. But that's a good, not a bad, thing. It's cheaper to run a Web site than it is to run a store. So if you can "migrate" some transactions from the premises to the Web site, you save on costs. Maybe someday you'll even be able to shrink the size and number of your stores while increasing sales, thanks to the Internet. Banks prosper because they've automated many transactions formerly handled by tellers. Stores will benefit from this, too.

First, though, you need to know what you want your Web site to do. For businesses, there are four main functions it can perform:

1. It can promote corporate identification and be part of your image-building by disseminating press releases, recent (favorable, of course) articles, product information and other marketing stuff. This is usually the way manufacturers use the Web, since to sell on it would be to compete with the retailers who carry their products. If a Web surfer is going to visit a search engine and type in your firm's name, the thinking goes, you want to make sure that he or she will get the official party propaganda in among everything else. This type of site is also a form of advertising, though not a particularly effective one yet, compared even with broadcast TV or print.

2. It can tell surfers what you make (or sell), give lots of information about your products and list (and link to) places where they can go to buy.

3. It can be a scaled-down on-line version of your stores, offering some of the products you sell—the more standardized ones, the ones most easily purchased from a Web site—just as a way of holding your place in cyberspace.

4. It can be an on-line version of your entire store. In fact, it can be the sole version of your store, if you are a pure-play—that is, on-line only—retailer.

To correspond with these four functions, there are four main reasons shoppers go to Web sites:

One is to grab and go. This is easiest at sites selling books and records—there's something in particular you're looking for, as a gift or for yourself, and you find it fast, buy it fast and split.

Two is to browse when you've got a few minutes to kill and are already on-line. You may buy something or not, depending on what you find. You can always use something.

Three is to do some info-loading, gathering specs and product reviews before you purchase, an event that may take place on-line or not.

Four is for those who don't wish to buy or even browse but need to get in touch with a company to ask a question about a product they already own, or to file a complaint, or to make contact for some other reason. These people are using the Web instead of the toll-free phone number most firms maintain, knowing that endless time on hold can be avoided by using e-mail.

Somewhere, at the intersection of those two lists, lie the purpose and potential of on-line shopping. Getting beyond the abstract, however, transactional Web sites are still in the shopping stone age. For the most part they're awkwardly designed, poorly structured and go against the way human beings move through any space, cyberspace included. Of course, they're still in their infancy. There aren't enough of them, and they haven't been around long enough, for clear-cut rules and standards for their design and operation to have been established. No one responsible for conceiving these things has thought through all the issues that come up whenever we perform the act of shopping. Some of that, no doubt, has to do with the fact that the designers are not the retailers. Five or ten years from now, the world of transactional Web sites will look quite a bit different, but for now they've got a long way to go. In fact, while discussing sites I've seen, I won't even name names, because I'm fairly sure all these on-line stores will be improved by the time you read this.

Here's one not-so-rare mistake, one that's almost inconceivable in the real world of stores: Many Web sites don't make clear what they can and cannot do. Using search engines such as Yahoo!, we were led to retailer Web sites where no retailing is done. This seems almost like a contradiction in terms, and certainly shows a lack of confidence or ambition. Nevertheless, these sites seem content for now to simply exist and put forth a little product information. Some giant retailers have sites where it is impossible to buy certain items, something that's guaranteed to frustrate shoppers. There are several Web sites devoted to new-car sales, but it takes awhile before you realize that you can't buy a car on-line. The sites put you through the drill of choosing what you want in your next automobile—make, model, color, options, cost and so on. But then, all the site does is inform a dealer near you that you're in the market for wheels—something that you could have accomplished on your own using a telephone and the newspaper. The instant you walk into a store in the real world, you know what it sells or services. In cyberspace, even this most elemental aspect is sometimes a guessing game.

The real-world rule about the need for a transitional zone just inside the entrance applies on-line. Once shoppers arrive at a site, they need a little time and space to orient themselves before being barraged with information or choices. They need to slow down, look around, get the lay of the land. If you put too many words on the home page, shoppers will miss a lot of them. If every possible choice is presented just inside the front door, shoppers will feel overwhelmed. But we've seen Web sites where the home page is almost a solid wall of type. We've seen pages where you have to choose from among dozens of options before you're even sure what can and cannot be accomplished at the site. A Web site has to be organized in stages, and the job of the first page is to simply tell the shopper where she is and to make the general layout of the "store" apparent. You have to know if you're in a vast, hangar-size megastore or a boutique. And you have to know where to find the entrances and aisles—how do I get to menswear, where is the product information, that kind of thing.

Sites have to be attractively designed, with enough white space to make the type readable. And the type has to be large enough to be seen under the less than optimal conditions of the average monitor. The same kind of thinking used by designers of signs and displays should prevail on Web sites, though it rarely does. The fact that most Web site designers are young and computer-savvy colors their design values, making it difficult for the rest of us. I've seen type on cybershopping screens smaller than the smallest newspaper classified ad.

In a Web site, as in a store, you have to be able to figure out where you're going and then get there with a minimum of guessing. This is the part that some Web sites screw up most royally. A fairly well-known grocery site was one of the worst where this is concerned. The first words you come upon after logging on is this mystery phrase: "Go back to all departments." Can anyone hazard a guess about what that means? To have this as the first possibility facing shoppers is lunacy. We decided to try to find baby diapers. Were they in the baby section? There wasn't one, at least not on the screen that listed the category choices. Was it in the kids' section? Nope, not there, either. It was in "nonfood and pet," if you're still with me. Once there, you saw the "baby care" section, in which you found diapers. There was also a full screen of baby food, each choice accompanied by a visual—a jar shown so small that the words on the labels were absolutely invisible. That was a common problem on this site—we came upon a graphic of a child's toothbrush so minuscule it looked like a toothpick. And when we clicked on the "gourmet food" section, the first item we were shown was a Power Bar. There was no picture of this delicacy—only a drawing of a camera, over which were superimposed the words "Image coming soon." Did that mean in seconds or in months? We're still waiting.

You should be able to navigate back and forth through a Web site using the site's directionals alone, rather than depending on your browser's "back" button. When you're "inside" the store, you should be able to do it all without leaving. But many sites break this rule. There's no lack of tiny, annoying glitches in the world of cybershopping. Even the best sites are guilty. At a CD Web site, we attempted to buy by clicking our selection but first had to puzzle out where exactly to click. It wasn't on the title, the artist or the CD cover, we discovered by trial and error—it was on the price. At the same site we loaded a few things into our shopping cart and then, at checkout, discovered that the cart was empty. Where did our CDs go? At all the CD sites, song lists are given for some albums but not others, and no explanation is offered, which leads you to wonder if maybe you're just not looking in the right place. You try to connect to a clothing chain's site, an error message comes up when in fact the site is simply too busy to let you in. Finally, at one clothing site, when something we ordered was out of stock, we were notified by U.S. mail!

Someday, I believe, cybershopping will have an added attraction: It will be fun. It certainly is not that now, which is a real problem. It needs to make up for its cold cyberness by using all the tricks at its disposal. Computers allow for all manner of interactive entertainment, but rare is the site that makes use of it. I'm amazed that no shopping Web site stars a living being on-screen to welcome shoppers, guide them through the site and answer questions. It could even be a creature with whom the cyberjockeys would feel comfortable—Max Headroom, say, or some other shopper-friendly android. Web sites will succeed to the degree to which they can overcome their limitations. One giant mass merchandiser's site uses absolutely no images of the goods it sells. Who would buy something without seeing at least a representation of it? No site at this writing, to our knowledge, uses sound at all, not even the ringing of the register to signal the shopper that the transaction has gone through. The possibilities for genuinely entertaining shopping Web sites seem to be endless. So why isn't anyone having any fun?

Of course, the cyberjockeys have their hands full just getting the sites to handle simple transactions. And it's better to have a well-run, up-to-date site that does a few simple things than a complex, ambitious one that isn't maintained properly. If you don't have enough staff to keep the seasonal goods section current, then don't have a seasonal goods section. If your server won't allow images to be loaded quickly, then don't use many images. If it takes forever to hear the audio clip of your president's latest speech, do without it. The *New York Times* recently did a study of e-mail reply time for business Web sites. It found that answering e-mail was, at most firms, a low-priority job, meaning that lots of shoppers sent messages thinking that they'd be treated politely, until they learned otherwise. Some of those companies would do less damage to themselves if they had never established Web sites. I mentioned earlier that I paid a visit to an automobile-shopping site that requested info about me and what kind of car I was trying to find. After I followed all the instructions, a screen came up and informed me that a nearby car dealer would call me within a day or so to follow up. A week later I finally got a call from the dealership's Web site clerk, who promised that I'd hear from one of the company's honchos within twenty-four hours. I'm still waiting for that call.

I also went to the Web site of a major national entertainment retailer and attempted to buy a videotape. I found it in a flash, easily, logically, and all was proceeding swiftly until I got to the payment page. There, I entered my credit card info, sent it along and got an error message—something about not having completely filled in the field. When I looked, I saw that I had filled in everything it requested. I tried again and got the same error message. I tried twice more and got it both times. I finally gave up on my purchase, but not before sending the site an e-mail complaining about the undeserved error message.

Nineteen days passed. Then I got an e-mail back informing me that my error was probably in typing the hyphens in my credit card number. Well, I e-mailed back, nothing on the page told me not to type them in. And the error message never mentioned a thing about hyphens. Only one day later I got a reply, in which it was pointed out that thousands of buyers had entered their credit card numbers correctly, the implication being that the problem was not in the site but in myself. I can only assume that the person on the other end of that e-mail exchange was a cyberguy, not a retail guy accustomed to dealing politely with the foibles and failings of customers. Maybe the real problem with on-line retail is that even as perfect as the cyberjockeys make it, it still must deal with non-cyberguys screwing it up.

The Self-Exam

EIGHTEEN

I sometimes turn our clients into amateur scientists by doing this: I'll force them to stand in one spot of a store with me for half an hour or so, just watching. It becomes a very Zen-like experience because if you simply look and don't move, you'll see things that are otherwise invisible. After five minutes you'll see things you missed after one minute, and after ten minutes you'll see things you missed after five. I'll stand with a client in the doorway, for instance, and ask, "Okay, what do you see now? What did that customer just do? How did that mother manage the door and her stroller? Why do you think that man looks so confused? What are those two people doing here—who's the shopper and who's just along for the ride? How did that woman interact with that display? Is she shopping it the way you thought she would?" And we'll stand there until the answers begin to reveal themselves, and the client finally understands why we do so much watching, counting, timing and videotaping.

At some basic level, all stores are alike, no matter what they sell or what kind of business they transact. Here, we're dealing with how people interact with the retail environment itself. On this plane, a bank is a video store is a supermarket is The Gap. The lessons apply across the board. I'd like to conduct an all-purpose workshop on how to perform a self-examination. And since this is a book, let's go to a bookstore.

We'll start by standing at the proper vantage point for evaluating any retail environment: half a block away. That's where the first issue arises—we can't see the place. We can see the building just fine, but there's no big sign or giant book or anything else to tell us we're so close to a bookstore. Now, its regular customers know where it is. But who knows how many others find themselves standing on this very spot, heads swiveling, trying to figure out where exactly the store is located. What's more, every day there are people walking down this street who might impulsively decide to drop in, but not if they don't know it's there. They might have half an hour to kill and start by searching for a coffee shop when suddenly they see the bookstore sign and think, Hey, I'll kill a little time browsing around in there—they may even have coffee! (And in fact, they do.) How many of those spontaneous shoppers is this particular establishment missing for want of a big sign clearly visible from all directions?

Okay, let's get closer—let's stand right outside. Here we can see the sign just fine. But what do we see in the windows? Well, books—what else? These are big windows, though, broad and high, and it's a fairly busy street, with lots of foot traffic and baby strollers and bicycles, the usual urban minefield, and if you can picture all this maybe you can see how objects the size of books might not be the easiest things on which to focus (especially since you're trying hard not to get run over by some speedy mom). There's a similar problem for window designers in drugstores, stationery stores and hardware stores: The merchandise is small, so it makes for lousy window displays. To make things only slightly more challenging, the plate glass has an anti-glare film on it, which makes it a little less transparent, and it's dirty, too, which adds to the obstacles facing the window shopper.

And books are already daunting enough in this department—unlike the people who bring us laundry detergent, say, or ice cream, book jacket designers don't like to think of what they're creating as a package for a product. To them it's more like a work of commercial art or a medium of literary expression, or some combination. As a result, a book's jacket isn't measured on the cruelly efficient terms used to judge most packaging. A book jacket may contain five different messages all competing for the viewer's attention. Here's one that features a title, a subtitle, the words "a novel," the author's name, the title of her previous book and a round sticker announcing that this work has been chosen for Oprah's Book Club. There's also a fuzzy image—two of them, in fact, one superimposed over the other in an artsy way. And the colors? Purple predominates, rendering all the type less than high-contrast. You try to absorb all that in the second and a half it takes to walk past this particular spot. Even the world's greatest window designer couldn't make this book visible from six feet away, which is the distance at which display windows should be capable of doing their job. In some industries, manufacturers consult with retailers to devise package designs that will do the most good in the store environment, but publishing does not. Overall, the entertainment media—compact disks and cassettes, videos, books—do a fairly poor job of creating packages with the merchandising function in mind. So until book jackets get better (or bigger), maybe the window should limit itself to big blowups of books or some other display scheme.

Okay, *now* we can go in. Books are not the easiest things to carry around, especially if you're holding several and you've also got a coat or a bag to manage. So some kind of basket is imperative. We've discussed this more than once, befitting such an important matter. But I'll say it again: If more shoppers can be encouraged to use baskets, all our research shows, sales automatically rise. Here, as in 90 percent of the stores I visit, the baskets are in a discreet stack just inside the doorway. A very bad idea. They're invisible. They should be moved farther inside, positioned higher, disseminated throughout the place, all of the above. As I've said, and keep saying.

Now we're inside the store (at last!) and the first thing we come upon, just to the right, is: calendars. In August. Does anyone buy next year's calendar in August? Probably not, yet here they are, a huge display of them occupying the right front, which is any store's prime real estate. In December, calendars here might be a good decision; in August, I suspect it shows the manager's unwillingness to move merchandise around as befits the cycle of shopping. You can tell this store's calendar display has been in place for a good long while—it's partly obscured by a few freestanding cardboard fixtures, recent arrivals, it seems plain. One actually blocks off a section of calendars, making it impossible to reach without rearranging the furniture, something most customers won't do.

Also right up front is a basket of fliers announcing the month's in-store author readings and other events. This is the right thing in the wrong place: No one walks into a bookstore and immediately begins reading promotional literature. That action would be totally incompatible with the main task of book-shopping—walking around and looking at books. And since you can't do both, shoppers are for the most part ignoring the fliers, which makes the store's intelligent marketing plan much less effective than it should be. It is futile to try to interfere with a shopper's natural task-oriented behavior, as we've seen over and over, in every type of store we study. If a bank customer is intent on filling out a deposit slip, to recall another example, she is in no frame of mind to read a brochure about vacation loans. In-store media needs to be placed where shoppers naturally pause in their travels if it's to have a fighting chance.

The final element of this bookstore's front section is the cash/wrap area. Here's where all the store's customers spend time standing still and facing the same direction. As we saw in our discussion of how shoppers perceive time, there's an art to making the most of such a fortunate moment, and this store has gotten it almost right—which counts only in horseshoes and hand grenades. For instance, there are several displays of impulse purchases up here—bookmarks, postcards and the like—but all are positioned just far enough from the line to be beyond the reach of shoppers idling there. As a result, the customers look bored and the fixtures are going undershopped. There's a rack of the upcoming week's *New York Times Book Review,* which makes perfect sense. But it's been placed at the far left of the cashier area, near the exit, meaning shoppers don't pass it until after they've paid for their purchases—too late. No provision has been made to entertain customers waiting in line; there's nothing hanging behind the cashiers to look at, no signs to read or displays of merchandise to consider. At the entrance to the cashier line would be a perfect place for those fliers that were languishing just inside the entrance, for once you've chosen your books you are free to read something else, and it's remarkable how shoppers in a bookstore line almost never look at the books they've chosen.

And now we're finally among the books. Here, as in most stores these days, the new releases and featured selections are kept on tabletops, a brilliant innovation for making the distinction between bookstores and dull old libraries, where everything is spine-side-out on a shelf (though even that is changing). This is a great system for showing books, but less than perfect from the perspective of shopping them. The clerk who stocks the displays does so as painstakingly as possible—she's arranging these tables to within an inch of their lives. As a result, shoppers are a little reluctant to just reach in and grab. They feel they'd be messing up someone's hard work. We've shot lots of video during bookstore studies, and you can see the reluctance in the way shoppers approach these piles. It's an example of how a good-looking display, arranged with meticulous care, can actually discourage the act of shopping. As we saw in Chapter 12, at the bagel store, in instances like this we advise clients to relax things a little—create spaces to suggest that goods have been taken, make objects slightly crooked or haphazardly arranged, anything to tell shoppers that it's okay to reach in there.

There's also another obstacle to taking merchandise from the table, one that becomes clear when you watch precisely how it must be shopped. The table holds maybe ten stacks of books, atop each of which is a plastic easel holding a copy of the book upright, so its jacket can be seen. No one wants to buy the book on the easel—it feels like a display, not merchandise; besides, it's probably been pawed a lot—so in order to take one from the stack beneath a shopper must lift the display copy, then with the other hand lift the plastic easel (or lift the book and easel, slightly awkwardly, with one hand), and then withdraw a book from somewhere in that stack. If the shopper is already holding something—a coat, a handbag, other books—taking a book from a table can be a complicated little stunt.

Still, lots of books are being grabbed here. In most retail settings, the longer a shopper holds something, the greater the chance that she or he will buy it. In bookstores, the opposite is true—someone browsing a book for sixty seconds is less likely to take it than someone who browsed it for thirty seconds. Surely, some bookstore browsers examine volumes expressly because they have no intention of buying them. You spy a book that looks important, or one that got a glowing review, so you pick it up, scan the jacket copy, check out the author photo, maybe read a page or two—almost as an *hommage* to the idea of the book and its author. Perhaps prolonged reading is how some shoppers talk themselves *out* of buying. Either way, this phenomenon is also due in part to the nature of bookstores—they're great places for idle browsing. It's a way of killing time that allows you to catch up on what people are thinking and talking about in the papers or on TV. You can't learn as much shopping a sweater rack. This also means that unlike other browsers, bookstore shoppers aren't necessarily motivated by the desire to buy. We researched a chain with mall and non-mall branches and found that mall shoppers were much less likely to buy than non-mall customers. This was especially true for men, and the reason seemed clear: These guys were just killing time while their wives or girlfriends or families were shopping elsewhere. Even the browsing style of these guys was different—in non-mall stores they entered and went directly to a section of the store. At the mall they walked in and meandered, seemingly purposeless. This is why bookstores are fleeing malls—the high rents aren't justified by the shoppers.

Beyond the tables of recent releases, we come upon the traditional bookstore setting—shelves, yards upon yards of straight wooden shelving, maybe six and a half or so feet tall. Wisely, sections here are grouped by shopper type, so, for instance, cookbooks, health, home and self-help—all, typically, "female" interests—flow from one to the other, while computers, business and sports are all adjacent. Each section is marked with an elegant little sign, but the signs are so elegant, and so little, that they are impossible to see from ten or twenty paces away, which is where such markers should reach. What's the point of a sign announcing "Photography" that's big enough to be read only when you're already standing in that section?

The problem with the typical bookstore arrangement of shelving is that it's unimaginative and awkward. Claustrophobic, even. How did tall, vertical arrangements of cases come to be the standard? Because that's how people store their books at home? It's a silly reason—imagine if housewares stores or clothing retailers adopted the same thinking. We'd be rooting through kitchen drawers to buy a peeler or through a closet to find a sweater. Narrow aisles formed by tall shelves are just about the worst display scheme you could dream up. There's a clear space-time ratio that we've seen in nearly all our research: The amount of time spent by shoppers in a given area is directly proportional to the amount of uninterrupted space (either actual or perceived) surrounding him or her. So if a section of a store feels roomy, and you can look in any direction and see off into the distance, you'll feel inclined to linger. Whereas if you are boxed in—or even if the architecture and the displays just make you feel that way—you'll want to move on in a hurry. Just watch how people browse bookshelves—rare and determined is the shopper who intently scans anything much above eye level or below waist-high. It's particularly difficult to see books down low, so you look only if you must. As a result, the books that are banished there by the luck of the alphabetical draw suffer. It's a ludicrous system: Is there any other store that allows the alphabet to dictate which goods are displayed where? Compact disks, you say? That's correct, but their displays don't suffer because of their horizontal layout, and maybe someone needs to try that for books. At the very least, stores should put some beanbag chairs or big pillows down there to make shopping the bottom shelves a little easier. Or, all books kept down there should be displayed face out and tilted upward a little, to give them a fighting chance to catch a shopper's eye. But even with that, the bottom shelves of a bookstore will remain one of the worst Siberias in all of retailing.

And now we've come upon the other great innovation of bookstores—chairs. If every store provided seating like this, the world of retail would be a whole lot friendlier for shoppers and their companions. Chairs have totally changed the bookstore vibe, making it into the much-sought-after "third place"—the locale that's not home and not job but still someplace where we feel comfortable spending time. And spending time in a store is usually a prelude to buying. But whoever positioned those chairs did so without sitting in them, for they afford no view of anything worthwhile from the store's perspective, no signs or displays aimed specifically at these customers. Anyplace where shoppers linger should be a communication opportunity, and this one is perfect for some prolonged sign-reading.

One last matter. Take a look at that wall, over near the information desk. What do you see? This week's *New York Times* best-seller list, or rather a grimy photocopy of it, taped up. Next to it is a rather grimy photocopy of the Modern Library list of the so-called one hundred top novels of the twentieth century. Have you ever seen a more pathetic display of such useful and interesting information? These lists should be reproduced large-scale and posted prominently in the front of the store. Record stores understand how we all love lists, and especially how shoppers use them as reminders. Bookstores tend to be clueless in this regard. Not only would I display the lists up front, but I'd also stock the books right under them. In fact, I'd offer a special deal on the top one hundred novels—a discount if you bought them all, and a good deal on a fancy bookcase to hold them. Will many shoppers bite? No, but a few will. Record companies package all of Mozart's music in huge boxed sets of more than one hundred disks, and they sell enough of them to collectors to make it worthwhile. Why have booksellers failed to identify or cultivate the idea of book collecting? They're missing a huge market, as record companies can attest.

I'd also tap into *the* powerhouse in bookselling today, Oprah Winfrey's book club. I'd stock all those books on one fixture also, and offer a package deal if you bought the collection. How many shoppers will buy the whole thing? Not many, but a few, I have no doubt. Publishers and booksellers are so preoccupied with how to sell one $27 book at a time that they fail to devote any imagination or energy to the hundred- or even thousand-dollar sale of creatively packaged merchandise. Too often, bookstores merchandise and sell the way publishers publish instead of how buyers buy. Considering how independent booksellers have always been in such close touch with the tastes and habits of their customers, this feels like a tremendous oversight. Perhaps it can also be a way for independents to survive and even prosper in a world where big chains and on-line sellers now dominate.

As I started this chapter by saying, at some level all stores are alike, with functions all must fulfill. It follows, then, that retailers can learn from one another even when their particular categories are vastly different. For example, in that bookstore we visited—and in almost every bookstore I've ever seen—no attention is paid to giving shoppers headed for the door a parting message, some good reason to return soon. Video stores excel at this via the board where upcoming video release dates are posted. Why don't bookstores tell shoppers that, say, the new Stephen King novel will be in stock in exactly one week? Such a fixture hung over the cashiers would also give those bored people standing in line something to think about.

There's also something video stores can learn from bookstores. The latter make great efforts to provide shoppers with more than just merchandise—they host author appearances, book discussions, reading clubs, events for children and so on. And the bookstore-cafe is so commonplace it's almost a cliché. Why don't video stores sponsor discussion groups for film buffs, or appearances by authors, newspaper critics or film scholars? A video store could host a Martin Scorsese Club to study the director's oeuvre and guarantee repeated rentals of his older movies and even those of his influences. Everyone is a movie maven nowadays, and video stores can take advantage of that just as bookstores cater to the literate among us. There's another thing the book world does that the video world should emulate. Video box designs are regulated by legal agreements between the movie's producers and its stars; as a result, the boxes all bear the same visual as the movie poster—a bad idea, for what worked large usually does not do well when shrunk down to the size of a video box. Video retailers must insist on the freedom to redesign packaging to suit the video shopper's needs. In books, the paperback's cover is almost always different from the hardcover's, giving a book a fresh look and taking advantage of good reviews. Videos should also get new boxes a few months after their initial release, to tie in with the star's or director's latest hit, for instance, or to boast about the video's popularity.

The lowly convenience store has quite a lot it can teach other retailers. Convenience stores successfully took on the supermarket industry by a foolproof strategy: They made themselves very available and very convenient. C-stores took special advantage of the changes in women's lives, which is always a smart idea. Women with full-time jobs made the big weekly shopping expedition a thing of the past for many American families. People staying single longer also contributed to that trend. As a result, we now make more grocery shopping trips and buy fewer items each time. And we're always in a hurry. All of which plays to the C-store strengths. They charged more than supermarkets, but that was acceptable, baby boomers said, in exchange for so much convenience. C-stores also can teach a lesson or two when it comes to media placement. If you're standing in line to pay for gas, your eyes go to one of three things—your car (to make sure no one's stealing it), your cash (to make sure you're getting the right change) and the clerk (because we always look at people). C-stores take full advantage of those natural sight lines, carefully positioning signage and displays of impulse goods to intercept your gaze.

In fact, once supermarkets finally woke up and realized they were being hurt by the C-store industry, they retaliated by going to the heart of the smaller challenger's appeal. As we noted in Chapter 6, a mainstay of supermarket design was that dairy cases were stationed in the rear, so shoppers were forced to walk by all the other merchandise to reach the staples. Now, some have created miniature C-stores way up front, offering milk and a few other necessities where shoppers can grab them, pay and be on their way—in the so-called shallow loop instead of the long trek to the back of the store. A big problem for supermarkets was that shoppers began to equate their hugeness with their seeming inability to innovate or excite. Now, many have gone boutique—where once you had a giant, undifferentiated store you now see a collection of smaller, shoplike departments, like the bakery cafe, in-store bank branch or drugstore complete with pharmacist, herbal remedies and other specialty products. Supermarkets have responded to the working woman's burden by going into the meal replacement business, so you can buy your chicken from the butcher counter or the rotisserie, your lettuce from the produce section or the salad bar.

Supermarkets have also done a lot with the store-brand trade. Once upon a time these generics were for the budget-challenged only. Their austere, institutional-style packaging only reinforced that notion. Today we have the contradiction of generic brand names, store-owned brands that are packaged to look as luxurious as anything else on the shelves. In some cases, the store-brand packaging veers dangerously near to trademark infringement, so closely does it knock off the big brand-name design.

The other retailer that has benefited from the C-store's lessons is the drugstore, especially drugstores owned by national chains. Today they sell everything from food to housewares to cold sodas and beer—just like a C-store. Many are open late, even twenty-four hours, which also cuts into the C-store's appeal. Drugstores have lessons of their own, of course. They've expanded their mission by appealing to the healthy as well as the ill. Drugstores are now a source of vitamins, herbal remedies, nutritional supplements, and books and magazines on health and fitness. In other words, they're serving people who wish to take their health into their own hands, a good idea in the perilous age of managed care. Savvy drugstores take advantage of the changing doctor-patient relationship in another way, too—they promote the presence of the pharmacist, whose experienced counsel sells a lot more vitamins and home cholesterol kits than any minimum-wage clerk will ever move. This is a potent reminder of how hungry shoppers are for contact with knowledgeable, caring store employees.

Fast food has quite a bit it can teach. The first lesson is that if you appeal to the tastes of children, they'll bring their parents along for the ride. This may have contributed to an overall juvenilization of American taste buds, but at least we get a national cuisine out of it. Fast food also excels at creative package deals (food plus movie tie-in toys), dynamic signage (a short, telegraphese sign in the window, the whole story at the register) and images over text (digital menu boards and pictures of food instead of words sell better to children, older people with bad eyesight and recent immigrants with a shaky grip on the language). The industry has practically perfected the drive-thru, though it still gets a few details wrong, such as failing to provide a menu board specifically for the second and third cars in line, so that diners can decide what they want before they reach the microphone. In one study we did, 18 percent of drive-thru customers said they were confused at some time during the process, which is why it still takes longer than it should. Fast food also can teach the rest of retailing something crucial about suggestive selling. In one study we did at a fast-food restaurant, having a clerk simply ask customers if they wished to upgrade—"supersize"—their drinks succeeded a whopping 47 percent of the time. The moral is that most salespeople stop trying and suggesting too soon, losing sales of accessories and add-ons, many of which are high-margin items. The rule should be that staff keeps selling (gently, of course) until the shopper says no.

What can banks teach the rest of retail? They are a form of retail, though most of us fail to see them that way. Certainly they exist and operate at ground level, the same as any store, and the principles of human anatomy and behavior still hold, whether we're "shopping" in a bank, a Banana Republic or a Burger King. Signs are still signs; we still move in response to certain aspects of architecture and design. Banks even sell things—every service a bank performs or financial instrument it offers produces a fee or interest owed. All of retail can learn from banks this guiding principle behind automation: You no longer have to provide a service if you can train customers to perform it themselves. We love ATMs for their convenience; banks love them because they turn every customer into his or her own teller.

For the most part, however, banks make lousy retailers. Back in the early '80s, many of America's biggest banks believed that by now they'd be pretty much out of the retail banking business. The future was in big corporate lending and private banking for rich clients. But that future never quite panned out—a few big customers weren't able to generate the same kind of profits as many little customers did. So banks are stuck in the world of retailing. That's probably why they get so much wrong. We do a great deal of work for banks here as well as in Europe, South America and Australia. And there are lots of good, smart, customer-minded retail bankers I can name—just not enough of them.

What do banks do wrong? The failure starts with the most basic elements, like operating hours. Name another store open only from 9 a.m. to 5 p.m. Monday to Friday. It's ridiculous. Yet banks still think of branches as unwanted costs rather than opportunities to meet customers face-to-face and find ways—income-generating ways—to serve them. Banks offer services tied in to the most important parts of our lives—home mortgages, retirement savings, car loans, education accounts, IRAs, it's a long list. Yet, according to a recent survey I read, Americans don't list banks among their top five sources of information and advice on finance, much less the implication of life changes. Considering that we automatically keep most of our money in banks, this is a spectacular failure. Bankers should be greeting us at the door just to get our attention. But do you know which bank employee has the most customer contact? At an Italian bank branch where we measured just this, the startling answer was, the uniformed guard. The same is true of many American banks. Customers just walk in, see him sitting there conspicuously and ask him for information or directions. And typically, he is an employee of an outside security agency, not of the bank. In most bank branches, it's easy to find the executive of the highest rank—his or her office is the one farthest from the front door. This is the kind of retail thinking that goes on in banks today. As we've discussed earlier, banks do a horrendous job with signs and other in-branch media. Almost none of it is positioned in a strategic fashion—it's just nailed up or dumped wherever there's space, with no thought given to what customers will be doing or thinking about when they come upon the sign or brochure rack.

When you do find yourself in the presence of a branch officer, the desk arrangement tells a great deal about the relationship between you two. He or she is on one side of the desk, you're on the other, and the computer monitor screen, which displays all the most intimate facts of your financial life, faces toward the banker and away from you. She's looking at something grim, judging by her expression, and don't you just wish you knew what it was? We performed a study of HFC Bank in Great Britain that taught us an important lesson: The closing rate of loans goes up, and the time required to close them goes down, when banker and customer sit next to each other rather than face-to-face over a broad expanse of desktop or table. It's a simple matter to create work-stations where banker and customer can both feel at ease. One such configuration uses a computer monitor on a swivel, so everybody gets a peek; the other simply places the chairs side by side, so banker and customer go through the process together, as a team, rather than as adversaries facing each other down.

In the end, even the bank's greatest innovation, the ATM, works against it. As I heard an executive of Chase Manhattan say at a recent industry gathering, the current buzzword in banking is "relationship," but in order to conduct any relationship the first thing you need is a place. ATMs actively discourage customers from ever entering a bank branch, meaning that the bank has no reliable way of meeting its clientele or selling it on any of its services. Which is deadly, at least in retailing.

Final Thoughts

NINETEEN

If ten years ago you told me that someday I'd be a generally acknowledged expert on how women shop for cosmetics—and by dint of having spent countless hours observing them do just that—I'd have called your shrink. Ditto if you had predicted that my firm would be a leading authority on the dynamics that govern the fast-food drive-thru line. In fact, I'm still a little discomforted when, in a corporate conference room, I hear myself being deferred to as the senior researcher. Most people who spend their lives in retailing do so thanks to some merchant gene. Still, I'm grateful to have found a path to it. My colleagues and I have been bitten by a strange bug—none of us are businesspeople, yet we spend an awful lot of our waking hours untangling the problems and issues that beset the world of shopping. We can't walk down a shopping street or read a restaurant menu without deconstructing the experience and trying to figure out how it could be improved. The merchants in my neighborhood are tired of all the free advice I proffer. When my significant other and I go on vacations, she has to remind me to turn off the automatic store-analyzer device in my brain. Even then

I'll end up leading us into a mall, just to poke around a bit. Unlike Margaret Mead, I don't have to go to the other side of the globe to perform a little fieldwork.

For most scientists, the exciting part of research is the exact moment of discovery—finding the missing bone fragment that explains everything, witnessing the lucky accident in the petri dish. Many times the secret lies in something we've seen before but whose significance we've failed to recognize. An example in our work is the boomerang factor, which I discuss in Chapter 6. The idea that shoppers frequently fail to walk completely through a store aisle, from one end to the other, is a painfully obvious one. Yet we had been studying stores for more than a decade before it occurred to us to quantify that behavior and weigh its implications. We wonder how something so important could have eluded our attention, but the truth is that we are still inventing the basic tools of our research. There is much left to do.

The science of shopping is a hybrid discipline—part physical science, part social science and only part science at all, for it is also partly an art. But it is always a practical field, concerned with providing information that can improve the retailer's edge and cut the odds of making a wrong decision. Much of our value lies in our ability to go beyond merely collecting data to make good educated guesses about what it means and how best to respond. While I can say that most of the time we have been proven right in our interpretations, we have been wrong sometimes, too. And so we keep searching. Even our most senior management people spend ninety nights a year on the road, devoting their weekends to stores, banks, restaurants and malls all over the world. It's been hell on our personal lives, I assure you.

Even with all that, the truth in the science of shopping is transitory. The basic facts of human anatomy remain, more or less, but the store itself and the tastes and behaviors of the shopper continue to evolve. Just as the farmer of 1900 had more in common with his agrarian ancestors of a millennium before than with his agritechnician grandson of 1950, the merchant of 1900 would have a lot of catching up to do today. If we look back just to the '70s, we see that many of the leading retailers of the period are gone now or greatly diminished. Korvette's, Woolworth's, Crazy Eddie, Montgomery Ward, all now consigned to the history books, and many others will follow shortly. Might Wal-Mart stumble, will Starbucks fade, will Marks & Spencer ever go global? It's a changing world. In the olden days, the adage held that with the right product at the right price at the right location, success was assured. Today you need that nailed down just to survive. Everybody is competing with everybody else, so the threat can come from any direction. It is dangerously narrow-minded for a store owner to believe that competition comes only from others in his or her category. In truth, retailers compete with every other demand on consumer time and money. Recently we've been hired to study patrons in movie theaters, which just reminds us that two hours and $8 spent in a cinema are forever lost to the rest of retailing. Likewise, if the experience of spending twenty minutes of unused lunch hour browsing in a computer store is more enjoyable than visiting a bookstore, then it becomes likely that some software will be sold—and impossible that a book will be. The era of the visionary retailer or the manufacturer king is over. In the twenty-first century the consumer will be king. Just as fashion now comes from the street up, the world of retail is about following shoppers where they are going.

First and foremost, shopping follows social change, and woe to the businessperson who fails to comprehend. Without a doubt, the major social change playing itself out during our time has to do with the lives of women. In his lectures, futurist Watts Wacker makes the point that, based on the current evidence, men are on their way to becoming exotic household pets. Retail must pay attention to how women wish to live, what they want and need, or it will be left behind. Even the enormous changes in the lives of men and children are merely in response to the lead taken by women. It pays to listen and be humble. Shoppers are fickle today, and their loyalty to brand name—whether of a product or a store—lasts only as long as the afterglow of the most recent shopping experience.

If bad results in one fiscal quarter send shock waves through a national retail chain, two or three sour quarters are lifeboat time. The best defense against complacency is to eliminate the distance between the floor of the store and the men and women who make the decisions about what happens there. The most intelligent management decree today is to push more responsibility and authority down to the store manager level. Senior brass must develop the tools for teaching managers how to make sure the store is serving the shoppers. Last year I told a largely male executive group at Wal-Mart that I could tell the gender of the manager in any of their stores based solely on how recently the women's dressing room had been painted. I don't know if I am responsible, but in the past six months I've noticed that lots of Wal-Mart dressing rooms have gotten new paint jobs.

Even with all there is to be learned from the science of shopping, we recognize that there is room for a creative merchant to throw the textbook to the wind and break all the rules. In Toronto I visited a 400-square-foot store called No. 6. In that minuscule space the owner sold hats, dresses, jewelry, bags, shoes, scarves and music. His fixturing came straight from the Salvation Army store. That store is an absolute delight, a total triumph of energy over space and budget limitations. It's hard to go in there and not buy something. You'd think a basic tenet of retail would be that shoppers should be able to say the name of your store. But I have a friend who owns a highly successful shop called Mxyplyzyk, an intentionally unpronounceable appellation taken from a rather obscure character in Superman comics. It's a crowded store filled with an eclectic mix of products, from bathroom fixtures to books, and the price points roam all over the map. The checkout process is primitive and the receipts are handwritten. But I can't teach Kevin, the owner, a single thing about retail—he's invented a selling machine in his own image, and it looks as if he's having a great time with it. For all the science we preach, we realize that if you've got the moxie, you might have the moves.

As professional observers, we play a strange role in the world of commerce. I joke that I'm the only person in retailing who's delighted to witness shoplifting. It shows that we're able to confound the Heisenberg Principle and watch people in stores without altering their behavior. Some of my most vivid memories involve thievery. I remember studying the video of a well-dressed matron at the fragrance counter of Filene's on Washington Street in Boston. She repeatedly dispatched the respectful clerk on missions to distant parts of the department while she loaded her tote bag with bottles of perfume from atop the counter. Actually, we commonly see well-dressed shoplifters buy one product, then steal another. At a drugstore in Spartanburg, South Carolina, our trackers kept finding individual disposable diapers (clean ones) tucked into odd corners of the store. The mystery was cleared up when they saw a shopper filling a half-empty diaper box with large jars of a pricey headache remedy. Our most pathetic shoplift sighting involved a father who tucked a screwdriver set into his sleeping infant's diaper.

But our job is like that of the crew on *Star Trek*—we're there to ob-serve and report but not interfere. We preserve the privacy of those we videotape, as a way of keeping faith with our ultimate patron, the shop-ping public. Given that my roots as a researcher are based in public ad-vocacy, I am very sensitive to questions of invasion of privacy in our work. I was appalled when one of the first major magazine stories on Envirosell called us "supermarket spies." We all accept the techniques of social science field research when they are used to study a rural mar-ketplace in Papua New Guinea. So why should our investigation of a mall in Minnesota be held to a different standard? At any rate, the sci-ence of shopping knows a great deal less about individual consumers than does your average direct marketing consultant, who can summon up any American's name, address, phone number, marital status, credit record and purchasing history in a flash.

Some colleagues have suggested that by writing this book I run the risk of giving up all our secrets—that a company could read these lessons and skip hiring us. But this book is only a start in a certain direc-tion. A business that pays attention to its customers probably already practices many of the things I discuss in this book. Many of our clients tell me that our work serves as an affirmation of beliefs they already held. It's always more satisfying for us to work with companies that are headed in the right direction. The other common observation is that most of our recommendations are more like fine-tuning than drastic overhaul. Which is true—you can move a sign two feet away, or slightly adjust a product's shelf arrangement, and have a large impact on what happens at the register. When you implement a dozen little changes throughout a store, you sometimes find you've improved an awful lot. As I like to say, in a world where marketing focuses on strategy, tactics are being ignored.

For example, I mentioned in Chapter 1 that older women were being ill served by drugstore cosmetics sections, where less-than-glamorous products such as concealer cream were stocked down near the floor, literally forcing shoppers to their knees. In fact, we had collected some video showing older shoppers crawling in order to browse the category—images that were truly poignant, I think, and ultimately effective. Today, most cosmetics planograms have been changed to accommodate the mature shopper. Moving the products two feet higher has made a big difference in consumer comfort and also in sales. We recently were hired to study how people shop for flowers at a supermarket in Australia. Sales in the department were much lower than anticipated until we saw why: The method of display—large plastic vats holding many flowers—was mystifying to shoppers. No one could figure out how much the flowers cost or whether they were sold by the bunch or the blossom. And masses of blossoms in large vats gave shoppers no sense of what the flowers would look like once they got them home. In other words, the simplest matters had not been sufficiently thought out. The display was especially forbidding to the occasional flower buyer, which is most of us. A few small changes were made—individual bunches were displayed in front of the large vats, prices were more clearly marked—and suddenly flowers were flying out of the store.

The fact that a minor alteration can bring a major improvement should come as no surprise. After all, science is by and large the study of very small differences. Critical truths are discovered that way. Charles Darwin went about measuring the length of birds' beaks, which is pretty small work even by our standards. But from his studies came a fundamental shift in our theories about living things and why they thrive or fail. Darwin's main finding sounds like common sense, too—the idea that successful organisms are the ones that best adapt to their environment. In stores, something similar happens, except that in retailing it's the environment that must adapt to the organism.

Twenty years ago I thought that if we could collect evidence to establish the link between amenability and profitability, we could create a viable commercial science. I'm enough of a realist to know that if you can take a public improvement and give it an economic payoff, the chances of it happening are great and the possibilities are limitless.

ACKNOWLEDGMENTS

Without the hard work, intelligence and diligence of Bill Tonelli, this book would never have happened. As listener, interviewer, organizer, editor and writer, his patience and interest never flagged. Over the course of this project he changed jobs and had a son, but never was without a smile, a good word and a positive attitude. Much of the perspective I have gained on Envirosell's work over the past twenty years has been from working with Bill on this project.

Glen Hartley and Lynn Chu have been my agents and friends these last two years. They are a rare couple, dedicated to thinking, truth and reverence for the printed word. I am grateful for their help in germinating and growing this book.

Alice Mayhew and Elizabeth Stein at Simon & Schuster encouraged and shepherded this volume to completion. Without their commitment, this past year would have been much more difficult.

Few careers and no businesses are built without help. Envirosell has been lucky in that we developed through the years a core of what we call Ambassadors—individuals who have been exposed to our work and have given us their wholehearted support. I wish to thank some of them for their assistance.

Richard Kurtz gave me a home and taught me the ropes of the research business. Richard still runs a small research agency in New York.

Alexandra Anderson Spivey pushed and protected. As an art critic, author and social observer, she taught me the basic lessons of how to survive in a city. No one could ask for a better advocate and a more giving friend.

Bonnie Predd sparkles. Big humor, cutting logic, good heart. We have followed her through her career from Waldenbooks to the U.S. Post Office to NationsBank.

Cal Mann started his career as a fisherman in the Gulf of Alaska. As an owner of Walden Partners, a PoP agency, he has chummed and baited the waters for us.

Mitch Wolf has retired to a series of Taco Bell franchises on the central coast of California. He runs, he bikes, he coaches. I remember him clad in pinstriped suits and a Wharton MBA, dispensing marketing topspin and good advice.

John Ryan is the luckiest good person I know. His company has changed the face of retail banking across the world. His gentle manners and warmth are testament to virtues not often associated with immensely successful businessmen.

Peter Hoyt is the publisher of *PoP Times,* the leading trade journal of the merchandising industry. He has been a tireless Envirosell advocate, pushing people and good ideas our way. I thank him also for being an early reader of this book.

Peter Katz entered my life when my business was a hazy mess. Without his early encouragement I would never have embarked on this journey.

Charlene Stern runs a bank marketing agency in Berkeley. When she was head of merchandising at Wells Fargo Bank, I heard stories of how tough and demanding she was. I am grateful that from our first meeting she understood what we were trying to do.

Doug Leeds is the chairman of Thomson-Leeds, one of the world's leading merchandising companies. His grace and mentoring have meant much to me personally and professionally. As a veteran of the PoP industry, his support and counsel have been invaluable.

Wendy Liebmann is the principal at WSL Strategic Retail. She is one of the wisest and funniest retail analysts I know.

James Lucas is the research director at Frankel & Company, McDonald's promotion agency in Chicago. When clients become friends it is best done carefully. As a fellow refugee from academia, Jim's ability to see what we could do helped to broaden our capabilities.

Wilton Connor is an inspiration. His packaging company in Charlotte is uniquely impressive. His example has taught me about courage and how to trust your instincts.

Giusi Scandroglio is my partner in Milan. Her friendship and hospitality have transcended good manners and good business and made me feel like family. Her innovations and suggestions about our methodologies and practices have been seminal in our development.

Alberto Pasquini is the chairman of PoPAI Italia and partner in Creativity, a major European design agency. His tireless and insistent advocacy is the origin of our Italian office.

Jean Pierre Baade is an authority on the history of merchandising in France. He also owns a design and marketing agency in Strasbourg. His support has been important in our European efforts.

José Luis Nueno is a professor of marketing at the IESE, the Graduate School of Management in Barcelona. His judgment and knowledge of European business and retailing have been invaluable.

There have been many others: Carol White at the Advertising Research Foundation, Joel Granoff at Compaq, James Adams and Lisa Hudson at Retail Concepts, Carrie Strader at Hewlett-Packard, Robert Gorrie at Gorrie Marketing Services in Canada, John Lombardi at Revlon, Margo Weitekamp at Neutrogena, Carmen Spofford at Federated, Allen Klose at Blockbuster, Pam Horwitz at NARM and Jed Horowitz at Video Pipeline, and probably more than a few whom I will have neglected to mention.

The media world has been very attentive and kind. *The New Yorker*'s Malcolm Gladwell wrote an embarrassingly flattering story on Envirosell and me personally, called, surprise, surprise, "The Science of

Shopping." David May and Patti Renton on the publishing side of *The New Yorker* have been very supportive. Cathy Black at Hearst Publications; Kate White, the editor of *Cosmopolitan;* Kathy O'Connell and Mary Noonan at *48 Hours;* an assortment of characters at National Public Radio and many others have treated us with understanding and interest.

Eric Larson wrote the first profile of Envirosell for *Smithsonian Magazine.* After reading Eric's piece, my father told me he finally understood what I did for a living. For that alone I am grateful.

No life is complete without friends and family. My significant other, Sheryl Henze, has been a patient reader and editor. Jeff and Christine Hewitt, Rip Hayman and Barbara Pollitt have cheered faithfully from the sidelines, as have Francis, Savie and Lisa Underhill.

Finally fulfilling a promise made twenty-five years ago, I wish to say thank you, Paula Kartus. I hope you have had a good life so far.

—New York, October 2, 1998

INDEX

About the Author

PACO UNDERHILL, urban geographer and retail anthropologist, is the founder of Envirosell, a research and consulting firm that advises a blue-chip collection of Fortune 100 companies. He has been profiled in *The New Yorker* and *Smithsonian Magazine* and has written for *American Demographics* and *Adweek*. He lectures widely and lives in New York City.

21100296

658.8
UND

Underhill, Paco.

Why we buy : the
science of shopping